Des Wilson has been President of the Liberal Party 1986–1987, Chairman of its General Election Committee, and a member of the key Alliance Election Planning Group.

A journalist who has written columns for the Guardian and the *Observer*, he is also Britain's best known campaigner on social issues, having been the first Director of Shelter, the organiser of the CLEAR campaign on lead in petrol, Chairman for four years of Friends of the Earth, and the founder and currently the Co-Chairman of the Campaign for Freedom of Information.

BATTLE FOR POWER

Des Wilson

SPHERE BOOKS LIMITED

First published in Great Britain by
Sphere Books Ltd 1987
27 Wrights Lane, London W8 5TZ
Copyright © 1987 by Des Wilson

TRADE
MARK

Set in 10 on 11½pt Monophoto Melior

Printed and bound in Great Britain by
Richard Clay Ltd, Bungay, Suffolk

To Jane

CONTENTS

Author's Note

This is an account of a year in British politics, and of the 1987 General Election, but particularly of a critical year for the Liberal Party and its alliance with the Social Democrats.

My vantage point has been the Presidency of the Liberal Party for 1986–1987, the chairmanship of its General Election Committee, and membership of the Alliance Joint Strategy Committee and the Alliance Planning Group, the small team put together by David Owen and David Steel to plan and manage the Alliance general election campaign.

For all that, it is an individual view. And a Liberal view. In my experience there is no definitive view of politics. Another with the same access to the inner workings of the Alliance but with a different political perspective could legitimately tell the story entirely differently. 'Truth makes on the ocean of nature no one track of light – every eye looking on finds its own.'

Nor does it delve into party or Alliance history, philosophy or policy more than is necessary to tell the story, for this is largely (if not entirely) *a diary of the happenings of the year itself* – of the last-grasp policy-making, the political manoeuvrings and the campaigning in the run-up to and during the General Election. There is, however, a sub-plot, namely the developing debate within the Alliance about what to do if no party won a clear majority at the General Election, and whether, after the General Election, the two parties should merge.

I considered at length what would be legitimate to report and what would be an abuse of my privileged access and involvement in the Alliance leadership. I decided the only hard and fast rules were to be as open as possible about my intention to write the book (for instance, the whole Alliance Joint Strategy Committee was told) and to report the behaviour and words of others on the basis of the kind of fair and reasonable treatment I would expect were the roles reversed. Thus, it would be improper to report exactly what was said on some occasions, but it would be fair to indicate, if necessary, that feelings were running high at a given point, that there was argument and controversy. After all, anyone who believes you can avoid difficulties or differences in any political party, let alone in a coalition, is naive. Partnership in politics is all about resolving difficulties and differences, and this book tells how people from vastly different political backgrounds, and often of vastly different personalities, have had to work together to do that. If I reveal mistakes by, or weaknesses of, those who are colleagues and friends, I do so knowing my readers will recognise that such failings are not exclusive to our party or the Alliance, but are gloriously and/or ingloriously human.

In any case, I believe the story of the Alliance is a proud one – of the idealism and self-sacrifice of many hundreds of decent people putting themselves on the line for their communities and country; and of a political force having to fight with limited resources and contend with an outrageously unfair electoral system and yet, by a combination of unshakeable faith, ingenuity, and hard work, providing the country with a credible alternative to the two-party system.

Finally, I should explain why the book is written in the third person.

I did not want to write a book full of I's. I felt that if I did my own importance would be exaggerated. I was in the centre, and had some influence in the Alliance some of the time, but my influence or power were limited compared with others. Also, because of my high profile in what had to be non-party political pressure groups during the first half of the 1980s, I had maintained a fairly low profile within the Liberal Party, and came fairly late to the heart of Alliance politics; as a result I often felt, especially in the earlier days, a stage removed – a participant, but sometimes a bemused one, sometimes an alarmed one, more interested than I was myself (at least in this context) interesting.

The problem was resolved for me by a man I greatly admire, John Arlott. Talking on television about his plans to write an autobiography, he said this:

> 'I don't like first person singular writing . . . in the last ten years the word "I" has only twice appeared in my copy . . . if I wrote an autobiography, I would want to try to write without the use of the first person singular and I think it would be a help if someone wrote an autobiography by the means of standing back and referring to himself in the third person. And I think you would come far nearer the truth if you did that. It is easier to say *he* did this than it is to say *I* . . .'

What was good enough for John Arlott was more than good enough for me.

That left just one remaining question: who would, then, be the author of this book? This, too, was resolved for me by a *Guardian* writer. The day after my keynote speech to the Liberal Party Assembly, Hugo Young, referring to my unusual route to the Liberal Presidency, wrote:

> 'He was an outsider coming in, and offering an outsider's judgement.'

So our author, the Outsider, later to become the Insider, was born.

Who's Who

The Alliance

Alliance Strategy Committee (overall planning and strategy of the Alliance – twelve leading members of each party – met monthly, chaired alternately by David Owen and David Steel).

Alliance Campaign Committee (smaller version of the above – took over for the duration of the General Election campaign – met weekly).

Alliance Planning Group (in effect, the 'executive' arm of the above committees, it directed the campaigning activities of the Alliance from November 1986 until the General Election and advised the leaders during the Election. Met weekly before the Election and then daily – alternately chaired by Owen and Steel, it consisted of John Pardoe, Lord Harris, Des Wilson, Polly Toynbee, Paul Tyler, Roland Freeman).

The Liberal Party

The Assembly (combination of annual meeting and main policy-making forum of the party – lasts a week, usually mid-September).

Party Council (meets three times a year to oversee the running of the party and take policy decisions between Assemblies – Chairman 1986–87, Des Wilson as Party President).

National Executive (responsible for the administrative and financial management of the party – meets monthly. Chairman 1986–87, Tim Clement-Jones).

Policy Committee (responsible for guiding and interpreting party policy, and for negotiating joint policy with the SDP – meets monthly. Chairman 1986–87, Alan Beith MP).

General Election Committee (planned and directed the Liberal Party General Election organisation-met monthly. Chairman 1986–87, Des Wilson).

Association of Liberal Councillors (ALC) (organisation of Liberal councillors and those involved in Liberal Party community politics – ran the local government election campaign. General Secretary, Margaret Clay).

Liberal Parliamentary Party (to June 1987)

David Steel (Leader)
David Alton (Chief Whip)
Paddy Ashdown
Alan Beith
Malcolm Bruce
Alex Carlile
Clement Freud
Geraint Howells
Simon Hughes
Sir Russell Johnston
Archy Kirkwood
Richard Livsey
Michael Meadowcroft
David Penhaligon (until December 1986)
Stephen Ross
Elizabeth Shields
Cyril Smith
Matthew Taylor (from March 1987)

Richard Wainwright
Jim Wallace

SDP Parliamentary Party

David Owen (Leader)
John Cartwright (Whip)
Rosie Barnes (from February 1987)
Mike Hancock
Roy Jenkins
Charles Kennedy
Robert Maclennan
Ian Wrigglesworth

Liberal Party

Des Wilson (President and Chairman of the General Election
    Committee 1986–87)
Paul Tyler (Chairman 1984–86, and then member of APG)
Tim Clement-Jones (Chairman 1986–87)
Andrew Ellis (Secretary-General)

The Social Democratic Party

Shirley Williams (President 1984–87)
Bill Rodgers (Vice President 1984–87)
Dick Newby (Secretary-General)

The Prologue

An election is called . . .

It came as an anti-climax. If the Prime Minister had, on May 11, 1987, not announced that the General Election would be held on June 11, she would have caused a political sensation. The date had been widely predicted for weeks and the Tory leadership had fuelled rather than dampened the bonfire of speculation. The Budget in March had been well received, if not ecstatically; the Prime Minister's trip to Moscow in April had been a public re- lation's triumph; the 'on the surface' economic indicators were all promising, interest rates were falling, inflation appeared to be under control, and there was a possibility that the number of unemployed would fall to less than three million in June. And Labour, the Tories' traditional enemy, were in desperate trouble. The last ten opinion polls had averaged 41.7% for the Conser- vatives, 30.4% for Labour, and 23.5% for the Alliance, and the latest, a Harris poll for ITV's *Weekend World* had the previous day put Conservatives on 44%, Labour 33%, and the Alliance 21%.

To add to all this the senior Ministers who had met at Chequers that Sunday had been able to review the results of elections on the previous Thursday, May 7, for 12,000 councillors on district councils in England and Wales – the Conservatives had per- formed surprisingly well, winning 37% of the votes, with Labour 29%, Alliance 26%, and others 7%.

It did appear that the Conservatives were set to repeat their landslide victory of June 1983.

But there were differences . . . considerable differences . . . at least seven of them:

First, while the opinion polls looked promising, the Tory position in 1987 was in fact substantially weaker than it was when the 1983 election was called. As a Gallup poll would show later in the week, compared with its poll taken immediately after similar local authority elections in June 1983, the Conservatives were down 10% and the Prime Minister's rating was down 6%. Almost all other comparisons between current polls and similar ones at the time of the 1983 General Election were adverse. In both the 1979 and 1983 General Elections the Conservatives had lost support during the campaign itself; this time they could not afford to do so. On the other hand, the Alliance was beginning the 1987 General Election campaign at the level of support it achieved on polling day on 1983, and, unlike the Conservatives, the Alliance, and previously the Liberal Party, had increased its support during past campaigns.

Second, there was the volatility of the electorate; support for the three parties had risen and fallen in a bewildering way over the past few months as Britain's political climate had become as variable as its weather. There was much uncertainty. Another opinion poll in this week was to show that 22% of those who said they planned to vote Conservative were open to changing their minds during the campaign; the figure was 27% for Labour 'supporters' and 39% for Alliance 'supporters'.

Third, Labour's 1983 campaign had been a shambles, and its Leader unfit for the challenge; it now had a highly professional set-up, and a Leader in Neil Kinnock who could well surprise everybody once the battle was under way.

Fourth, there had been substantial regional variations reflected in the May 7 local election results and thus it was likely that the opinion poll figures for the country as a whole would not necessarily be reflected in the numbers of parliamentary seats won.

Fifth, there would be no Falklands factor this time; the Prime Minister's popularity rose dramatically after the Falklands war and few doubted that it was a critical contributor to her landslide victory in '83.

Sixth, there was the fact that Margaret Thatcher was seeking a record third endorsement by the electorate; the British voters had become accustomed to making a change at fairly regular intervals; putting the Tories back once more would go against the grain.

And, finally, there was the spectre that must have haunted the Conservatives most, the fairly recent phenomenon of tactical voting – the possibility that Labour and Alliance supporters would choose to vote for the candidate most likely to beat the Conservatives, and by so doing make fools of the pollsters. If, as was possible, the best the Tories could achieve was around 39% to 40% of the popular vote, then there was a substantial anti-Conservative majority; if they stuck to party allegiances the Tories would probably be safe, but yet another opinion poll finding was that around 20% of voters were now considering using their vote tactically.

Perhaps the bookmakers were right to make the Tories 8–1 on. Despite all the above qualifications, this *was* the message of the opinion polls. Yet odds-on favourites did not always win, otherwise there would be no bookmakers, and favourites had lost general elections before; the last to do so was Harold Wilson who entered the 1970 Election at the same time of year with the same confidence only to find that in the last days of the Campaign the ground moved from under his feet and that after polling day it was not he, but Edward Heath who occupied 10 Downing Street.

There was also more at stake in this General Election than any since the Second World War. In the past eight years Margaret Thatcher had transformed the country; some argued for the best, and others for the worst. When she took office only 7% of the electorate owned shares; now the figure was 20%. When she took office there were more than 13 million trade union members in Britain; there were now less than 10 million. For the first time ever there were more shareholders than trade union members. She had humbled the trade union movement with a combination of restrictive legislation and resistance to strikes, her most notable triumph being the defeat of the miners in 1986. At the same time, she was engaged in a programme of privatisation of nationalised industries, but with the guarantee that employees and considerable numbers of small investors could buy shares. By allowing council tenants the right to buy their own homes, and by directing housing policy and finance behind home ownership, she had dramatically increased the number of 'people of property'. There were plenty of other indicators of the material wellbeing of the majority (car owners, for instance, had increased from 54% of voters to over 66% in her years in office).

But there was a downside. Unemployment in those eight years had more than doubled – at one point tripled – as manufacturing industry had declined. The nation's wealth had been increasingly concentrated in the south-east of the country. Unemployment in the north was double that in the south. But the real division was between those whose circumstances ranged from comfortable to affluent and those who were comparatively poor. Thus the poorest fifth of the population owned less than 7% of the national income while the top fifth owned nearly 40%. The income of a poor family with two children had in real terms increased by only 2.6% between 1979 and 1986, whereas the income of a well-off family had increased by 21%. Taxes had been cut at the expense of necessary public expenditure and there was a rapidly developing housing crisis, the country's infrastructure was falling into disrepair, and there were daily reports of fresh crises in hospitals and schools caused by lack of resources. The Thatcher solution to the complaints of the middle class about education and the health service was to increase the opportunities for opting out into private health care and private education, thus further distancing rich from poor.

Now she wanted to become the first Prime Minister to win three consecutive terms so that she could continue her crusade to crush socialism and establish a private enterprise society beyond the capacity of any successor to change.

For Neil Kinnock and the Labour Party this was perhaps the last chance to frustrate Margaret Thatcher's ambitions, to re-establish democratic socialism, even to save the Labour Party itself, for many believed that if Labour lost this election, we would never see another of its leaders in Downing Street.

The Thatcher–Kinnock struggle would bear little relation to those of earlier adversaries like Heath and Wilson, for the latter two had competed to demonstrate their worth to manage the country within a broad consensus on both domestic and foreign issues. Labour may have developed the welfare state in the years after the Second World War, but the Conservatives had nurtured it too; the Conservatives may have been more hawkish on defence, but the armed services would admit they saw little practical difference in the policies of a Conservative or Labour Defence Secretary. Labour may have nationalised a number of industries, but few were re-privatised by the Conservatives. In fact it had been the Conservatives who nationalised Rolls-Royce when it looked like folding up. The Conservatives may have made life easier for the get-rich-quick merchants in the City, but they had not noticeably suffered under Labour. Of course there had been differences, but they were often exaggerated for political reasons, and were often more the stuff of political rhetoric and ritual than of reality. It could not be more different now. There were huge and fundamental differences between the Conservatives and Labour on economic policy, on the social responsibility of government, and on defence and foreign affairs.

Had Labour defeated the Tories in 1983, it would not have been difficult to reverse the thrust of Thatcherism; she would have probably retired, and possibly under a different Tory leader the consensus could have been re-established. It would be much harder if Labour were re-elected in 1987 and impossible if she continued for another four years. That was what was at stake between these two parties.

But then there was the Alliance, backed by a quarter of the voters in 1983 but thwarted by an unfair electoral system and only a minority party in the House of Commons, neither in debt to vested interests nor bogged down by doctrine, increasingly an attractive alternative for those who wanted a balance between the emphasis on individual freedom and enterprise of the Conservatives and doctrinaire socialism, who wanted to live in a society where people could do their own thing but also share their well-being with those who needed care, who despaired at the way the country was being divided and polarised, who wanted new people running a different kind of government.

For the Alliance there was the realistic possibility that it would gain more of the popular vote than Labour, and thus replace it as the main opposition party in the country and therefore enter the 1990s with a real chance of power. Thus, for those who believed that a Conservative victory was a foregone conclusion, the General Election offered an alternative attraction — the battle for second place and for control of the centre-left of British politics.

Nor did the sub-plots end there (we now begin to see why even a General Election beginning with one party so well-established was so eagerly awaited by the political cognoscenti), for there was, of course, the possibility that Labour and the Alliance could together pick up sufficient support during the General Election campaign to stop the Conservatives achieving an overall majority even if they did have more parliamentary seats. This would create a 'hung parliament' with all of the possible scenarios that would arise from that eventuality.

The days were over when the only question was 'who will win'? Who would come second? Would any party achieve an overall majority? If no party did, what would happen? Would one try to govern without a majority, introducing a few popular policies, and then calling another general election when it stood a better chance of winning? Would the party with the most seats but without a majority make a deal with one of the others? Even form a coalition?

Finally, for the two Davids . . . David Steel and David Owen . . . there was also a lot at stake. Steel had devoted his ten years as Leader of the Liberal Party to re-alignment of the left and to the achievement of what now seemed possible . . . the replacement of Labour by a Liberal-led left-of-centre party. Owen had turned his back on a brilliant career in the Labour Party, culminating in becoming Foreign Secretary at thirty-eight, to help create the Social Democratic Party; if that sacrifice, if all that he and his colleagues had put at risk, was to be justified, the alliance with the Liberals had to make substantial gains at this General Election. As they met with their senior advisers and managers to finalise plans to seize the initiative in this first 'phoney war' week before the General Election campaign began in earnest on May 18, they were entitled to feel confident. They were beginning the General Election far stronger in the opinion polls than in 1983, and with the local authority success behind them. Their campaign was well-planned and professionally prepared. There was unity on the manifesto. The two headquarters teams were merging together well in the Cowley Street headquarters of the SDP. (Admittedly the telephones weren't working, the photocopier had broken down, and they were short of typewriters, but these problems could be solved!)

Like racehorses trained for one big day and one big race, they were fit and ready and impatient to go. For them it would climax four years of increasingly comfortable partnership since Owen took over the leadership of the SDP from Roy Jenkins after the 1983 election, and in particular it would climax nine dramatic and hectic months since those now far away days of last autumn, of Eastbourne 1986, and the week that fell apart . . .

The Liberal Party

Eastbourne – the week that fell apart

It was more like a hot summer's day than early autumn. The sun shone upon the white cliffs of the Sussex coast from a clear blue sky, and the beaches and beauty spots between his home in Brighton and the town of Eastbourne were alive with day-trippers. The Outsider steered his car off the main road and parked on a cliff top near Beachy Head, overlooking Eastbourne and the English Channel. Even from this distance he could see the detail of the neat little pier, and his destination, the white-stone Queen's Hotel nearby.

He paused for only a few minutes, his desire to bask in the warmth of the moment proving no match for his need to be at the scene of the action, and then he drove down the hill and onto the seafront. From Beachy Head the town had appeared to be dozing in the mid-afternoon sun, but at sea-level Eastbourne was all bustle. There were Liberals everywhere. Liberals carrying luggage into hotels. Liberals transporting leaflets and exhibition equipment to the Winter Gardens. Liberals hurrying to fringe events – a teach-in on defence, a commission on Europe, a workshop on 'balance of power', a party to launch the youth campaign. Liberals queueing at the Queen's Hotel to register for the Assembly. Liberals gossiping in bars, and plotting in corners. And also Liberals just strolling on the front, greeting old friends, speculating on the week ahead, and sporting their brand new delegate badges amid the old folk out for their Sunday afternoon constitutional and day-trippers rejoicing in the fact that they could still swim in the third week of September.

For a town like Eastbourne a party conference is a major event and a considerable boost to the local economy. There would be more than 2,000 Liberal delegates during the week, and at least the same number of non-delegate visitors — media people, exhibitors, lobbyists, and observers from business, from pressure groups, from embassies, and even from the other political parties ... all spending money. Then there would be the publicity for the town. And the drama, for the Liberal Assembly may be a mixture of reunion, debating club, party political broadcast, public demonstration and revival meeting, but as at the other party conferences, this is where the real stuff of politics can be experienced ... the ambition sensed, the swords of ideology crossed, the moments for instant fame seized, and, sometimes, real history made.

The Tories still talk of 1963, when Harold MacMillan resigned because of ill-health in the middle of a conference. It resembled an American convention as the party launched itself with unrestrained enthusiasm into a unprecedented open battle for the vacant leadership. The Labour Party still remembers Hugh Gaitskill in the early '60s responding to the Party's new unilateralist policy with his promise to 'fight, fight, and fight again'. More recently there was Neil Kinnock's dramatic 1985 attack on Militant, one that newly established his authority as a party leader and confirmed the defeat, at least for a time, of the Party's extreme left.

Liberals still talk of the Assembly speeches of Jo Grimond, most memorably his 1963 claim that the Party was 'marching towards the sound of gunfire'. Or of the Southport Assembly dominated by the scandal over Jeremy Thorpe, who insisted on making a brief platform appearance despite pleas to him to stay away. Or of Bournemouth in 1984, when despite an impassioned plea from the floor by the Party leader, David Steel, the Assembly voted to make it Party policy to send Cruise missiles back to the United States.

Eastbourne, however, has a particular place in the hearts of many Liberals, for the last time the Assembly was held there, in 1970, the Party passed the resolution that launched it on the community politics route to increased popularity:

'In determining the organisational strategy to achieve Liberal aims, this Assembly endorses the following objectives as of prime importance:

1 A dual approach to politics, acting both inside and outside (established political institutions).

2 A primary strategic emphasis on community politics; our role as political activists is to help organise people in communities to take and use power, to use political skills to redress grievances, and to represent people at all levels of the political structure.'

That Eastbourne Assembly followed a shattering result for the Party in the 1970 General Election. The comedians of the day would quip that you could get all the Liberal MPs in a taxi or a phone box. The Outsider, then director of *Shelter*, recalled having a meeting with David Steel at the House of Commons on the opening day, and then driving him to Eastbourne, Steel to participate in the Assembly, the Outsider to speak at a fringe meeting. At one point, as he took a corner at speed, Steel had protested, 'Careful, you've got a sixth of the Parliamentary Liberal Party in this car.'

The Community Politics resolution, moved by Tony Greaves, the iconoclastic northerner, driving force for many years of the Association of Liberal Councillors, (ALC), and scourge of the Party leadership, marked the emergence towards the end of the idealistic '60s of a fresh generation of Liberals committed to winning power from the grassroots upwards and to building links with radicals working in the kind of pressure groups The Outsider was involved in.

Much had happened to the Outsider in the intervening sixteen years. In 1970 he was still a member, albeit disenchanted, of the Labour Party. It had been hard being a member of the Labour Party when you discovered you weren't a socialist. So he had increasingly been directing his energies to voluntary action, initially with Shelter. Shortly after that Eastbourne Assembly in 1970 he concluded nearly five years with the housing campaign and returned to his trade of journalism. In 1973 he joined the Liberal Party, and was almost immediately thrown into a by-election as Liberal candidate for Hove. He lost on the same day that Alan Beith won Berwick-on-Tweed. After contesting the seat a second time in the general election of February 1974, he concentrated on his career for a number of years until a fresh impatience to act, rather than report the actions of others, coincided with a call from the environmental movement, first with the CLEAR campaign on lead pollution, and then as chairman of *Friends of the Earth*. Environmental protection, he found, was more often than not obstructed by secrecy; so in 1984 he launched the Campaign for Freedom of Information. Thus, while a Liberal now for many years, he had exercised his liberalism largely beyond the frontiers of the party.

But, like the party itself, he too owed much to Eastbourne, for it is questionable whether he would have become a party member were it not for that 1970 decision and the way the party subsequently developed on twin tracks, one maintaining a radical presence at the centre of British politics, and the other developing a fresh and practical approach to politics at the grass roots.

Undoubtedly had anyone told the Outsider and his passenger on that September day in 1970 that in 1986 they would sit side by side at a Liberal Assembly, one as President-Elect, and the other celebrating his tenth year as Leader, they would no doubt have called for men in white coats! But that was what lay twenty-four hours ahead as he now put aside these memories, booked into the Queen's, the headquarters hotel, registered as a delegate, and then strolled round to the Congress Theatre where on Monday afternoon he would deliver what would, in effect, be the Assembly keynote speech. For a few minutes he stood on the platform, drew comfort from the protective solidity of the lectern, tested the microphone, and took in the awe-inspiring proportions of the hall, with its three tiers and 1,700 seats, deserted, apart from a few radio and television technicians perfecting the sound and the lighting.

Then to the press room, already, even on this Sunday afternoon, filling up with some of the 500 journalists and technicians who would cover the Assembly. There were rows of tables, typewriters, telephones, the computer technology of the Wapping newspapers contrasting with the battered typewriters of the *Guardian*. There were television monitors to relay the proceedings from the conference hall to the press room. And there was a separate little theatre for press conferences, where he now joined the team who would field questions at the eve-of-Assembly press conference in half an hour's time – the Assembly chairman, Roger Hayes, a tall, laconic Councillor from Kingston-upon-Thames; the Party's recently appointed Secretary-General, Andy Ellis; the retiring President, the Cornish MP, David Penhaligon; and Chief Whip in the House of Commons, the Liverpool MP, David Alton.

They decided to open the press conference by stressing that the Assembly would be the launching pad for the Liberal election campaign. They would claim the Party was in good shape – that since the 1983 General Election it had made 181 net gains in council by-elections, scored 37.2% of the votes compared with 33.7% for the Tories and 29.7% for Labour at parliamentary by-elections, and that its present showing in the opinion polls was a satisfactory lift-off point.

So, at 5.30, the press conference took place. The room was packed, the journalists listening patiently if somewhat sceptically to Roger Hayes spell out this positive message. But it was obvious they saw no news in this. So all the questions were about the defence debate to take place on the Tuesday: would the party endorse the leader's position? The panel played what in cricket would be described as a straight bat ... 'no problems expected'.

Yet the press conference theme had not been contrived. It *was* the plan not only to use the Assembly to launch the election campaign to the country, but also to gear up the party itself, and the first step was a meeting of the General Election Committee in a small room in the Queen's Hotel that evening. Paul Tyler, who was to work more closely with David Steel, was retiring as chairman and it was now decided that The Outsider should replace him. The group – Tyler, Lord (Geoff) Tordoff, Phil Harris, Tim Clement-Jones, John Piggott, and Andy Ellis – plotted the use of fringe meetings during the week to alert the party to the need to prepare, and to brief it on plans. The Outsider, it was decided, would address candidates the following day, and there would be a fringe meeting for General Election planning on Wednesday.

From there the group went to a full meeting of the National Executive in a larger room at the Queen's where its decisions were confirmed.

By now the headquarters was packed. Flustered bar staff were desperately raiding each other's stocks to meet a demand they clearly had not anticipated. The hotel reception and delegate registration desks were still surrounded by Liberals arriving from more distant constituencies, from Scotland and the North or from the west of Wales. And the fringe meetings continued. Bermondsey MP, Simon Hughes, who probably speaks at more fringe meetings than anyone else, was addressing the Victoria Suite on 'Rethinking Childcare'. Alex Carlile, the Party's Home Affairs Spokesman in the Commons, was at the Sandhurst Hotel, talking about the 'Penal crisis and criminal justice'. The Queen's suite of the headquarters hotel was over-flowing with first-time delegates attending their own traditional eve-of-Assembly reception.

The Outsider had had enough of meetings and now went to his final engagement of the evening, dinner with David Penhaligon, who tomorrow would introduce him to the Assembly. David was accompanied by his wife Annette, and the three were joined by the SDP President, Shirley Williams.

By the time they returned to the lounge at around 11 o'clock the fringe meetings were at last over, and the reunion was well under way.

It was, someone was later to recall, like the launching party for the *Titanic* – everyone in high spirits, a sense of history in the making, yet no one anticipating the calamitous way the story would end.

The Outsider fought his way past the happy crowd to the stairway. He had decided to call it a day.

Monday

On Monday the sun still shone and Eastbourne looked just like a seaside town should look. After an appearance on BBC Television's *Breakfast Time*, he had breakfast with Andy Ellis.

The nineteen-stone Secretary-General of the party had packed more electioneering experience into his thirty-four years than almost anyone else in British politics. He had become involved in the Liberal Party while at Cambridge in the late Sixties, befriending Colin Rosential, now Liberal leader on Cambridge City Council, who shared the Ellis passion for politics and the railways. As a boy Ellis was a train spotter and to this day was a walking British Rail timetable, able to tell you exactly how to travel from A to B anywhere on the network. 'My knowledge is a bit more sketchy outside the UK,' he had been known to confess to astonished recipients of his off-the-cuff guidance on how to travel from Maidstone to Penrith including the changes and a rough idea of the waiting time at each station.

Ellis read mathematics at Cambridge, his feel for figures proving invaluable for interpreting canvassing returns later on. He also became involved in student politics as chairman of ULS (Union of Liberal Students), hitch-hiking relentlessly up and down the A1 and around the country, spending many nocturnal hours thumbing lifts at roundabouts, all in the cause of promoting Liberalism at universities. He was also a key member of the community politics movement.

He then attended the hardest of all political schools, local politics in Newcastle upon Tyne, where with an old printing machine and a second hand duplicator he set himself up as *A ELLIS: Typing and Duplication Services*, a low cost and, it has to be said, low income operation he maintained for a number of years while fighting Labour for council seats. In 1974 he was the agent for Newcastle North in the General Election, and in the second election of that year was the candidate for Newcastle Central.

The reputation that he was to build as Britain's supreme by-election organiser had its lift-off point in Newcastle in 1976 when Ted Short resigned his seat. The Liberals were at a low ebb, just 6% in the opinion polls at the time, but just the same the stock of the Labour Party in the north-east was such that they took no risks, fixing the by-election for only twenty-two days after Short resigned. In a campaign run from his little printing works Ellis achieved a 19.5% swing away from Labour and came only 1,800 votes short of a spectacular win.

He was elected onto the County Council in 1977, leading a team of four on a council of over 100. Ellis then, as now, saw the Liberals as *the* radical voice in local politics. He attacked Labour (of the T Dan Smith era and afterwards) as 'a right wing, centralist, uncaring organisation, interested only in power'.

It was really in 1981 with the arrival on the scene of the Social Democratic Party and the famous by-elections involving Roy

Jenkins at Warrington and Glasgow Hillhead and Shirley Williams at Crosby that what had always been diverting political sideshows became major political events with all three parties moving in huge resources. By-elections were of particular importance to the Liberal Party, and more recently to the Alliance, because every success added to their momentum, reminded the public that there was a third force that was capable of winning on a larger scale, and achieved for the Liberals and latterly the Alliance publicity that until close to the '87 Election it was not given in the day-to-day political coverage from Westminster. On the basis of the Newcastle result, Ellis was chosen by the Liberal Party as its By-elections Officer, and now began a ten year 'career' as by-election specialist. Wherever one took place, Ellis was there, either Liberal liaison man if it was a Social Democratic by-election, or campaign manager if it was a Liberal one. He was in Bermondsey when Simon Hughes won. Perhaps his most remarkable result was in Brecon and Radnor where two or three days beforehand he predicted the result down to a handful of votes. He also masterminded the two by-elections that on the same day in 1986 led to the election of the only Liberal woman MP, Elizabeth Shields, in Ryedale, and saw Chris Walmsley fall just 100 votes short in West Derbyshire.

Over those years he won the unstinting admiration of the party and the political commentators, not least for his skills in interpreting canvass returns and predicting the actual results. If Ellis said it could be won, it could be won. If Ellis looked pessimistic, you knew the news was really bad.

Ellis was that unusual combination, a politician who cared about the broad principles but who was also happy to be buried in the detail. He virtually re-wrote the Liberal Party constitution, and was deeply involved in the lengthy negotiations between the Liberal Party and the SDP on the allocation of seats each would contest at the General Election. Now in 1986 he had moved from Vice-Chairman of the Party to be its professional Secretary-General and was deeply involved in building up a regional structure to strengthen the Party's campaigning in every part of the country.

Tall and heavy (he, in fact, lost over three stones fighting the 1986 by-elections and looked a lot healthier as a result), Ellis had become a familiar and popular figure at every party event. His activities may have led to a developing political reputation, but they had not made him any money, hence his reputation too for sartorial eccentricity – the subject of many a good-natured joke in Assembly satirical reviews.

The Outsider and Ellis worked well together and on the rather nervy morning of the former's big speech it was natural for him to want to start the day by chatting to Ellis over bacon and eggs (and in the case of the latter, sausages and sauté potatoes and toast and whatever else he could pile onto his plate, for the Ellis physique owed not a little to the Ellis appetite).

The Outsider had decided not to look at his speech any more before he delivered it. He had spent weeks mulling over its contents, trying out different drafts, testing them on friends, and he was now committed. He wanted to come to it fresh.

Some weeks earlier he had decided on his themes: He knew it would be his first appearance as chairman of the General Election Committee, and decided there needed to be a powerful political opening, an attack on the other parties of some originality, and an affirmation of the radicalism of the Alliance. He decided to condemn the other parties together rather than separately, as those who had shared power – 'the unholy alliance of the past'.

He would then stress that the Alliance was concerned not just to gain power but to change the nature of the political system itself. He would condemn the double standards and self-service of the old party politicians, and then spell out Alliance plans for giving power to people.

He would remind his audience of his links with community action and the pressure group movement, and spell out some of the lessons for the Alliance from that experience.

And he would define the Alliance as the party that was aware of the close proximity of the 21st century and the need to look ahead to its problems and possibilities.

The speech in his pocket, he joined Jane, his wife, and some old friends for lunch.

In the meantime, David Steel was arriving at the hotel and, after taking possession of his suite on the second floor, was holding the traditional first-day meeting with his colleagues in the Parliamentary Party. Elsewhere the Assembly Committee was considering the resolutions and amendments for the defence debate to come on the Tuesday. It was at this point that the circumstances were created for the disaster that was to occur.

The two meetings should never have taken place at the same time. Ideally, the Leader and Parliamentary Party should have been represented at the Assembly Committee, as they were entitled to be, by both the President, Penhaligon, and the Chief Whip, Alton. At least one of these powerful figures should have been there with a brief to persuade the Assembly Committee to produce amendments to the defence resolution that would fairly express any party reservations without being seen as a major rebuff to the leadership or an act of disunity with its Alliance partners. Instead, the Assembly Committee were left to their own devices. One member, Gordon Lishman, was to recall 'whatever it believed it was doing at that meeting, it had not been lobbied. It did not have representatives there from any section, including the parliamentary party, who were briefed to argue a case. There were no battle lines drawn at that point. And there was little political content to the debate about what amendment to take. There were, of course, some underlying individual preferences, but basically the decision was 90% management and 10% politics.'

So, while the MPs were meeting elsewhere and, by neglect of their rights to representation, were denying themselves any involvement, the Assembly Committee chose two amendments. One of them was to turn what was on that Monday such a happy Assembly into one of the most unhappy in memory.

But more, much more of all this later, for the Assembly *was* in happy, even exuberant, mood as it gathered at 2 o'clock to be welcomed by David Penhaligon, its retiring President. Robin Day, the veteran BBC commentator, commented to viewers on the light-hearted, almost festive spirit compared with the SDP conference the previous week.

The Outsider made his speech and was content. He had said what he wanted to say and it had been satisfactorily received.

Now it was the turn of David Owen.

And now, too, it is time to reflect on the background to his speech and all that was to come this week – above all, on the difficulty the Alliance had experienced in reaching accord on defence policy and, in particular, whether or not when Polaris became obsolete in the 1990s, it should be replaced.

To this issue David Owen and the Liberal Party had come from different directions.

Contrary to repeated misrepresentation, the Liberal Party had never adopted what is known as the 'unilateralist position' but Assemblies over many years had passed resolutions pressing for steps to reduce the dependence of the super powers on nuclear weapons, and for a policy (negotiated within NATO) that did not involve Britain having its own nuclear deterrent.

In 1960 the Assembly reaffirmed its belief that attempts by Great Britain to become an independent nuclear power 'do not contribute to the maintenance of world peace, do not add to Britain's own security . . . therefore, calls upon Her Majesty's Government to cease forthwith any further independent manufacture of nuclear weapons . . .'

Even earlier that year, in February, Liberal MPS tabled an amendment to a defence motion in the House of Commons calling on the government 'to abandon its policy of attempting to create an independent nuclear deterrent'.

In 1961 the Assembly called on governments to cease nuclear tests forthwith, and on the governments of Britain and France to renounce all future tests. In 1964 it re-affirmed its belief that British policy should be based on the promotion of measures of disarmament and arms control. In 1979 Party Council declared its opposition to the stationing of Cruise missiles in the UK. In 1980 Assembly 'reaffirms its total opposition to an independent British strategic nuclear deterrent and the purchase of Trident missiles; it condemns successive Labour and Conservative governments for spending vast sums on the modernisation of Polaris without Parliamentary authority . . .' In 1981 Assembly reaffirmed its opposition to the deployment of Cruise missiles and 'commits the Liberal Party, as a first step, to reject and campaign against the siting of Cruise missiles in Britain'. In 1983 the Party Council called upon the government 'to take the initiative in proposing that the USA and USSR in Geneva negotiate a mutual and verifiable freeze on the manufacture and deployment of all nuclear weapons to be followed by progressive and agreed reductions in existing stockpiles'.

Then in 1984 came a now famous Assembly debate on a resolution entitled 'Uniting for Peace'. This reaffirmed 'the Liberal
Party's opposition to the maintenance of an independent British
nuclear deterrent' and committed the Party to a step by step
process of disarmament which included cancelling Trident
forthwith, including Polaris in arms control negotiations, and
the removal of Cruise missiles from British soil. It was in this
debate that David Steel took on the radical left of the Party and
lost. There were two points at issue – whether Polaris should be
retained but put into any disarmament negotiations, and whether
Cruise missiles should be sent back from whence they came.
Steel won on the first point, but lost on the second. During the
debate Paddy Ashdown made a brilliant and probably decisive
speech opposing the retention of Cruise missiles. The Outsider
spoke a few minutes before Steel, arguing that the party should
hold its existing line on rejection of Cruise. Just because Thatcher
had allowed them to come was no reason why they should be
allowed to stay. Steel went down onto the floor to argue passionately for including them in arms negotiation talks now that
they were here, but he was narrowly defeated.

The party was by no means completely in tune with CND, but
its abhorrence of nuclear weapons and its preference for a non-
nuclear Britain had been consistently re-stated over the years
and was forcibly re-affirmed at Bournemouth.

David Owen, on the other hand, was aggressively multilateralist. A former Foreign Secretary, he had departed the Labour
Party partly because of its inclinations to unilateralism. He firmly
believed that Britain's possession of nuclear weapons made it
safer especially while there was an inbalance in conventional
forces. He also believed that if Britain lost its nuclear status it
would lose its status in the world generally. And he took that
status seriously – his critics would say he took it too seriously.
Owen had never been in any doubt that unless circumstances
changed radically, we would need eventually to modernise and
then replace Polaris. Not only did he hold these firm beliefs, but
he actually took pleasure in discussing the various nuclear
alternatives, often insensitive to the fact that when you talk with
evident interest about weapons you can easily sound to others as
if you would actually like to use them.

There was, therefore, always likely to be real difficulty between the Owen-led SDP and the Liberal Party on this issue. Bournemouth did not help. But even before that 1984 Assembly, Owen and Steel had decided to set up a Commission to try to resolve the differences in defence between the two parties. Its brief was 'to examine British defence and disarmament policy in the context of Britain's membership of the NATO and the European Community, and to make recommendations in time for consideration by our respective parties at their annual conferences in 1986'.

They chose as chairman John Edmonds, not a member of either party, but a former Foreign Office man with a record of high-level involvement in defence matters, including being the Head of the Arms Control and Disarmament Department for three years, and Leader of the UK delegation to the Comprehensive Test Ban Treaty Negotiations in Geneva for another three years. Another non-party member was General Sir Hugh Beach. The party members were carefully chosen to represent the spectrum of positions within the two parties. For the Liberals, Paddy Ashdown and Brian May, two of the Bournemouth victors in the Cruise missile debate, were balanced by Christopher Mayhew and Laura Grimond, both firm multilateralists. Richard Holme was there – inevitably – and, once he became the party's defence spokesman, so was the successor to Jo Grimond as MP for Orkney and Shetlands, Jim Wallace. The SDP team was led by their defence spokesman, John Cartwright, and included Bill Rodgers, a former Labour Minister.

Liberal radicals, concerned that there appeared to be no democratic formula for determining Alliance policy, were deeply suspicious of the Commission. Its members had been chosen by the Leaders; was it not, therefore, just a device to manipulate the Parties into acceptance of their line? Why could not a similar exercise be conducted by the two democratically-elected Policy Committees?

Yet there was sense in the Commission. It *was* well-balanced, and it did create the opportunity to draw in outside expertise. Of greater importance to Liberal doubters, there were rumours that the Commission was leaning more towards Liberal inclinations than those of David Owen. Liberals were being advised 'don't knock the Commission ... it's looking promising'.

And so it was. Within the Commission a consensus was developing around a range of views, notably:

- There should be a stronger European pillar within NATO, intended to achieve a better balance of power between Europe and the US on defence responsibilities.

- NATO should develop policies that would be obviously defensive, based on the concept of minimum deterrence, and with greater reliance on conventional forces. NATO's military commanders in Europe should plan on the basis that nuclear forces should not be used and would not be needed.

- In addition to a comprehensive review of Britain's defence priorities, in order to deploy capabilities and resources properly, there should be a wider European review, intended to achieve more effective combined use of European forces, reserves and equipment and closer cooperation in the research and production of new equipment.

- Trident should be abandoned.

- Britain should resume a more positive and active role in the process of arms control and disarmament, including working for such measures as:
  (a) Deep cuts in both Soviet and US nuclear weapons stockpiles
  (b) The inclusion of British nuclear weapons in nuclear arms control negotiations
  (c) A moratorium, while the talks on these cuts took place, on new deployment. 'Britain and her allies should be studying the freeze concept including appropriate verification'
  (d) Strengthening of the anti-ballistic missile treaty
  (e) Pressure for an agreement to halt the deployment of intermediate nuclear missiles and to eliminate missiles already deployed by both sides. Pending negotiation of this agreement, Britain would take the initiative for a limited term moratorium on further deployment by the West. (This meant no more Cruise missiles for Britain)
  (f) A withdrawal of battlefield nuclear weapons from the zone extending 150 km from the east-west divide in Europe

(g) Promotion of an agreement on neutral and balanced force reductions in Europe

(h) No support for President Reagan's Strategic Defence Initiative (STAR WARS)

All of this was welcome to Steel as an attractive proposition to put to his own Party, and much of it was not too difficult for Owen to accept, although he disliked the word 'freeze', believing the concept to be unrealistic. How could you achieve consensus on what constituted a balance at any one time? How could the Americans be asked to accept a freeze when they perceived themselves to be in an inferior position?

But the real crunch was Polaris. The rumours (subsequently proved to be correct) were that the Commission had concluded that no decision need be taken now on whether or not Polaris should be replaced. It would support the maintenance of Polaris as a European deterrent for the next decade – well beyond the end of the next Parliament – but saw no reason why anyone should decide about replacing Polaris until they saw what happened in arms control and disarmament talks, in the developing relationship within NATO between Europe and the United States, and in the range and costs of the technical options for a European minimum deterrent, and until they could better assess the changing views of European allies about whether European defence required a new British nuclear capability.

Even to the committed multilateralists on the Commission, like Mayhew, this made sense. So it did to Steel.

To Owen it sounded like a fudge.

Still, it was possible that after Owen and Steel had received the report of the Commission and had the opportunity to discuss it with its members, that Owen could have been persuaded that this was a reasonable compromise, and that the Defence Commission proposals as a whole represented a viable defence policy for the next General Election. Then in early May reports started to appear in newspapers that the Liberals had 'won' on the Defence Commission. An article in *The Scotsman* shortly after David Steel had given an informal interview to its Political Editor appeared to confirm the rumours. In a fateful decision, partly in anger at these reports, Owen concluded that this part of the

Commission's Report would have to be torpedoed before its publication. On May 17 at the SDP 'Council for Social Democracy' he did just that.

On whether or not Britain should remain a nuclear weapons state – i.e. modernise or replace Polaris – he made it clear that 'this is the question on which we will need to make up our minds *before the next election*'. No leader of any political party could stand before the British electorate and refuse to answer the question. The others were clear – Mrs Thatcher believed in Trident; Mr Kinnock would cancel Trident, decommission Polaris and disown Britain's nuclear deterrent. The Alliance must be clear too.

'I must tell you bluntly that I believe we should remain a nuclear weapons state. If we are to carry conviction in our decision to cancel Trident after an election, we ought to be prepared to say that we will find a replacement for Polaris, unless there has been such a massive reduction in nuclear warheads on the part of the Soviet Union and United States that we would feel it right in negotiations to give up our nuclear weapons.'

He hammered home the point (and at the same time he hammered the Commission):

'Certainly you should know quite clearly that I definitely do not believe that I would carry any conviction whatever in the next election were I to answer – on your behalf – on the question of the replacement of Polaris, that that would have to depend on the circumstances of the time. That would get and deserve a belly laugh from the British electorate. That sort of fudging and mudging is what I left behind in the Labour Party. The electorate are entitled, at the very least, to know whether we will take steps to share the costs and responsibilities of a European contribution to defence when Polaris comes to the end of its life. That decision, and the decision to keep that option, will have to be taken during our five year period of government. There are no ifs and buts about this issue. My message is clear. Conviction politics must not become a monopoly of Mrs Thatcher. The SDP was founded on convictions, better than the convictions of Mrs Thatcher – and we should not be ashamed of them or run away from them.'

Given all that was to follow that summer, and what was to follow at the Eastbourne Assembly, it should be stressed that *it was at this point and as a result of this speech that the Alliance split on defence.* Furthermore, it was not a split between Liberals and Social Democrats, it was a split between those in both parties who shared either the Commission view or the Owen view.

All hell now broke loose.

Bill Rodgers, one of the SDP's founding Gang of Four, and a major contributor to the Commission, wrote an article for *The Times* flatly contradicting Owen's speech:

'When the Polaris missile system comes to the end of its life in the late 1990s, should it be replaced? This is not a question of principle and ought not to be a test of political virility. It is a matter of cost and opportunity — set against the changing international scene.' He continued that the decision should be taken only in the light of a thorough and up-to-date review of alternatives and the international situation. 'It is surely sensible to postpone a final decision on Polaris replacement while these matters remain in the balance. This is not a fudge. There's no deceit or humbug in admitting an open mind until a review has been completed. The real fudge is to say unequivocally that Trident should be cancelled but that Britain should remain a nuclear weapons state.'

As a final crack at Owen he concluded: 'Certainty is not always a virtue. Nor is conviction itself evidence of truth. The Commission's report is not an exercise in evasion and compromise. It sets out a credible policy that both Social Democrats and Liberals should support.'

In the meantime, Shirley Williams, another of the four SDP founders, was voicing her fury at Owen's initiative. 'It does not follow that what the Leader said is the same and identical with the policy of the party,' she said in a radio interview. 'The present policy of the SDP is that the party is willing to replace Polaris under certain circumstances but not irrevocably doing so.'

Two SDP Commission members, John Cartwright and James Wellbeloved, attending the last meeting before publication of the report, insisted on the addition of an introductory letter of explanation from the Chairman. When the report was published on June 5, Edmonds' introduction duly stated: 'Since we completed our work, there has been a lot of misleading speculation about the report's conclusions. As a result, certain members of the

Commission wish it to be made clear that in their view Britain should in present circumstances remain a nuclear weapons state and that they are willing to replace Polaris. Some other members believe that present circumstances do not justify the replacement of Polaris. I must stress, however, that all members agree that a decision on whether, and if so how, to replace Polaris should be made on the basis of the criteria we have set out.'

And so the report was published on June 5. It contained only one note of dissent, by Brian May, of Chelsea Liberal Party, a retired civil servant who now spends most of his time at his main home near Brussels, and who is the author of *Russia, America, the bomb and the fall of the Western Europe*. May concurred with most of the report, but dissented from its attitudes to the United States and to the Soviet Union. It missed, he wrote, a rare opportunity to put itself in the vanguard of an identifiable historical movement – namely the 'slow divorce' taking place between the United States and Western Europe. It was, in a nutshell, too pro-American. He also could not accept the report's perception that the Soviet Union was expansionist while the West was only engaged in mutually beneficial cooperation. It was, also in a nutshell, too anti-Russian.

If David Owen had chosen this moment to express his reservations, he could have been open to counter-argument, but not to criticism that he had acted destructively. He was just as entitled as anyone else to comment on the report, maybe more entitled. But, because of his pre-emptive strike at the Polaris section, the report stood no chance of achieving the two Leaders' objective – namely to reconcile different views on nuclear defence. It was even more damaging than that; it unveiled considerable differences of opinion within the SDP leadership about their responsibilities in coalition with another party, and it fed the distrust of many Liberals about Owen's reliability as a partner.

As John Lewis wrote in the *Sunday Telegraph*: 'The issue far transcends differences over whether Britain should replace Polaris . . . with a bitterness not present before, Dr Owen is being accused by the Liberals – and some leading members of the SDP – of undermining the whole principle of coalition on which the Alliance fights.

'Mrs Shirley Williams, Mr Bill Rodgers, and Mr Roy Jenkins,

are all highly critical of the way in which Dr Owen appears to have pre-empted the report . . .'

Hugo Young, writing in the *Guardian*, also put the defence row in the context of the Alliance and coalition politics.

'Dr Owen's private discourse these days never fails to expound on the virtues of coalition . . . his election strategy rests squarely on the promise of give and take (yet) a splendid but destructive row now impends, which could, at its worst, leave the Alliance looking as erratic and non-credible in 1988 as Labour did in 1983.

'This, if it happens, will have come about because of Dr Owen's overbearing determination to be seen as a conviction politician. A true coalitionist would find a way of moderating his convictions, especially when these are shared by few Social Democrats, and where a defensible modification has been presented on a plate. . . . quite why an avowed coalitionist should insist on (conviction politics) is probably to be explained by reference to psychology rather than political calculation. But as a result, an explosive device is about to be detonated.'

David Steel was appalled. Temperamentally the opposite of Owen, a striver for consensus whose convictions tended to be on the broadest thrust of policy rather than on specifics, Steel had been impressed by the Commission report and would have enthusiastically welcomed it. Now he had to tell Owen that he believed the SDP leader's pre-publication activities had been disastrous. In particular, he rejected out of hand the suggestion by Owen that the two parties could, if necessary, contest the election as an Alliance whilst conceding that they differed on defence. In an interview with Brian Walden on *Weekend World*, he said, 'he (Owen) is right to say it is not the end of the world if that happens, but in my view it is pretty close to it. I don't think we can go into an election with one set of candidates saying one thing and another set saying the other. We are duty-bound to debate this report in manner which will reach a common conclusion before the election manifesto is completed.'

He went on to say that 'if we can't agree before we get into government, how can we agree when we are in government? That is what the electorate will want to know'.

Speaking the following weekend at a meeting of the Liberal

Party Council in Wigan which soundly defeated a Liberal CND move to rubbish the Commission report, Steel was even more cutting: 'In his first Conference speech as SDP Leader, David Owen invited people to tell him when he was talking nonsense. On defence matters I would never say that, but there is one question on which I felt bound to take up his invitation. The suggestion that we could live with SDP and Liberal candidates saying different things at the next election on defence is profoundly misplaced ... to be blunt, to have Liberal candidates saying one thing and SDP another would be unacceptable to me, and incredible for the electorate.'

He continued that the Alliance was a 'partnership which requires not surrender of principles but careful analysis of and respect for each other's wishes in the compilation of a solid and sound policy platform on which we can both stand with trust and confidence.

'I know that he was annoyed at press reports before publication. He had every reason to be. There is no reason for party triumphalism in our Alliance. But as I have pointed out to him from rather longer experience of the bed of nails which party leadership sometimes is, we must both expect to be angered by many press reports we don't like before we get to polling day at the next election. Precisely because we are two parties, we are obliged to continue — paradoxically — to have a closer unity between us than exists with either the Tory or Labour Parties.'

The media coverage, but perhaps more so the divisions within his own Party, and in particular his estrangement from the other members of the Gang of Four, must have led Owen to wish that he had handled the Commission's report in a different way. He and Steel now set about trying to recover the ground, their strategy being a European tour, calculated to both produce a lot of impressive television pictures over the summer, and at the same time enable them to show evidence at their party conferences in the autumn that there was European support for the thrust of their proposals — the strengthening of the European pillar of NATO, and a possible European deterrent strategy. As Steel had said at Wigan, 'I do not believe there is any future for us in competing with Mrs Thatcher in brandishing a British bomb in perpetuity, whatever else is happening in the world. A planned pooling of our resources with our neighbours is a far more attractive proposition.'

While the two Leaders were travelling in Europe, the two parties had to prepare resolutions for their respective conferences. The Joint Strategy Committee encouraged by Steel and Owen, had decided to promote similar resolutions for both gatherings, welcoming the Commission's report as a critical *contribution* to defence policy. Because the resolutions would not *finalise* defence policy and because it was assumed there was likely to be support for the broad thrust of the Commission report, it was hoped that these resolutions would produce lively defence debates but at the same time an appearance of unity between the Harrogate and Eastbourne conferences. (It is worth noting that a problem for the Liberal Party has been that the SDP conference always takes place first, and Liberals feel themselves to be put in a position where they either approve policy consistent with that of the SDP, or open themselves to the charge of 'wrecking the Alliance'.)

In welcoming the Commission report, the SDP resolution at Harrogate called for a 'full investigation of the practicality of a European minimum deterrent'. But a small shift at the SDP conference which was perhaps not adequately signalled to Liberals was caused by an amendment to the resolution; instead of the Torquay defence policy of the SDP being 'reaffirmed', it was recognised as the 'basis' of SDP policy. Its mover, Ben Stoneham, pointed out that simple reaffirmation of the policy would be an open invitation to the Liberal Party to reaffirm all its previous policies. By amending the resolution in this way, the SDP would create the flexibility for a solution within the Alliance and avoid the impasse which would otherwise annihilate them. Thus, as Geoffrey Smith, *The Times* columnist, wrote the following day, the signal flashed to Owen from his party was 'green tinged with amber'.

Smith commented on the proposal of the European minimum deterrent. 'The whole tone of the defence debate within the Alliance has been transformed by introducing a new phrase into the discourse ... no longer is it acceptable in polite Alliance society to speak of a British national deterrent. It is a minimum European deterrent that is now under discussion.' As a political device this was a 'brilliant idea to serve a political purpose', but would the trick work with the Liberals? 'The trick has certainly worked with David Steel, but that may be simply because he wants it to work. His concern is, above all, to find the basis for agreeing with the SDP, so that the Alliance can fight the election on a united programme.'

So the scene had been set for Eastbourne. Or had it?

Over the summer Steel had concentrated on persuading David Owen to 'cool it', and on finding common ground not so much between Owen and the Liberal Party, as between Owen and the Defence Commission. There had been two assumptions: first, that the Defence Commission was sufficiently acceptable to Liberals to produce a clear majority at Eastbourne on the lines of the resolution passed by the Social Democrats (and were it not for the suspicions engendered by Owen, it probably would have); second, that the publication of the Commission report had moved the debate from specifically Social Democrat or Liberal policy to Alliance policy. On this latter point Steel and a number of leading Liberal radicals, including some of his parliamentary colleagues, held an entirely different view and one that Steel had unfortunately not comprehended. Steel had increasingly come to act and think like a joint Alliance Leader rather than a Liberal Leader. For instance, when the Joint Strategy Committee, consisting of twelve senior members of each party, was set up, it was initially the practice for the Liberal team to meet for thirty minutes beforehand to discuss the agenda. Steel had cancelled the meetings, arguing, as he did later this week at Eastbourne, that 'we are either an Alliance or we are not'. To Steel, a gathering of the two policy committees was in fact one gathering to determine one policy. To many Liberals, and to many Social Democrats, probably including Owen, it was an on-going negotiating process from two clear positions.

Steel wanted the Liberal Assembly to pass what was effectively an *Alliance* resolution – just as he believed the Social Democrats had done beforehand.

But many Liberals saw Eastbourne as a last chance to establish a powerful *Liberal* position for the final negotiations with the SDP on the joint policy programme, 'Partnership for Progress'.

This basic difference of interpretation of the purpose of the defence debate at Eastbourne was, second only to Owen's miscalculation in rubbishing the Commission report in advance, the fundamental cause of the problems that were to follow.

Thus it was, that Simon Hughes, Archy Kirkwood, and Michael Meadowcroft, signed a report, *Across the Divide*, published on the eve of the Assembly that began from the position that 'the Liberal Party must make a strong, Liberal contribution to the debate within the Alliance. We should not be reluctant to make that contribution. To do so is not to be divisive. It is to recognise that a strong Alliance cannot be built upon a compromise which is the lowest common denominator between two weak positions, but, rather, requires a combination of two strong parties to argue and agree on the best points of two clear sets of policy.' According to the three MPs 'we as Liberals need to be clear amongst ourselves before we can reach agreement with our allies'.

Thus there were two conflicting positions, each revealing the nature of the protagonist. Steel hoped, perhaps even believed, that the Liberal contributors to joint policy discussions would be approaching the issues almost afresh – definitely not as defenders of a party line. This was hardly surprising, for Steel was, in any case, no respector of Liberal defence policy (having suffered Assembly rebuffs on the issue more than once), and his mind was also now concentrated on the General Election campaign. He had one over-riding concern – to end the internal debate and concentrate everyone's mind on campaigning for votes. In mountaineering terms, it was almost as if Steel was setting off on the final assault on the summit, while the three MPs, and many others in the Liberal Party, deeply concerned to promote specifically Liberal values within the Alliance, were still establishing the base camp – namely the policy that would unite the parties for that assault.

(There was later to be bitter recrimination that the three MPs had not properly advised David Steel of their plans, or given him a chance to dissuade them from publication of *Across the Divide*. In fact, they had asked Archy Kirkwood to have a word with Steel in Ettrick Bridge (they are neighbours) but Kirkwood's wife had been taken to hospital on the critical weekend and it had slipped his mind. It was, they claim, 'a cock-up, not a conspiracy').

This, then, was the background to the not unfriendly and yet reserved welcome the Leader of the Social Democratic Party, the Right Honourable David Owen, received when he rose to speak at Eastbourne that sunny Monday afternoon.

It was a clever speech, and typically Owen. He had been advised to avoid the defence issue in order not to be provocative; in fact he devoted nearly thirty minutes to the subject. You could put it down to arrogance, except that it was at least in part calculated to cater to Liberal sensitivities. Perhaps he had listened to Shirley Williams' Harrogate speech the week before, because his theme was less the need for defence, and more the need to balance defence policies with initiatives on arms control. 'It is the balance between the two which is fundamental.'

He went on: 'If our European partners see us firm and clear and committed to our defence posture, then they will listen to us on our disarmament posture. Then the British government's position in NATO will have weight and clout, and on many occasions carry the day. But if they see arms control and disarmament is just put up front to cover a lack of determination, and lack of resolve on conventional arms, or our nuclear deterrent, or commitment to NATO, we will not count for much and our voice will not carry weight.'

He then launched into a lengthy and intricate lecture on the international negotiations taking place. As *The Times* was to say in a leader the following day: 'some of his hearers will have doubtless found it irritating. It certainly had elements of the pre-examination revision class where the teacher's only interest is in the scholarship boys.'

From the platform you could see the Assembly struggling to maintain attention. Some looked bored; some undoubtedly did look irritated; but many listened intently. It was masterly in the sense that it was a speech deliberately intended to lower the temperature, to demonstrate knowledge, to intimidate opponents (unless, they too, knew their stuff) , and yet with its emphasis on disarmament to counter the impression of Owen as a man never happier than when talking about the relative destructive capabilities of weapons. But it also had the virtue of taking its audience seriously – OK, you want to talk about defence, then let's really talk about defence!

It was a speech delivered without notes. It was, as always

with Owen, not intended to ingratiate but rather to impress. It was a success in those terms. And a small number who had planned, if they felt it necessary, to storm out, were left bewildered in their seats.

So the opening session was over, and the Assembly moved on to reaffirm Liberal concern for the Third World, and then to discuss worker involvement in British industry. And then to tea. To a walk in the sun. To drinks. And to chat.

The Monday evening meeting of Parliamentary candidates tends to be the one fringe meeting that David Steel addresses during the Assembly week, and the Outsider was due to speak with him, Steel on defence, and the Outsider to launch himself as chairman of the General Election Committee. Steel's speech had been telegraphed as a clarification of his position before the Tuesday debate on defence. Thus the room was uncomfortably packed, not just with candidates, but with media, and the Party Leader and his fellow speaker sweated together under the television lights.

Steel argued for the pooling of resources in a proper European defence community. 'I want to assert that the Liberal Party has a wholly proud record of logical and coherent argument on defence. In the 1950s we sought to restrict nuclear military capacity to the two super powers. We did not succeed. The British government disagreed and sought independent nuclear status. So did the French. The Party faced up to these unwelcome developments by deciding in 1984 not unilaterally to abandon the Polaris deterrent, but to use it to help multilateral negotiations. However, we now face the prospect that we might abandon our deterrent capacity unwittingly, through obsolescence, leaving France as the only European nuclear power.'

The French position could not be ignored. 'If we choose to abandon *our deterrent*, we would not achieve a non-nuclear Europe. Our next-door neighbour would still have a nuclear force over whose future scale, deployment, or negotiated abandonment we would have absolutely no say.'

Pressures of cost had created a new atmosphere in Paris which could be explored. 'By pooling British and French nuclear resources on behalf of Europe we could exert a stronger influence on the cause of disarmament . . . we could also achieve minimum deterrent capacity not only at a much lower level of both risk and cost than Trident, but even at a lower level than the present Polaris force.'

He said this was not an attempt to elevate Europe into a third nuclear superpower, but the proposed policy would end the dominance of NATO policies by the American President, open the way to reduced nuclear stockpiles and reduced costs, and bring Europe closer together on defence in accordance with consistent Liberal policy.

The Outsider read Steel's speech later. On paper it was not too bad. At the meeting it did not work. In that hot and overcrowded room he simply could not hold his audience who seemed hungry for a different speech. Maybe it suffered from the lack of a lighter touch at the beginning. Maybe they resented the overpowering presence of the media, and the feeling they were being used as a stage army. Maybe they wanted a comparison with Owen – more idealism, a feeling that their Leader at least was not just obsessed with defence. Perhaps some wanted to be made to feel their opinions mattered, rather than the Leader coming and laying down the line. Whatever the reason, it was not a success.

You can judge a speech partly by the questions that follow. Do they pick up on details? Do they reveal an audience drawn to what the speaker is saying and wanting to know more? After he had spoken entirely on defence, Steel received only two questions on the subject – one was: 'Why do we have to spend so much time talking about defence when people on the doorstep are talking about the health service, housing, and crime?' The question drew applause; it, and the lack of other questions on defence, may have been taken by Steel to indicate that the candidates were content. The Outsider had an uncomfortable feeling that this was not the case. The audience was muted. There was a feeling of unease.

His own contribution and the meeting over, the Outsider decided to end a day that had started so many hours and speeches earlier by calling in at the ALC reception. So did Steel. To be honest, they had little choice, for both knew they could not be effective without the support of the Association of Liberal Councillors, and that says much about that grouping within the Party.

The ALC had taken over a whole hotel, and the basement was packed with party personalities munching sandwiches and fighting their way to a totally inadequate and overwhelmed bar. Leeds councillor Maggie Clay, the diminutive but determined ALC boss and her predecessor, Tony Greaves, were surrounded by some of the other 2,000 Liberal councillors from around the country. Nobody was talking defence. Hung councils, housing, rates . . . these were their concerns.

The ALC was initially a small group of councillors set up to share experiences. Then came the community politicians, Lishman, Greaves, and the others who had emerged from the Young Liberals in the Sixties with the belief that the only way to achieve political power in Britain was to start at street level, then move to community level, then town or city level, and so upwards, winning confidence by working for people where they lived, and also developing an understanding of what they really wanted.

It was when the ALC obtained some money and some space in a former chapel at Hebden Bridge that the two strands came together . . . the focal point being their full-time worker, Tony Greaves, former chairman of the Young Liberals, and destined to be one of the party's most controversial members. Greaves, son of a policeman, an unmistakable figure with his shiny near-bald head and woolly jumpers, built the ALC up into a powerful force, nurturing local authority liberalism so that the party steadily increased its numbers of councillors from one set of local authority elections to another. Maggie Clay, who had only recently succeeded Greaves, was another key figure, as was Trevor Jones from Dorset. It was the ALC who picked up the idea of the hard-hitting, newsy, Focus leaflets, pioneered by the other Trevor Jones in Liverpool, and now distributed artwork and ideas to thousands of candidates all over the country.

Partly funded for a number of years by the party in London, ALC had now taken over the organisation of local authority elections for the party.

But ALC had also become a major leftish lobby within the party with the ability to produce votes behind candidates for party office, or to win support for radical resolutions. As a result relations with the Westminster leadership tended to be volatile. Tony Greaves, in particular, was never one to couch his thoughts in diplomatic language, and was a constant thorn in the side of the leadership. He drove David Steel to fury when in the 1983 election he publicly announced that part of the Alliance manifesto was not really Liberal policy, thus providing the opposition with some useful ammunition.

Greaves still wrote an egocentric but readable column in *Liberal News*, combining this with being a councillor in Pendle, and running the party's publications company. A gruff and prickly character, he was also humorous and warm-hearted, and an indefatigable worker. He had perhaps allowed the media to set him up occasionally as a focus for discontent, but under him, and subsequently Maggie Clay, the ALC had become a force to be reckoned with, hence the presence of Steel and other senior party figures at their late-night, overcrowded 'do' at Eastbourne.

Steel went back to the Queen's Hotel for the nightly meeting of his MPs who were considering the defence debate. The main resolution would be not dissimilar to the Harrogate one, with its emphasis on defence and disarmament, support for the creation of a stronger European pillar within NATO, and its welcome of the Joint Commission report as *a contribution* to Alliance policy. Of the amendments available to it, the lunchtime Assembly Committee had chosen two. One, to be moved by Leighton Andrews, asking that the resolution should be used with past resolutions as the basis of Liberal policy in negotiations with the SDP, was acceptable to the MPs and had also been accepted by a Policy Committee meeting earlier in the evening. The other amendment posed problems. The last words of the main resolution stated that the Assembly welcomed 'closer cooperation in defence policy and procurement between Britain and its West European partners, to develop a more effective British contribution to the collective defence capability of the European pillar of NATO'. This second amendment now added the words 'provided that such a defence capability is non-nuclear'. This amendment was interpreted by Steel as unilateralist or bound to be perceived by others as such.

There are to this day conflicting views of what happened at that Monday night meeting. Some Liberal MPs, loyal to the Leader on the issue, claim they were given no indication by others, such as Meadowcroft and Hughes, that they would be opposing the platform line. But the pro-amendment MPs believed their position had already been clearly established by the publication of *Across the Divide*. Simon Hughes also believes to this day that it *was* made clear that he and Meadowcroft would probably speak for the amendment, and says that there was not the slightest attempt to dissuade them from doing so.

At this point Steel and the majority of the parliamentary party still believed they would carry the day, and they concurred with the Policy Committee decision to field Jim Wallace to open the debate and Malcolm Bruce to close it, and to play the whole affair low key. Steel, perhaps mindful of his failure to sway the Assembly at Bournemouth, or perhaps believing it would not be necessary, showed no inclination to speak.

There was no consideration of persuading the movers to withdraw the amendment, or of tactics to rally support for the platform the following day.

This is crucial – *no attempt was made at that meeting to set about managing the Party to achieve the result the Leadership wanted.* Of course, this can be interpreted positively. It could be said that, unlike other parties, the Liberal Party is genuinely democratic, that there is no attempt at manipulation of, or dictatorship to, the Party on policy. This would be more convincing if the Leader did not have a veto on the Party manifesto, and if on other occasions he had not made it clear that he would simply take no notice of an Assembly resolution. No, it was not for these idealistic reasons that no plans were made by the MPs to manage the debate and achieve the required result. The real reason was lack of contact with their party. Those responsible for party management, for leadership, were not in touch with what was happening in the hotel bars and the fringe meetings, where resistance to the unamended main resolution was being developed. By their failure to sense the mood of the party, their failure to be represented at the Assembly Committee meeting and try to influence the choice of amendments, their failure to organise a vote-collecting initiative the following day, their failure to consider the nature of the speeches that would need to be made, they had made themselves vulnerable to defeat.

Two who did not share the complacency were Archy Kirkwood and Simon Hughes. They walked back to their hotel that night together. Kirkwood was deeply troubled. He had been an aide to Steel in the House of Commons many years earlier, had moved to Ettrick Bridge with his wife Rosalind, to assist the Leader there, was a friend and a neighbour, and in 1983 became, with Steel's help, the MP for the neighbouring constituency. Kirkwood had formed with Hughes and Meadowcroft a kind of caucus on the left of the Parliamentary Party, and faced now the prospect of opposing Steel the following day. He was, he told Hughes, not prepared to do it demonstrably. He would not speak, and he would vote at the back of the hall.

Hughes left Kirkwood at his hotel, and walked on. He now knew he would speak. And he knew what it meant.

The son of a brewer for Whitbread, Hughes had been raised in Wales, achieving a series of scholarships to quality schools before going to Cambridge, where he joined the Liberal Party. Also an active Christian, he worked in youth clubs as well as in London Liberal politics until in 1982 he achieved a record swing in Parliamentary history of 48% to snatch Bermondsey from Labour at a by-election. He held it comfortably in 1983. As MP for an inner London working-class constituency, Hughes inevitably found himself taking a different line from colleagues in rural seats, and his recent election as President of the Young Liberals (succeeding the Outsider) had confirmed his status as a leader figure on the left of the party. But Hughes had really taken off at the Dundee Assembly in 1985. A brilliant speech in the housing debate won him a standing ovation, and it was generally felt that an equally dazzling winding-up speech in the Northern Ireland debate saved the platform from defeat. This time, however, he would be seeking to defeat the platform and, if he succeeded, would capture the position on the left that Paddy Ashdown had won with his anti-Cruise speech in 1984 and subsequently lost by his unconvincing attempts to reconcile his own views on the issues with those of the leadership.

In an article published some weeks later, Hughes explained his position in the Eastbourne affair: 'I feel [my decision was] at least partly justified by my duty to keep faith with those hundreds of friends or colleagues whose attitude I shared and who felt their views or values were at risk of being eroded away, unargued. This was a time when they needed support from "their leaders", not silence. Of course the risk was that if we won (but not if we argued our case and only just lost) I should be accused of breaking faith with other colleagues and undermining the authority of my Leader. But surely one is not expected to argue another's position as well as one's own?'

Thus did Hughes argue to himself as he walked home that night.

Back in the Queen's, the party continued, journalists and lobbyists now freely mixing with Liberals and inevitably drawing closer together, one happy band of voyagers, as the ship that was the Liberal Assembly steamed further away from the rest of Britain. All seemed well. The captain was in his cabin, the passengers judged the first day of the cruise a success, the sea was calm and the stars bright in the sky.

The iceberg was still some fifteen hours away.

Tuesday

For the Outsider, Tuesday began well. His speech had been well reported, the high point being a complimentary article by *Guardian* columnist, Hugo Young. He could not have hoped for a more generous judgement from such a source. He penned a note of thanks and then went to breakfast with Peter Riddell, the *Financial Times* political writer. The morning he spent working in his hotel room and then lunched with journalists from *The Times*. Richard Holme was also there and the two walked back to the Assembly together.

Along with Tordoff, Ellis and a few others, Richard Holme had for years been one of the key 'managers' of the Liberal Party. As far back as 1968 Holme was arguing for a re-alignment on the left and with Steel and Pardoe took part at that time in the launch of a short-lived organisation called the Radical Alliance. Its aim was to bring radicals from the Labour and Liberal Parties together on common ground and also to attempt to attract radicals from outside party politics. The Outsider had been involved.

In the '70s Richard Holme became an indispensable unpaid aide to David Steel, writing speeches, helping with day to day responses to political events, and undertaking a lot of the 'fixing' behind the scenes. Despite being President of the Party for a crucial year as the Alliance was developing, and also the candidate for Cheltenham, he was better known to the insiders of politics than to the public. Hardly a day passed when he was not seen having lunch with one writer or another, promoting the current leadership line.

For his pains, Holme for a while became a kind of hate figure for the Party's radicals. This was partly because he was seen as too pro-Alliance in the early days when there were still many Liberal doubters, and partly because Holme's wheeler-dealing in Westminster and Fleet Street meant that he became rather remote from the grassroots. 'What is Holme up to?' was the question. In fact, the party had been unfair to Holme. Holme was an enthusiast to the point of fanaticism about politics, an indefatigable worker, and extraordinarily generous. The number of words he had self-effacingly written for Steel over the years must be beyond counting. And despite the scepticism of radicals, Holme was by no means on the right of the party. A campaigner for constitutional reform, he also embraced green issues. The key to Holme was that he wanted to win. He would spend hours poring over the opinion polls, looking for every sign of hope, and hours more hyping up the results to journalists so that they could be presented as positively as possible.

Despite his rather military bearing, and a fairly short fuse, he was a warm character, more than able to see the funny side of his experience at the Harrogate SDP Conference when he had, in the early hours of the morning, slipped out of bed and across the corridor to the loo only to hear the bedroom door lock behind him, leaving him trapped in the middle of the hotel stark naked. Only by removing a vase from a small table on the landing, and covering himself with its cloth, was he able to obtain help. But now Holme was nervous. Articulate and persuasive in private, he had always been a less effective public speaker. He was confident of being called in the defence debate and was beginning to feel the weight of the responsibility – the more so because when he speaks he is assumed by many to be speaking for Steel. As the two walked down the main street of Eastbourne, Holme read his speech aloud. His listener felt apprehensive. Holme had written his speech in relatively small handwriting on sheets of lined paper and, even allowing for the difficulty of reading it while walking, was clearing having difficulty following it, or in putting any emphasis behind the words. The Outsider felt that Holme would be at a considerable disadvantage. And yet it was too late to have it typed, so he felt it best to keep his doubts to himself.

In the hall a debate had begun on an ALC resolution entitled, 'After the General Election'. The ALC intention was to establish guidelines for the handling of a balance of power. They wanted Alliance negotiators to make their top priority a change in the way Parliament worked and the way the country was governed. They should not enter into negotiations over ministerial positions until satisfactory arrangements had been made over working practices and policies 'taking into account the wide range of relationships possible between parties, from former coalitions to far more limited arrangements'. They wanted the negotiating team to consist of not only the two Leaders but also representatives elected by the two Parliamentary Parties. The ALC also wanted consultation with the national Officers of the Party throughout the negotiating process, and the negotiations to be reported back to the Parliamentary Parties for approval and decision throughout.

Maggie Clay, who moved the resolution, had already made clear in an article in the *Guardian* the previous week that she differed from the two Leaders who wished to enter into negotiations 'without a shopping list'. Clay had written that the Alliance would need to have a package of key demands worked out in advance and clearly known to the electorate. 'They have the right to know, if a balanced parliament does result, exactly what the Alliance will demand.'

The debate was stolen by David Alton. The previous week the SDP conference had been told that it would be 'foolish to tie the hands of the two Leaders in advance of negotiation', but Alton, who the Outsider believed had cleared his words with David Steel, now said 'we are not prepared to barter for Cabinet seats and Ministerial limousines in return for dropping demands for electoral reform. . . . Any decision to sacrifice electoral reform in any temporary deal would be a gross betrayal, not worth a candle.'

He also developed a point that Steel had made on many previvious occasions, that Liberals would find it difficult to enter into a coalition with Margaret Thatcher. 'It would be easier for a lion to become a vegetarian than for Mrs Thatcher to change . . . a precondition of any negotiation is that she despatches herself to Dulwich the moment the election is over.'

Had the defence debate not followed, this would have undoubtedly been a well-reported part of Assembly week, for it represented a firm declaration by Liberal rank and file that it was not happy to respond to David Owen's plea to both Parties: 'Trust us'. This was not just because of a suspicion of what Owen would settle for, or even a suspicion that if Owen and Steel were negotiating together, Owen would prevail over Steel, but arose from ALC experience on more than 100 councils where Liberals or the Alliance held the balance of power. They felt they knew a bit about negotiating and they wanted their experience taken on board.

The Party was, however, waiting to deliver a more controversial message to the two Leaders, for Jim Wallace was now at the rostrum, opening the defence debate. Wallace, youthful-looking, decent, earnest, and with a developing reputation for being an effective operator in the Commons, would rarely have to make such a critical speech. The hall was now packed, with at least 100 delegates having to watch the debate on television sets outside. Paul Hannon, former Assembly Committee chairman, who had won praise for his chairmanship of the defence debate in Bournemouth in 1984, was once more in the chair, assisted by Geoff Tordoff. On Hannon's right, his customary place during the week, was David Steel, and on his right, the Outsider.

Most of the front row of the platform was made up of Members of Parliament, all supporters of the Steel line, the one unilateralist being the Young Liberals' chairman, Felix Dodds. The conflicting positions were better represented on the back row of the platform where there were a number of younger, radical Liberals.

Wallace urged that the non-nuclear amendment be rejected because the Assembly would be demolishing the key and carefully-constructed proposal about Polaris in the Defence Commission's report: 'we would be foreclosing one possible and important option, and rendering pointless the initiative with our European allies which David Steel and David Owen are pursuing.

That initiative is not an attempt to put together a third super-power; rather it offers the clear possibility of a reduction of the existing levels of nuclear weapons.'

But John Smithson, the uncompromising Yorkshireman, who had been active on the left of the Party for more than twenty years, and who moved the controversial amendment, would have none of it. The idea of a European deterrent was a 'monstrous betrayal' of Liberal principles. An Anglo-French bomb was as unacceptable as a British bomb.

Party vice-chairman Leighton Andrews, already assured that the platform would back his milder amendment, attempted to anticipate the publicity that could follow a defeat for Steel on the other one. 'We read about a split between Steel and activists. No one is more of an activist in this Party than David Steel. There is no need for the debate to be presented in this way.'

He was yet another who believed the debate was about the Liberal position for negotiations with the SDP. 'Today we are sending signals – signals to our negotiators on Alliance defence policy that they must not be timid – signals to our SDP colleagues that the policy must be stronger on disarmament.'

The impact of the Andrews speech was somewhat undermined by an extraordinary entrance by Cyril Smith.

Smith, a big man physically and in personality, had stormed out of the Parliamentary Liberal Party and mainstream Liberal politics three years earlier at Harrogate, after the Assembly had refused to respond to his protest that he had not been allowed to play a sufficiently central part in the 1983 General Election. Smith, backed by Alton and Hughes, had promoted the idea of a Deputy Leader of the Party, only to see it rejected by the Assembly. The last straw for Smith was that he was not called by Paul Hannon, also chairing that controversial debate. With maximum publicity, Smith picked up his ball and went home, making it clear that he would no longer play a full part within the Parliamentary Party and would not act as a policy spokes-man.

Smith had also indicated that he would probably not stand for Rochdale at the next General Election, although many Liberals took this with a pinch of salt. During the past few months he had begun to send signals that he could be wooed back, and had accepted involvement as the head of a team to launch a particular assault on Labour seats where the Alliance held second place.

Steel had been particularly anxious to encourage Smith back into the fold and to persuade him to stand in Rochdale once more, so a bargain had been struck whereby Smith would be given a special fifteen minute slot to address the Assembly on the Wednesday, ostensibly to report on his campaigning unit. Even that was not sufficient for Smith. Choosing the debate when the hall was packed and the tension greater than it would be at any other point of the week, he now proceeded to make a spectacular entrance from the hall. Everybody else on the platform simply went round the back, climbed a few stairs, and unobtrusively slipped into their chair. Not the Rochdale Giant, who lumbered slowly across the front of the hall, surrounded by photographers, temporarily reducing even the defence debate to a sideshow, and then disappeared to eventually reappear on the platform to what was admittedly slightly less enthusiastic applause than he may have hoped for.

Leighton Andrews abandoned the uneven struggle for attention and made way for Ruth Addison-Coleman, who as Ruth Addison had once chaired the Young Liberals. In those days she had been a constant critic of the Leadership; now she made a surprising and impressive speech, calling for unity. The defence resolution was not ideal, but it was a useful step on the way. 'I am sad that there are some people who will minimise the broad areas of agreement in the report. This is the old politics – better to fail in ideological purity than to win and have the power to do something about it.'

Steel applauded enthusiastically, as did the row of MPs at the other end of the platform – Alton, Wallace, and Smith.

Paddy Ashdown began by expressing considerable scepticism about the Steel–Owen initiative. He said, he found the balance of the argument 'is for me compellingly with those who believe the long term role for Europe is to develop the non-nuclear option.'

At this point all that Ashdown had said was good news for the non-nuclear campaigners. But, as if disturbed by the applause that followed, he abruptly changed tack. 'If therefore the amendment were to indicate that whatever happens in the *short term* it is the present view of the Assembly that we should not be establishing a new European independent deterrent in the *long term*, then I could not stand here opposing it ... but the amendment goes much further than that ... no matter how you read it, it has to mean that we preclude from our discussions with our European partners in the short term, not only a new generation of deterrents but the current Polaris deterrent as well.

'However you put it, fellow Liberals, recognise this – passing this amendment will damage further discussions between our leaders and the French.

'Those discussions should continue. It is the job of the Party to open doors; do not slam them.'

Ashdown, who had received a standing ovation at Bournemouth two years earlier, now received muted applause, and none from the Young Liberals who had cheered him so lustily at that earlier Assembly. It was a speech the Yeovil MP would regret. He had alienated his personal constituency in the party and gained not a vote for the platform.

Immediately after Ashdown came Tony Greaves, beginning with an exchange of jokes with Paul Hannon and then setting out to destroy the Ashdown position. Greaves made a clever speech – he acknowledged that the world moved on and that 'things change', but then said that values and principles were constant: 'This is a debate about values and principles and the soul of the Liberal Party. If we abandon those what is our contribution? We might as well go and join the SDP.'

Richard Holme followed. He could rarely have been less convincing. Stumbling, as the Outsider had feared, on almost unreadable notes, while on the platform David Steel began to look increasingly desperate, Holme stressed that he also found the notion of a Eurobomb incredible, but that was not the object of the exercize anyway. The amendment would make it impossible for the Alliance Leaders to talk to their European allies. But as a debating speech it was a disaster. In fact, the cumulative effect of Paddy Ashdown's word play and the unconvincing performance of Holme was counter productive to their side – by comparison with the assurance of the anti-nuclear debaters they lost points rather than won them.

It was becoming increasingly clear that the debate was being lost on the floor. The Outsider could feel Steel's growing depression and suddenly his vulnerability, and was wishing fervently that he was anywhere except sitting beside the Leader on the platform. This was one of his few differences with Steel. He had never wavered in his opposition to Britain having any nuclear weapons whatsoever and had consistently voted within the Party for the non-nuclear strategy, and had opposed Steel over Cruise missiles at Bournemouth. He had never believed in the deterrent theory; what kind of argument was it that a weapon was safe because nobody dare use it? Even if the super powers had been deterred from using nuclear weapons they had not been deterred from vastly increasing their numbers and their destructive power; in what way had that made the world a safer place? Nor did the deterrent theory offer any guarantee that a mistake would not occur. Nor could it be argued that Britain was a safer place for now having nuclear weapons on its soil, particularly when those weapons were under the control of another power. Furthermore, the country was already paying the price of its involvement in the nuclear arms race – for instance, bearing its share of the cost. On the other hand, he was not particularly impressed with the amendment. He did not feel it was particularly necessary. And he could see the political implications of defeat for the Leader. He was also becoming more aware, every minute, of the negligence of all in the party leadership, including himself, that had precipitated this confrontation. Yes, he too was culpable; he had been so preoccupied with working on his own speech for the Monday, he had abandoned the defence debate to others. It is probable that he could have made no difference, but that was not the point – he had not tried.

He had warned David Steel as they sat together before the debate that he would be abstaining. This had not worried Steel, who found it a considerable advance on having his President-Elect opposing him, but now the Outsider realised just how uncomfortable his position was. Above all, as he sensed Steel's growing distress, he felt an almost overwhelming desire to throw his personal support behind him and yet the Outsider also knew that he had credibility with Steel's opponents on the issue; by maintaining at least neutrality at this point, by not abandoning his support for the non-nuclear position even if he did not vote with them, he could possibly, as the new Party President, play a vital role in reconciling the different groups at a later stage. Yet would that do? Were there not many in the Party who looked to him for a lead? He was suddenly too aware of how, perhaps like the Assembly itself, he was unprepared for the moment.

At the rostrum Simon Hughes was now delivering the killer blow. He told the Assembly the Party had to enter the negotiating process asserting a Liberal view. The Assembly was about reaffirming traditional Liberal policies.

'Paddy was wrong – Tony Greaves was right ...' ... passing the amendment did not preclude discussions with the French.

But the Party should have no truck with a Eurobomb – 'a Euro-nuclear bomb mountain with twelve fingers on the button'.

It was an extraordinary speech, not particularly logical, not particularly fair – words following each other at speed, almost tripping over each other, points made in short jabs and thrusts – almost as if a highly intelligent speaker was tripping up over his own feelings, and all the more moving and impactful for it.

He appealed to David – 'Leader David' – to abandon the policy. 'We have never voted for an independent deterrent. Not only must we not do so now, but our policy must be to do so never.'

The speech received an emotional response. The Young Liberals, who had elected Hughes as their President to follow the Outsider earlier that year, were on their feet, cheering. On the platform, Dodds rose to his feet, as did a group of five or six in the back row. There was no applause from David Steel.

But if Hughes had left Steel looking sad, his deputy, Alan Beith, now raised his spirits.

The Outsider had been increasingly impressed by Beith. The dapper little man who, as we have seen, had won his Parliamentary seat at a by-election in November 1973 on the day the Outsider had lost his own by-election battle in Hove, had subsequently become the Chief Whip, and developed the reputation for ruthless control of the Parliamentary Party, and of being to the right politically. Despite being a nimble debater, articulate and impressively reasonable, Beith had made little impact beyond the Party and the House of Commons. And yet, the Outsider had seen him perform brilliantly on more than one occasion. He recalled his folksy and effective speech at the eve of poll rally in the Brecon and Radnor by-election, and his sound performance at a difficult meeting during Ryedale by-election. And he had found him a well-balanced contributor in Committee discussion. Beith, he suspected, was more of a heavyweight than he had so far demonstrated, and now at Eastbourne he made a brilliant speech, the first really incisive one from the platform.

He began by commenting to laughter that if ever he was on a capital charge he would hire Simon Hughes to defend him.

He then talked of the changing world, the fact that you could no longer treat the United States with the same confidence and equanimity as he, for one, could have done six years earlier.

Effectively he pulled rank on the younger Hughes by referring to his international experience: 'I wish Simon had been with me when I met Mr Gorbachov earlier this year. Gorbachov would find some aspects of this debate difficult to understand. What he would not understand is the idea that anybody would expect to influence him by reducing their capability in advance of any offer he made. He simply would not understand that at all,' he said to loud applause.

Beith made it clear that he, himself, did not want an independent British nuclear deterrent. 'It's not British, it's not independent, and it's not a deterrent.' But, he said, European defence had to be inter-related. 'We are only twenty miles from the coast of France. There is a nuclear armed power over there. We can't pretend they don't exist. They'll still be there whatever we pass this afternoon, and we have to find ways of replacing narrow, nationalistic concepts of defence, with the idea that Europe as a whole is seeking to defend freedom and the values of democracy.'

It was a telling point and well applauded. David Steel was clearly uplifted by the speech.

Beith, too, stressed that to pass the amendment would destroy the chances of developing European policy. He argued strongly that the European initiative created a situation where the Americans could not dominate NATO – a position that became profoundly more unhealthy every year.

The first speaker to refer to concern outside the Party, Beith said there was massive interest outside the hall by people who wanted to know what was on offer to them. 'They reject by a massive majority Mrs Thatcher's attempt to escalate the arms race by the Trident programme. They simply do not believe there is any sense in Labour's attempt to say "throw the Americans out but we'll somehow benefit from American nuclear defence". That seems to be either immoral or absurd. And they are saying to us: "Can you agree between yourselves, can you produce a coherent policy, and is that policy one which gives us the security of knowing that what we lose from our armament is negotiated away, and that what initiatives we take are multilateral and clearly based on the attempt not to simply rid the world of our nuclear weapons, but to rid the world of Soviet nuclear weapons as well?".'

And so the stage was set for Michael Meadowcroft.

The MP for Leeds West had been around Liberal Party politics for many years. He had worked at Liberal Party headquarters. He had been active in the ALC. He had written innumerable pamphlets and became a party philosopher. He had held many of the senior party offices. And the news of his election at Leeds West had been one of the high points of that dispiriting 1983 election night. Meadowcroft was also a member of CND and a consistent advocate of the unilateralist approach. At the same time, he was one of those who, more than most, respected the way the Liberal Party had become an extended family to many of its members, and saw himself as a conciliator within the party. Conciliator? Why, then, was Meadowcroft ready now to throw his weight behind what would be seen as a divisive amendment? The answer lay in his determination, consistently demonstrated, that the party's democratic machinery should always be used. Meadowcroft's constant complaint had been that policy was increasingly made by Steel and Owen, or in ways that did not involve the processes established over the years. Meadowcroft was not satisfied that the party had had the opportunity, or would have another opportunity, to debate defence policy properly as it had evolved, and to express its view. Meadowcroft, as he had demonstrated in *Across the Divide*, did not see this as a divisive debate for the Alliance but as the final stage in establishing the message that Liberals would then take into Alliance discussions.

Meadowcroft now began by repeating once more the line adopted by all on the anti-nuclear side of the debate – that it was the role of Liberal Assembly to make Liberal policy. That policy must be rooted in Liberal values and intellectually sustainable. He said the arguments against the amendments had failed on both counts.

Countering the suggestions that the amendment was a unilateralist one, he cleverly claimed that his complaint about the amendment was that it was not unilateralist. He put once more the emphasis on passing the amendment as a negotiating weapon.

It was left to Malcolm Bruce, the MP from Gordon, to wind up the debate on behalf of the Policy Committee (and, in effect, the leadership). This he did competently as always, stressing the commitment to arms reduction. He attacked the positions of Labour and the Conservatives. But alas for Bruce, the Labour and Conservative Parties had become irrelevant to this debate – the fight was between the two positions in the hall. Bruce continued reading a speech that was articulate and well-reasoned, but he was sticking to the game plan devised at the Parliamentary Party meeting while the game itself had changed. There had been nineteen speakers, and, as all the commentators acknowledged the following day, it was the pro-amendment debaters who had clearly won on the floor. What the situation called for was a spectacular debating speech, taking the other side on, providing an answer to the question in the hearts of so many in the audience: 'Can I support the Leadership and at the same time preserve the Party's principles?' Bruce (to his later distress) was unable to provide that reassurance.

The vote took place, and the amendment won by 652 votes to 625.

As the result was announced by Paul Hannon, Steel turned to the Outsider and laughed humourlessly. 'It was close,' he said. From the hall came a mighty roar, as the Young Liberals led the cheering and clapping. The Outsider looked at them sadly. It was a bad moment. His heart was with their ideals, but the celebration was inappropriate. A point had been made – maybe it, or a similar one, had to be made – but a heavy price would be paid.

He followed Steel off the platform across the now crowded tea room and exhibition space, and into the press room where a press conference had been fixed. Steel kept calm, 'It was an irritant, rather than a setback,' he told reporters. He understood the Assembly's impatience for a non-nuclear policy — it was a healthy impatience. It would still be possible for him to continue his European discussions.

Party conferences these days are, with the exception of the big debates such as the one on defence, as much about what happens outside the hall as in it, in particular the scores of fringe meetings in hotels up and down the seafront. And the parties. The main one at the end of the defence debate was hosted by TV-AM in the Queen's Hotel. It was packed and all the talk was of the defence debate. At this point no one was panicking. Steel had handled the press conference well. The position seemed manageable. The Outsider returned to the main hall, taken over for the night by the team who organise the annual Assembly satirical Review. This had become increasingly professional over the years, although he felt this year that the usual (and generally well accepted by their target) cracks at David Steel appeared more numerous and less funny. Meadowcroft and Archy Kirkwood were, as always, playing in the band, Meadowcroft's own jazz band. The review ran over its time and the other Members of Parliament assembled for their regular evening meeting without the two musicians. It was to be a meeting those present would always remember.

David Steel may have been upset by the result of the debate but he is not a vindictive man, nor one to censor the expression of genuinely held convictions by members of his Party. Obviously disappointed at the result, he was not in acrimonious mood, and simply said that matters had not been made easier but that a defence policy could still be hammered out. He felt that those who had broken ranks with the Parliamentary Party had been naive. They did not understand the political consequences of their actions or the way they would be portrayed in the media.

The others were in less generous mood. They felt betrayed. Elizabeth Shields criticised Simon Hughes and Michael Meadowcroft for behaviour that was inconsistent with the spirit of Alliance unity that had helped her win the Ryedale by-election. The temperamental David Alton was furious, claiming the three MPs had published *Across the Divide* without proper consultation with the defence spokesman and had not kept in touch with the Parliamentary Party about their plans. Alton, now Chief Whip, was all for establishing rules of collective responsibility for the Parliamentary Party.

Alex Carlile, one of those who had been most severe in his judgement of Paddy Ashdown at Bournemouth two years earlier, now took an equally hard line on the latest dissenters, as did Russell Johnston, a dedicated European and multilateralist, who had been glowering at everyone since the debate ended. He and David Steel's old friend and sponsor, Lord Mackie, now weighed in. Steel had been a Mackie protégé years back when the latter ran the Scottish Liberal Party, and at recent general elections, whilst Steel had travelled the country, Mackie had done much to look after Steel's own constituency campaign. To him this was treachery, no less, and this normally genial man stormed onto the attack. Johnston was equally severe.

By the time Simon Hughes arrived at the meeting after delivering yet another speech on the fringe, some were baying for blood. Hughes is a remarkably cool customer in these circumstances. He voiced his sorrow that the others were upset, but said he had the right to speak in the debate. He acknowledged that more collective responsibility should be introduced (Stephen Ross: 'It's a bit late now, Simon.')

When the two musicians arrived, Meadowcroft weighed in by condemning the whole way the defence policy had evolved, making his now familiar points about party democracy.

Having listened to the unhappy debate, Steel wound up by saying they were now stuck with the issue for the rest of the conference and that he would have to change his speech drastically. He had wanted to talk about the major social issues of housing and education but he had no choice now but to return to defence.

When the meeting broke up in the early hours of the morning, it was left to Beith, Alton and one or two others to hammer out a line for the media the following day. The declared intention was to play it cool, following the Steel line of saying it was an irritation, rather than a major disaster.

Wednesday

But somewhere between 1 and 2 o'clock in the morning and 7 or 8, David Alton went completely off the rails. Perhaps it was what he read in the morning papers. The headlines must have confirmed the worst fears: 'Alliance pact is shattered', said *Today*. 'Ban the Bomb vote shatters the Alliance', said the *Express*. 'Liberals rebuff Steel over nuclear policy', said the *Guardian*. 'A policy in pieces', declared *The Times* editorial. 'Nuked – Steel's defence deal wrecked by his Party', reported the *Daily Mail*. 'Bad day for the Alliance', said the *Financial Times*. 'No nukes Libs beat Steel in big vote', declared the *Daily Mirror*. 'Steel's defeat is not merely a personal set-back. It has also created a chasm, which may prove unbridgeable in the structure of the Alliance,' said the *Telegraph* in a leader. 'The electorate will draw its own conclusions about the viability of the Alliance in the aftermath of this vote. A house which is half nuclear and half anti-nuclear is a house divided against itself.'

The *Guardian* leader said: 'The nine words "provided that such a defence capability is non-nuclear", represented a serious defeat for David Steel especially, and for David Owen. They had invested so much personal effort and conviction in the pursuit of the opposite resolve that there could no shrugging off or re-interpreting yesterday's roll call.'

The *Guardian* confirmed that 'one notable feature of the defence debate was the almost total lack of reference to the SDP. This was a Liberal debate about Liberal policy, and speaker after speaker stressed the supremacy of Liberal values over political necessity.' The *Guardian* then concluded: 'Before yesterday's vote the prospect was that the electorate would be offered a three-way choice at the election ... nothing is that clear today. The Alliance, experiencing the reality of members and conferences, has a lot of work to do.'

It was an appalling press. And it followed similar television coverage the night before. Whatever *Liberals* cut off from the world on the good ship Eastbourne felt the debate had been about, and whatever *Liberals* felt had really happened, *the world* outside had been told that the Alliance had split down the middle on defence – that the ship so festively launched on Monday had somehow torpedoed itself and was all but sunk.

This was what confronted David Alton that Wednesday morning, but whether it triggered his actions is hard to say. What is beyond doubt is that Alton proceeded to compound the problem by accentuating the divide within the Party. He missed no radio or television opportunity to attack the dissidents and those who had voted with the majority. He briefed journalists similarly. At a press conference he actually waved the different headlines around in front of the cameras to show how the Party had been damaged. The Outsider, who happened to arrive in the press room while Alton was having his conference, could hardly believe his eyes or ears. Surely the way to play it this morning was to cool it, to stress that the Leader was not overly perturbed, to emphasise the positive, that the Party had actually approved 90% of defence policy, to stress what steps could now be taken via the Policy Committees to establish final Alliance defence policy, etc. Alton was doing the opposite – throwing oil onto the flames.

Inevitably the Alton line came back to the Party as they started to arrive at the conference hall, and the result was increasing acrimony between the different sides. It was, to quote words to be made famous later in the week, 'a breath-taking misjudgement' on Alton's part.

In the hall, the conference debated education and steps towards greater racial justice, and then just before lunch came the appearance of Cyril Smith. The Outsider had to admit it worked. The Party was bruised by the un-Liberal-like ferocity of some of the overnight inquests and by the media coverage, morale was low, and the barn-storming speech by Cyril Smith was an antidote to be enthusiastically absorbed. The man who stormed away from Harrogate three years earlier, criticising Steel's leadership, now declared the same Steel to be the best political leader in Britain. Building up to a climax, he announced that he would, after all, 'carry the banner' at Rochdale in the general election.

It was outrageous, but the hall rose to applaud as its spirits had risen, and everyone went to lunch happy.

That night Meadowcroft, Hughes and Kirkwood were all due

to speak at the Liberal News Rally, the main fringe meeting of the week, together with Paddy Ashdown, the Outsider and others on the party left. The Outsider had founded the Liberal News Rally at Bournemouth in 1984, basing it on the idea of the Tribune Rally at the Labour Party conference – one event during the week when the detailed discussions of fringe meetings made way for an out-and-out rally with an emphasis on radical ideas. Thus the presence of the three dissenters was no coincidence – Meadowcroft and Kirkwood had spoken at the two previous rallies, and Hughes had been asked nearly a year back. Ashdown was also a regular speaker. The defence issue was barely mentioned, but the Outsider took the chance to shore up Steel, reminding the Party that it could not pat itself on the back for the tolerant nature of its debates if it was then to bay in triumph over the defeat of its Leader. Also, he argued, no matter how idealistic one's politics, occasionally one had to dirty at least one's fingernails, if not one's hands, and Steel was often put in the position of having to dirty his own on behalf of the Party. This called for recognition and not holier-than-thou criticism. The Outsider had been provoked to this speech as much by the cutting nature of the review the previous evening as by the insensitive celebration by some of the defence debate decision.

In the meantime, the atmosphere around the Leader's suite on the second floor of the Queen's was becoming gloomier. Unfortunately, Steel was hearing mainly from one side of the Party, who were reinforcing the sense of betrayal instead of encouraging a more philosophical view. There was cause for foreboding about what was happening to the Leader's speech.

Thursday

Another busy morning for the Outsider. At 7.30 a.m. he had to appear on the *Today* programme, and then live on the BBC TV at the opening of the day's transmission, together with Holme and Jim Wallace. He was less satisfied with this. He began with a criticism of Steel's advisers only to catch the eye of Holme, who looked suitably disconcerted, all the more so when David Dimbleby turned to him and said 'Well, you are one of these advisers, Mr Holme.' Afterwards, he said he could have kicked himself, but Holme was relatively philosophical, although not happy about the Outsider's passing reference to 'the Steel camp'. Holme said it made Steel sound under siege.

The Assembly was now debating nuclear energy. This had been trumpeted by the media as another likely Liberal rebuff for the SDP, but once more the party was in difficulty simply because the SDP Conference had taken place earlier. If it was to take its own individual line it would inevitably be portrayed as creating another split. In fact the difference between the two parties was not that great; it was not that the SDP were pro-nuclear power, more that they needed more convincing than the Liberals that it should be abandoned. It was an impressive debate, with a number of speeches in support of nuclear power, although there was clearly an overwhelming majority for the resolution to phase it out.

But the debate that should have been the major one of the week, on 'Partnership for Progress', took place in the afternoon. At stake was the approval or rejection of the major policy document, prepared by a team from each Party, from which the election manifesto would ultimately be produced. Altogether thirty-three speakers took part. It was a debate that evidenced the unity that now existed within the Alliance, but the media did not want to know. The only story on Thursday, and in particular for Friday's papers, was the division on defence.

Steel flew by helicopter to London to take part in a *This Week* interview with David Owen. He then returned to participate in *Question Time* live from the Assembly arena. At the same time, the Outsider had dinner with journalists from the *Guardian*, before proceeding to appear live on *Newsnight*.

At about midnight he found himself in Steel's suite, being upbraided by Richard Holme for repeating his criticism of advisers on the air. 'Everyone knows it means me,' said Holme. Holme looked so distraught, surrounded by bits of paper as he worked on the Steel speech, that although the Outsider was actually pleased with the interview, he had no heart to argue with him.

In any case Steel then arrived, and he, Holme, Alan Watson, and the Outsider briefly discussed the Leader's speech. Steel made it clear that he believed he needed to re-assert his authority for the benefit of the outside world, and that he would have to jettison much of the speech he had intended on domestic policy and take a tough line with the Party.

The Outsider said that Steel was entitled to say what he felt about defence, but the bulk of the speech should still be about other matters. 'I don't care whether you speak for two hours, what matters, is that no less than sixty-one minutes of it is about other political issues and no more than fifty-nine minutes of it about defence.'

He argued that it was possible for Steel to make his points without attacking the Party, but there was little sympathy for him in the room. He left the team to it, retiring to bed, deeply concerned by the mood in what he still found himself thinking of as the Steel camp – for in its isolation at this moment this is what it had become. It was now clear that no one would be able to influence further what Steel planned for the morrow, except those already around him, and they – especially with Holme leaving for America – were totally committed to the hard line.

Friday

After a rather unsatisfactory appearance on TV-AM when he could offer few positive views about how the defence problem could be resolved, the Outsider gave an interview to IRN, and then went to the first of two breakfasts, one with Paul Hannon to discuss how he should introduce Steel later in the day, and then a promised appearance at a breakfast hosted by Paul Tyler. He then spent the morning dealing with correspondence and packing. After lunch he made his way to the platform, where the Party was beginning to assemble for the final session. The mood was tense. The small gathering behind the platform did not like the sound of what they had heard about the speech. Not that this was a lot, for it had been decided not to release it to the press until Steel was actually on his feet. This merely added to the tension.

So concerned was he about the Steel speech, the Outsider had forgotten that his own moment was about to come. The speech of the Party Leader is traditionally preceded by the induction of the new President, who receives an ancient copy of Milton's *Areo-pagitica*, presented to the Party by its 1947 President, Isaac Foot, and signed by each successive President and held by them as a token of their position. Perhaps because he had been preoccupied and not anticipated the moment, perhaps because of the warmth of the cheer for the incoming President, he was moved as he signed the book, shook hands with Penhaligon, and then took the Chair of the Assembly for the first time.

'Twice this week in newspapers I have been described, not unkindly, as an Outsider,' he said. 'I believe this is because my route to the Presidency has been more one of campaigning for Liberal causes beyond the frontiers of the Party. I can only say I have never felt more an Insider than I do today, and it is a proud and happy feeling.'

The Insider then thanked Penhaligon for his service as President of the Party and took care also to refer to the MP's wife, Annette. Penhaligon was warmly applauded. It was a moment the Insider would feel particularly pleased about later in the year, for tragically it was to be Penhaligon's last appearance at a Liberal Assembly, and he thus departed to what for him must have been a heart-warming ovation.

Now the Insider asked the Assembly what kind of man would make a suitable Leader for the country in the 1990s. One, he said, who should be free to speak for all of the people, not one class, or one part of the country. One with compassion and an instinctive sense of justice. One whose concern for the wider world could restore our international standing. One who would encourage long term responsibility. One whose own decency and tolerance would set standards of behaviour in public life.

And he came to a paragraph he had drafted with care: 'One whose Leadership of their own Party is based on the self-confidence that will allow others self-expression – who knows strong leadership is not reflected in docility but the full involvement of members – who knows a great leader creates more leaders, not more followers.'

He called on David Steel. And then Steel was there, threading his way between the two front rows on the platform, still sufficiently in possession of himself to remember to stop and shake hands with Rosemary Cooper, soon to fight the Knowsley North by-election, and to shake hands with the Insider and say 'Congratulations on becoming President of the Party'.

But the Leader intended to come to the point with his audience immediately. 'One of the traditional sports of party conferences is guessing the lengths of the Leader's ovation. I don't advise anyone to take a bet on that this afternoon.' And he made it clear he didn't care much how his speech went down with the party: 'People outside understand that applause is no substitute for getting our programme right.'

So to defence: 'I must tell you bluntly that two related characteristics of our debate on Tuesday disturbed me, one was the sight of the Liberal Party reverting to a habit which I thought we had kicked ten years ago, of being seen sitting in a corner polishing and burnishing our policy to get it nice and pure and shining, in the context of the ideal world we would all desperately like to see, rather than dealing with the real harsh world in which we live.'

The hall was still. The Assembly now knew this was not to be a happy occasion.

'It is one thing to declare our goal of ridding our country, our continent, our world of nuclear weapons. That we must assert with all the passionate intensity at our command. But if we are ever to be in a position to influence our destiny in that direction, we must also convince the electorate that we have carefully thought through the painful steps we must take to reach that non-nuclear goal. Declaring the objective is not enough. The objective is not a policy.

'The Chernobyl cloud drifting over Europe and over parts of Britain carrying its dreaded fallout in the wind should have taught us, if we didn't know it before, that you cannot create nuclear free zones by putting up signs on the lampposts of Lambeth. Our Assembly resolution as amended is the equivalent of one of these signs.'

There were shouts of dissent from the hall. The audience, previously united in their attention, were now divided in their response. Some were roaring their approval, others were stunned by the words. Steel was shaking but determined: '. . . and it will convince no one that we are capable of advancing from where we are now to a genuinely nuclear free world. So there is no point in trying to blame what happened on the press.'

He wanted intellectual consistency and intergrity in our policy. 'One delegate said yesterday that the trouble with this Assembly was that it had too much heart and not enough head. Well, by God after seven years of this benighted government the country needs a party with a lot of heart, and I am proud to lead it. But it needs its head as well.

'The second point which troubled me was the no doubt well-intentioned but completely misguided belief that in some way it was this Assembly's task to accentuate the few remaining points of difference with the SDP in order to 'strengthen my hand' in manifesto discussions with David Owen. 'That is a breathtaking misjudgement.'

Once more there were cries of dissent, for this was the crux. Speaker after speaker opposing the platform on Tuesday had stressed that the debate was establishing a *Liberal* policy, and had talked about the need to strengthen our negotiators with the SDP and constitutionally they were right. A Liberal Assembly made Liberal policy. It was the role of the Policy Committee to negotiate Alliance policy.

But Steel was concerned with the political realities, not the constitutional niceties. He forged on:

'We are either in alliance or we are not. We must live and breathe the Alliance. It is unthinkable that we enter the election with two defence and disarmament policies. But neither David Owen nor I are prepared to arrive at any election policy as a result of some botched up bargaining process. We wouldn't convince the country. We wouldn't convince you. We wouldn't convince ourselves. We will arrive at our election policy by applying our common judgment to the problems which will face the next government on taking office. We will have our repeatedly stated goals firmly in view as we do so.

'I am reported as being angry with this Assembly. My emotion is not that of anger but of profound frustration that what you hope for and what I hope for, namely electoral victory for Liberalism and the Alliance, may have been temporarily and unnecessarily put at risk.

'Yesterday, two events took place which sent a clear signal to the electorate that we are on our way again. The first was your overwhelming endorsement of our joint Alliance document,

"Partnership for Progress", and your massive vote of confidence in the democratic procedures by which we will determine our manifesto for the election – involving the policy committee, the parliamentary party and the candidates. Both David Owen and I are well able to move forward on all policy issues including defence on the basis of that document – that is a clear message I give to you, the SDP and the electorate.

'The other event of yesterday concerned David Owen. We had what the *Sun* would call secret talks in London – watched by about seven million people. It was a good meeting, confirming my belief that the bonds of our Alliance will hold. Neither of us subscribes to the doctrine of infallibility of party leaders – at least I don't, but nor does he. No one should be worried by differences in style, or even occasionally of opinion between David Owen and myself. The reality is that this relationship will work and will hold. The two leaders and the two parties are growing steadily closer.'

Turning now to the specifics of defence and disarmament, he argued that 'if we are to get reductions in the missiles pointed *at* this country as well as those based *in* it, the Russians must know that we would be able to maintain, and if need be update our nuclear capability, until such time as these negotiations succeed. If we are not so prepared, we might as well follow the Labour party's logic and abandon the nuclear deterrent system unilaterally, hoping that out of the goodness of their hearts the rulers in the Kremlin will kindly destroy theirs. In the '70s there was a party leader in Denmark who achieved some limited success for a while by arguing that he would save costs and reduce taxes by withdrawing his country from NATO and installing a taped message in Russian at all his country's airports saying "we surrender". Denis Healey's tape is a good deal longer but its message is basically the same. Liberals place a higher value on the defence of liberty than that'.

He re-iterated opposition to Trident but also his support for retention of a minimum deterrent capacity no higher than the present Polaris force. 'I believe we can achieve this through collaboration with our European neighbours. Nothing in that is designed to create a new European super-power, or a Eurobomb, or a committee of fingers on the button, as some have sought to suggest. Securing greater European cooperation to get better value for money in defence, to promote world disarmament, and to switch global resources to development, is wholly in tune with the European ideals of this party, which we have proclaimed consistently since the 1950s.

'My two parliamentary colleages who spoke against the policy resolution, both said that a non-nuclear Europe was a final aim and that their amendment was not intended to frustrate the efforts we are making to find an effective European policy. Very well, we shall go on doing so.'

He then spelt out the choice he wanted the electorate to have:

'The Conservatives will make an eight-fold increase in Britain's nuclear firepower. The Alliance will maintain a minimum deterrent and only until the success of arms control negotiations renders it unnecessary.

'The Conservatives will starve conventional forces of the equipment they need in order to find the money for Trident. The Alliance will safeguard the real interests of our army, navy and air force by sharing costs and equipment with our European partners.

'The Conservatives will lock Britain into us technology for another generation, through the purchase of Trident and through British participation in the Star Wars project. The Alliance will contribute to a stronger European effort in high technology, from which Britain as well as our partners will benefit.

'The Conservatives will leave Britain over-dependent on the judgement of whoever occupies the White House. We haven't forgotten the bombing of Libya. The Alliance will place defence within the wider European context, through which we will also pursue concerted economic and industrial recovery.

'The Conservatives will continue to frustrate every initiative for disarmament as they have for the past seven years, particularly if British nuclear weapons are involved. The Alliance will use the whole weight of British government power and influence to bring about comprehensive arms reductions.'

Then, at last, Steel moved on to education and housing, speaking about the latter with some passion. And then on to South Africa. And increasingly the Assembly was being pulled round behind him. He began to build towards a stronger finish.

There was still hope. But then there came a most unfortunate phrase. Steel had been making the point that Liberals were being effective at local authority level. 'But Britain as a whole is not a Liberal country, and we connot convert it to one until we achieve power.' He then said: 'I am not interested in power without principle. But equally, I am only faintly attracted to principles without power.'

Probably Steel did not intend it as it sounded, for he went on to emphasise that 'without power all our resolutions, all our idealism, and all our passion will remain mere intention, mere hopes, mere dreams ... we will do nothing, achieve nothing unless we can first gain power and then use it wisely'.

But to a Party so deeply committed to principle, and abhorring the other parties for having none, it had been an unhappy phrase.

Steel concluded by emphasising the two-way committment between leader and Party, and that, 'together we have made a commitment to the people of our country, and they require us to keep it'.

In re-reading Steel's words, they do not come across on paper as a too harsh attack on the Party. They seem reasonable. And yet in that hall and defiantly delivered their impact was devastating. The assembled were told by the headmaster that the exam results were not good enough, and the majority didn't like it and didn't think it fair.

The Insider's pleasure at his own reception earlier had been replaced by the wish, for the second time that week, that he was not there. He knew that it was for him to give a lead to the Assembly in applauding its Leader, but he could scarcely do so, for he was convinced that if there had been a defence debacle, it had been the fault of the Party leadership and its managers, including himself, and not the Party itself.

The tragedy was that the Insider was not only impressed himself by Steel's argument on the specific issue but he felt that many in the Assembly were impressed too. Unfortunately they had not heard it from the Leader when it really mattered on Tuesday. He had either been too confident of success or too afraid of defeat. It was equally tragic that it had to be a speech that was so unfair to the Party that showed some of Steel's best qualities – his courage, for not even the conviction that he was right made it an easy speech; his professionalism, for it was, in its delivery, a magnificent performance; his clarity, for whatever one's views on the contentious issue, it was beautifully structured and argued; and (once he abandoned defence and talked about the underprivileged) his genuine compassion and anger at the indecency and unacceptable injustice of poverty.

Yet in order to create the right image in the media the next day, Steel had turned on the Party, had punished it for his and his colleagues, (including the Insider's) own mistakes.

'Breath-taking misjudgement' that they thought the debate was about Liberal policy and about the Liberal position for negotiations with the SDP? At what point during the debate, or prior to the debate, was the Party told otherwise? A defence policy no more valid than a sign on a Lambeth lamppost? Or a position consistent with party policy evolved over the years? Why, if the decision was that bad, were commentators who were sympathetic to Steel forced to admit in their reports that his case had been hopelessly lost in the argument on the floor?

Where was *organisation* in the failure to put together a campaign to win the day? What was *leadership* about? Was it about convincing a few columnists in a few heavyweight papers, or re-establishing personal images, or was it about sending the troops away enthused, and happy, putting the best possible light on any difficulties and divisions?

Yet the Insider did not feel angry, except at his own culpability; about the Leader's speech he felt sad. Steel almost fell into his chair at the end of the speech, trembling with exhaustion. He would, the Insider guessed, always believe that he had done what he had to do. Thank heavens this was not the Labour Party – thank heavens this was the Liberal Party and even in its distress it would forgive. And the standing ovation *was* genuine enough. The Party *wanted* to send its Leader away in good heart. The Party *wanted* to undo the impression of disunity. The Party *had* responded to much of the second part of Steel's speech. It *had* been a brave and impressive performance, and, if he wanted to demonstrate authority, authority of a sort he *had* demonstrated.

But everyone was to say they had never known such a depressed finale to an Assembly week as the muted celebrations that Friday night.

So ended the Eastbourne Assembly of 1986. It had been a week that had begun so well and then fallen apart. It had been a week that had been unfairly represented and interpreted to the outside world, sadly by Liberals as well as the media, for it had not split the Alliance; it had at worst merely created a temporary hiccough. No one doubted that an Alliance defence policy would emerge. Further, it went on throughout Wednesday and Thursday to reinforce Alliance unity on a broad range of issues but this was lost in the media concentration on the so-called split. Yet, as the opinion polls were soon to show, the message that emerged from Eastbourne was that the unity the Alliance presented to the British people was a fragile one and in response the people showed the opinion pollsters that their support for the Alliance remained fragile too.

The Insider climbed wearily into his car and drove back up the hill from Eastbourne on the way to his home in Brighton. As he had on his way to the town that previous Sunday, now so many memories away, he paused and looked down. The sun was still shining as it had done six days earlier. He knew the shadow that lay over the town was only in his mind – and also that one other thing had changed. Personal to him. He was no longer the Outsider. He was President of the Party, he was Chairman of its General Election Committee. He was the Insider now, with responsibilities to the party that had to be shouldered at a desperate time.

The Liberal Party
and The Alliance

From Eastbourne to the Barbican

On the Saturday after Eastbourne the Insider spoke to David Steel on the 'phone. A tired and disappointed Steel acknowledged that any benefit from the media coverage of his speech had been paid for by a drop in Party morale and a deepening of divisions within the Party. The two decided to meet at Steel's home at Ettrick Bridge in October. The Insider left for a week in the United States, and Steel for a well-publicised trip to South Africa.

The pending General Election had an inhibiting effect on the Labour Party Conference where there was a display of uncharacteristic harmony. However, the Labour leader, Neil Kinnock, confirmed his determination to pursue a policy of unilaterally abandoning nuclear weapons and closing down American bases, and the conference took place to a background of disapproving noises from the Reagan administration designed to encourage concern in Britain over whether NATO could survive such a policy.

Labour unfolded its latest symbol – a red rose.

The Conservative Party Conference was also a success. Ministers cast the best possible light on their records and announced a variety of measures in the areas where they felt most electorally vulnerable – unemployment, health, education. The Chancellor of the Exchequer, Nigel Lawson, made one of his few effective Conference speeches.

At a dramatic but ill-prepared summit meeting in Reykjavic, Soviet leader Gorbachev and Ronald Reagan appeared to come close to accord on sweeping reductions in nuclear weapons, but the talks foundered because the US President refused to abandon his Strategic Defence Initiative (STAR WARS). Nevertheless, for the first time a reversal of the arms race and even the elimination of nuclear weapons from the planet seemed at least an outside possibility. All three British political parties responded positively – but for different reasons. The Tories claimed that if there were a cut back, it would be as a result of their tough multilateral approach; Labour unilateralists claimed that their vision of a non-nuclear world had been proved to be credible; for the Alliance the rapidly changing circumstances created the chance to make a fresh start on defence policy.

On a more humdrum level (by these international standards), in the week of October 12 the Insider and the President of the Social Democratic Party, Shirley Williams, began their autumn campaign called 'People in Power', a barnstorming tour of major media centres to promote the Alliance as the Party that would break the system, putting people back in charge of their own affairs. Beginning on the Monday in Glasgow and Edinburgh, they went on to Leeds and Manchester on Tuesday, to Birmingham on Wednesday, and to Norwich and Cambridge on Thursday.

The Week October 12 to 19

... with Shirley Williams on tour ... Liberals debate defence while the media talks of a summit ... Any Questions and on to Ettrick Bridge

It was an encouraging week. There were press conferences in the morning, university meetings at lunchtime, more media interviews in the afternoon, and public meetings in the evening. The university meetings were packed, and the public meetings well attended too. Shirley concentrated on the case for a Bill of Rights and Alliance proposals for decentralisation, and the Insider on the need for proportional representation and freedom of information.

He developed considerable respect for the bustling, determined Shirley. An experienced campaigner himself, he was disconcerted by the way she seized the initiative wherever they went by, quickly briefing herself on local issues and adapting her remarks to make them relevant to whatever interviewer or audience she addressed.

Shirley had a reputation for unreliability, and for arriving late, often without her papers. There was an SDP joke that when Shirley was searching in her handbag for her train ticket on one journey, and the inspector said 'Never mind, Mrs Williams, I trust you,' Shirley replied: 'You may not want to see it but I do . . . I've forgotten where I'm going!' The Insider found – at least on this journey – no justification for this reputation. He had welcomed the campaigning trip as an opportunity to become better acquainted with his fellow President, and he was impressed. He could see that the behaviour others assumed to be absent-minded, or woolly, was partly the result of taking on too much. Every minute in cars or on trains was taken up with dealing with correspondence, or writing articles, and at every destination there was a handful of telephone messages awaiting her. She was a woman of restless energy. The Insider had learnt to pace himself, and when speaking to audiences to hold a bit back for when it really mattered. But before every audience Shirley would stand, tense and slightly hunched over the lectern, giving her all, radiating energy as she argued her case. She was a one-pace, all-out woman. Every media opportunity was grasped. Every individual, no matter how humble, was given equal attention. She was at times like a woman possessed. And she made no secret of her passion to regain power. The Insider knew, too, of her reputation for being a ditherer, a charge dating back to the early days of the SDP, and at least in part related to her decision not to fight the Warrington by-election, but once more it was confounded by his experience of her on this trip (and subsequently). The Insider found she could see an opportunity and grasp it, often ruthlessly. Rather than being slow to act, his experience was that she was more likely to move too quickly . . . risking getting the wrong end of the stick and over-react, particularly when she herself was directly affected.

The two Presidents took every opportunity on their trip to talk to local Liberals and Social Democrats about Eastbourne and its aftermath. Activists were finding that in working class areas the row had had little effect, but that there had been a noticeable set back in middle class constituencies. There had also been some hurtful arguments within local parties. Everybody was anxious for an early solution.

While in Cambridge the Insider had received a series of

messages to 'phone reporters in London. On doing so he was startled to be asked to comment on a 'summit meeting' to take place at Ettrick Bridge at the weekend. He had not been looking at the meeting with Steel in this light, but was now informed that others would be there, in particular Jim Wallace and Simon Hughes, and that details had been released from Steel's office. He hastily telephoned Jim Dumsday, the Parliamentary Press Officer, to find out what was happening. Apparently the weekly *Liberal News* had reached journalists with a story about the meeting between the Party President and Steel, and this had spurred the Leader's office to release more details.

By Friday the newspapers were now full of the 'summit'. The *Guardian* claimed there was to be seven-day campaign by Steel to deal with the defence issue, concentrated on the meeting at Ettrick Bridge, the Policy Committee meeting on the Tuesday, the weekly meeting of MPs on Wednesday, and the National Executive the following Friday. *The Times* said Steel was 'gambling on bringing into line those rebel MPs who refused at the Eastbourne Assembly to back his quest for a European minimum nuclear deterrent, by downgrading the nature of that deterrent, by playing on the Alliance's disasterous post-Assembly performance in local elections and opinion polls, and by emphasising the anger of the wider Party outside the Assembly at what has happened'.

Liberal News carried on the defence debate. Alan Beith argued that in the aftermath of the breakdown of the Reykjavic talks, the area of difference within the party seemed both small in scale and remote in significance. He returned to the Defence Commission position that it would be foolish to make a final decision on Polaris. 'Any option we are likely to choose needs to be consistent with our objective of reducing, or at least freezing, the level of nuclear arms in Europe. One of the faults in the way the possibilities of Anglo-French cooperation were presented – and they remain only possibilities – was that the emphasis was too much on the hardware and not enough on the prospects of limiting total nuclear arms by joint targeting and of eventually shifting French defence policy away from its outdated disassociation of France away from European strategy.' But whereas Anglo-French cooperation in a strengthened European pillar was a political objective of real importance, the Anglo-French option in hardware could only be one of several possible alternatives to Trident if Polaris were to be replaced.

Beith argued that defence policy and defence spending needed to be firmly subordinated to foreign policy. Decisions on hardware followed decisions on strategy, not the other way round. 'One of the criticisms of the Leadership position at Eastbourne was a feeling that the hardware was being put first and that too great a reliance was being placed on a particular solution which had been far from fully explored. Our political priorities should be much more clearly visible. As it is, we have muddied the waters with the detail of our discussions.'

The main article in *Liberal News* was by Michael Meadowcroft, who defended the publication of *Across the Divide* and had this to say about Eastbourne: 'All of us want a united Party and Alliance. We are all prepared to go to great lengths to achieve unity. But if unity is gained by imposition rather than consent it is unlikely to survive scrutiny by opponents. It is difficult to jump from David Steel's speech at the 1982 Assembly – "There are some things we can do on our own. We can abandon the pretence of a British independent deterrent" – to his speech to delegates this year: "We now face the prospect that we might abandon our deterrent capacity unwittingly through obsolescence ... the country will want to know that we are ready and able to maintain and modernise our deterrent." It is not just that four years is a long time in politics, because on 23 April this year David said: "whether there should be any replacement at all for Polaris – I am inclined to think that there shouldn't be". To be loyal to him saying that in April is straightforward but I do need a little persuasion to be loyal to the opposite point of view in September.'

Meadowcroft described the 'lampposts in Lambeth' reference as 'drawing a caricature in order to deface it'. He referred to 'senior colleagues the day after the debate giving even greater coverage to the bizarre tabloid headlines – it was as distressing as it was impolitic'.

By mid-Friday the party was getting steamed up by the suggestions in newspaper stories about the Ettrick Bridge 'summit' that Steel's aim was to arrive at the Policy Committee determined to push his own option. Michael Meadowcroft telephoned the Insider. 'The Party is anxious to help – we'll go 95% with him at least – provided he doesn't try to steamroller it. If he tries to steamroller it we'll not just have a defence crisis but a leadership crisis.' The Insider said he couldn't see why Steel should not come to the Policy Committee meeting with his own suggestions but he agreed that the way the suggestions were put would be crucial.

The Insider found a growing pile of correspondence on his desk. There were conflicting messages. For instance, there were resolutions from local associations complaining about the vote at Eastbourne: 'This association thoroughly deplores the lack of responsibility displayed by delegates, some senior Liberals included,' started one, 'and urges that at all events in the eyes of the public those privileged to be present should be forcefully reminded of their duty to preserve the credibility of the Party in its quest for power. Whatever their opinion, however strongly held, dissidents should not be enabled to arrogate to themselves the right to jeopardise those hard and continuous efforts which have raised the stature of Liberals in many parts of the land, where Liberals have significantly advanced in spite of the odds ... at best it was a lamentable exhibition of naivety, and worst it was broadcast evidence of blundering inexperience.'

On the other hand, there was a letter from an old friend in the Party, and chairman of one of the Regions: 'Steel's speech has left very many of the older and longest serving members of the Party in a very low state of morale. His obvious misunderstanding of the Party and his attacks on our principles and most of all his own lack of interest in principles without power will take a long time in the healing.'

The Insider travelled to Sale on the edge of Manchester for *Any Questions*. On the train he carefully read the newspapers to anticipate likely questions, and jotted on small cards the points he could make in reply. It emerged during dinner with John Timpson and the other panellists – the Junior Minister for Industry, John Butcher, the Bishop of Manchester, and Ann Mallanieu, that the programme was to take place in a grammar school that would shortly be closed down as part of Manchester City Council's comprehensive policy. To his horror his mind went a complete blank on what the Party's policy on this was.

Politicians are expected to know a little about every policy area, both to deal with audiences at public meetings and with the media, but this, he felt, was the problem with politics – that politicians were forced to pretend to be authorities on every subject, surviving on superficiality, often adding to the sum of public ignorance rather than to its enlightenment. How much better it would be to simply answer the question 'I'm sorry, I'm afraid that's one of the policy areas I'm only loosely acquainted with and I've no worthwhile comment to make.' Unfortunately, when it came to *Any Questions*, this would not only be breaking the rules, it would render the game unplayable. He slipped away and telephoned David Alton in Liverpool, catching him just before he left home for a speaking engagement. A few minutes later he returned to the dinner table fully briefed.

After the programme, he found at his hotel a message to telephone Shirley Williams. She had come up with a hot tip from an 'inside source' that the next election would be in March. This, she felt, should add a note of urgency to the Ettrick Bridge meeting. He was sceptical. Politics is a process of endless rumour and speculation, and the sanest of people will sometimes believe the most unlikely proposition. March would hardly allow Nigel Lawson to introduce a pre-election budget, and would possibly rule out the Prime Minister's trip to Moscow. He felt that if it was the plan to make a run for it early in the New Year, May or June would be the earliest dates.

The following morning he drove from his Manchester hotel to Shrewsbury for a 'Green Briefing' organised by local Liberals, and then drove Simon Hughes to Scotland. Given less than four hours to arrive for dinner, they drove at speed up the M6 and then, in heavy rain, across the Borders to Ettrick Bridge. On the way they exchanged stories of Eastbourne and of the events of the past week. The 'summit' had come as news to Hughes too. He had heard it on the midnight radio news.

Steel greeted his two visitors warmly, and the three tucked into the roast lamb cooked by his daughter, a catering student (Judy was away), a bottle of red wine and plentiful supplies of malt whisky. The conversation continued until about 2.30 in the morning. They only briefly discussed what had happened at Eastbourne. The Leader was exercised about the poor communication on controversial Assembly resolutions. There had been no time to look at the defence amendments, to discuss them with the Assembly Committee or with their initiators, and to try and find common ground. His guests reminded him that the Chief Whip could have attended the Assembly Committee meeting, but nevertheless there did seem to be a timing problem and the Insider offered to raise the question with the Assembly Committee. They suggested Steel should receive a broader range of advice, both on policy issues and on Party thinking. Why could he not arrive at the Assembly on the Sunday night and have a gathering of people representative of key factions within the party, to discuss the coming week and get the feel of what resolutions were coming up and what the problem areas could be? Steel replied that the Assembly was for him a nightmare already, exhausting both because of its pace and because of the pressure he was under. Frankly, he said only half-jokingly, he would prefer not to be there at all, let alone arriving even earlier. His guests suggested that it could be less of a nightmare if he invested more time anticipating and eliminating problems in advance.

The three discussed the role of the Assembly, Steel arguing that the Assembly was the major showcase for the Party and that the rank and file did not seem to understand this. The Insider felt the Party did understand it, but it was also the chance of the rank and file to state their own views, and to influence policy, and that there would always be a balance to strike with no guarantee that the conference would not tip over one way or the other unless it was properly managed. By 'managed' he did not mean manipulated, rather that there was proper communication, and where possible, understandings reached that would be genuinely acceptable to the different parties to any policy dispute.

Detailed proposals on defence had been put off until the morrow, but Steel and his visitors discussed at some length how a revised policy could be made acceptable to the Party. Steel's plan was to promote it fairly firmly. He hoped there would be a special assembly to endorse it. The two urged the Leader not to be seen to be pushing it too hard himself. The more it could be seen to emerge from the Defence Spokesman and the Policy Committee, the more acceptable it would be. The Insider told Steel: 'I've talked to Liberals all over the country and I am satisfied that they want a solution, and they want it quickly, and it will be OK for you. To be frank, the one person who could screw it up is you. If you are seen to descend from Scotland with your policy, determined to foist it on the Party, it will be resented and resisted by at least a vocal minority.'

Instead, the matter should be dealt with as routine business at routine meetings. The Policy Committee, the Parliamentary meeting, and National Executive were all due to hold routine meetings, and there was a routine Council meeting on November 22 – if it was handled this way Steel would not be seen as pushing a policy onto the Party by special manoeuvres, such as a special assembly, but rather *the Party* would be dealing with the matter via constitutional channels in a calm and unexceptional way.

As they made their way to their different corners of the rambling Steel home, the Insider reflected for the umpteenth time since he had known his host just how easy it was to talk to him. You didn't have to talk in code to Steel. He listened well, and he talked directly, and there was rarely much room for misunderstanding. More than seventeen years had passed since the Insider had come to Ettrick Bridge for the first time. He and Steel had met in the late '60s, and the then relatively unknown Scottish MP had taken on the chairmanship of Shelter in Scotland. He had always liked Steel's sense of humour; he would laugh readily, and could laugh at jokes about himself. He had carefully developed the likeable, moderate image that had served the party well, but no-one near him had any doubts about his ambition, or that he would act ruthlessly if necessary. His critics in the Liberal Party who accused him of a lack of idealism based that charge on the assumption that if you were idealistic, you could only think in one way; take defence – Steel was as idealistic about the pursuit of multilateral reductions in nuclear weapons as the unilateralists were idealistic from their own perspective, but the gap between idealism and self-righeousness is a narrow one, and his critics did not concede this point.

For all his calculation and ability to play the long term game,

Steel could act impulsively, often when his patience was strained too far by a minority in the party, but for all that, he was normally inclined to find a solution acceptable to everybody, rather than just demand his own way. This should never be interpreted as lack of courage, however; that had been demonstrated on many occasions. In the early days, before his constituency majority was secured, Steel had refused to duck out of the anti-apartheid protests at the South African rugby tour, despite knowing that it would lose him votes. He had taken on abortion law reform knowing that it would be much misrepresented and opposed.

The Insider had always believed that both Steel and the Party had suffered from the fact that he spent a number of years as Chief Whip before becoming leader. As a result, he had been largely pinned down in the Commons, had perhaps become too much of a Commons man. He could not understand why Steel devoted so much time to meeting ambassadors and minor politicians from other countries and attending irrelevant receptions, and why the Liberal Parliamentary Party felt it necessary to waste so much time at the House of Commons voting when it would have no effect on the outcome, when they could be spearheading the fight in the country.

He knew Steel was not at home with the hand-shaking, baby-kissing, small-talking stuff of politics, but when he had accompanied the Liberal leader, he had observed how highly effective he was on walkabouts, in shopping centres, and at all sorts of informal gatherings. Steel could, whatever his reservations, rise to any occasion. Once, after a post-rally dinner with Welsh Liberals, Steel and the Insider left the restaurant by the wrong door and found themselves in the middle of about 150 members of bowling teams who were in Wales for an international tour, and were now combining some fairly heavy drinking with half-listening to a noisy cabaret. Before Steel could retreat, the compère spotted him and called him forward. Steel, unable to escape, responded brilliantly, with a couple of perfectly-judged jokes and, having arrived to a mixture of astonished applause and some jeers, left to loud cheers.

As a political leader, he had nearly all of the skills – judgement, a vision for where the Party was heading, the best touch with the media in British politics, a philosophical approach to the abuse and criticism that inevitably would come his way from opponents (and even some times from so-called friends), and professional skill with the major speech (even if he was from time to time less effective on minor occasions). He could occasionally be un-appreciative of the enormous voluntary input of many Liberals, probably less from ingratitude than a failure, from his West-minster perspective, to be fully aware of it. His lack of enthusiasm for becoming involved in policy creation meant, too, that he tended to let the Party do its own thing – set up policy panels, set off down a particular route, without offering some guidance as to where, in his view, it should all lead, and then, when he didn't like the result, he would seek to brush aside the product of a lot of dedication and hard work.

Parties always expect the impossible of their leaders, and leaders usually expect too much of their parties. The leader of the Liberal Party has enormous freedom of manoeuvre, if only because he has unequalled access to the media. You could argue for hours about the role of a leader in a party like the Liberal Party, but in the end it's all about the balance between *directing* the activities of the party and *representing* its policies and posi-tions. The Insider believed that the party provided Steel with the maximum possible freedom to direct; it had overcome its reserva-tions about the Lib-Lab pact, it had overcome reservations about the Alliance, and it had compromised time after time. In fact so much so, that it was arguable that the Leader had been spoiled, and thus over-reacted on the few occasions, usually to do with defence policy, when the party refused to follow his lead. Eastbourne had been a case in point. But his main failing was that he either did not always appreciate the need, or would not acknowledge the need to develop opinion behind him – by in-formal consultation, by ensuring that opinion-formers within the party were properly involved.

Yet, Steel was under no threat. There was no rival contender for the leadership and his skills were widely recognised and admired within the Party. He was not a loved Party leader, but there was a simple reason for this – he had no desire to be one, and made no concessions to attract affection. Likewise, for all his popularity with the public, he was not a populist.

He was at his most likeable in the company of just one indi-

vidual, or a small number of people, relaxed, expecting no concessions to his seniority, and quick to see any humour that was
there. You didn't have to spend more than an evening in the
slightly chaotic, homely and warm base of the Steel family at
Ettrick Bridge to see why the Leader commanded the loyalty of
those closest to him.

The week October 18 to 25

The 'initiative' on defence . . .

The following morning it was raining, but this did not deter the
Insider from taking a walk. As he left the house engulfed in a
massive borrowed windcheater and uneasily tugging the Steel
labrador behind him, he could hear the guffaws of the Leader
and Simon Hughes as they observed him from the kitchen
window. Hughes and Steel then had their own chat to (he
assumed) repair relations after Eastbourne. Shortly after he
returned, Jim Wallace arrived, and after a chat, the four went out
into the yard to be filmed by photographers and television crews.
After lunch Hughes had to leave for a speaking engagement in
Yorkshire, and Steel and Wallace settled down to finalise the
details of the defence proposal while the Insider prepared a
communiqué on the gathering. When he joined the other two he
had the chance for the first time to comment on the proposal they
hoped would resolve the conflict.

For the multilateralists, there was a promise that the Alliance
would be committed to NATO and that it acknowledged the
obligations of membership, including acceptance of allies' bases
on British soil. There was a promise to maintain (with whatever
necessary modernisation) the minimum nuclear deterrent until it
could be negotiated away as part of a global arms negotiation
process and in return for worthwhile concessions by the USSR.

For the anti-nuclear forces within the Party there was the
promise to 'freeze' Britain's nuclear capacity at a level no greater
than that of the Polaris system, the promise to give a much
higher priority to fostering the disarmament process which 'if we
are successful, would mean that a modernised minimum UK
deterrent in the mid to late 1990s need never actually be required',

the promise to seek a battlefield nuclear weapon-free zone in Central Europe, the promise to agree voluntarily to a freeze on nuclear weapons testing and encourage the USA to do likewise, the promise to withdraw British support from the Star Wars programme, and the proposal that, subsequent to the proposals in Reykjavik for substantial reductions in intermediate nuclear weapons, Britain should propose a moratorium on further deployment of these while there remained a possibility of further negotiations.

The Insider was encouraged. It appeared that Owen, while being reassured that we would maintain a minimum nuclear deterrent if it could not be negotiated away, was being asked to concede a freeze on the size of our nuclear capability, and throughout the document there was a shift of emphasis from solely defence to defence *and* disarmament.

In his capacity as Party President he then issued a brief report to the media. He had to deal with some extraordinary stories in the Sunday papers that Steel would threaten to resign unless a special assembly accepted his policy. One newspaper described it as a 'back me or sack me appeal to the Liberal Assembly'.

The Insider told the media: 'We were convinced, no one more so than David Steel, that we should seek to deal with the defence issue calmly and via the established decision-making processes of the Party. Jim Wallace has had a chance to discuss and reach accord with the Leader on proposals which he intends to put to the Policy Committee and the Parliamentary Party this week. We all still have an open mind on the question of whether a special assembly will later be necessary. That matter will be resolved by the National Executive.'

He was able to add honestly that 'suggestions in newspapers prior to our meeting that David Steel wished to bypass the Party or push his views with the threat of resignation are nonsense.'

So that was it. Some summit! Yet that Sunday night pictures of the four in Steel's front yard ranked high in the television news, and there was substantial publicity in the newspapers on the Monday morning. Recalling the rather chaotic nature of the conference, the Insider noted, not for the first time, the contrast between the disorganised reality of many political happenings and the more impressive picture that can be created for and/or by the media.

On the Tuesday morning the Alliance Joint Strategy Committee met. Steel explained the proposal that he was putting to his Policy Committee and Parliamentary Party, and said that he had shown it to David Owen who could live with it. Alan Watson pressed Owen on the point and was supported by others. It would be disastrous, Owen was told, if after the Steel initiative was taken, it was undermined by any action by him. Owen replied: 'It doesn't create any problems for me.' He went on to say he had put the crucial words to his National Committee and they had been happy with it. 'Freeze' was not 'a happy word' and it was an outdated concept . . . but he would not make a point of it.

While this was the most substantial matter before the Committee, another was the proposed structure for Alliance General Election planning. John Pardoe and Lord Harris tabled a paper proposing that when the election was called, the Joint Strategy Committee be replaced by a smaller Alliance Campaign Committee. In the meantime, there would be a small core group, the Alliance Planning Group, consisting of Owen, Steel, Pardoe, Harris, Tyler, Roland Freeman (one of Owen's PR advisers), Polly Toynbee and the Insider. The proposal was presented and accepted in a low-key way, but its endorsement was of critical importance to the two Leaders, who wished, via this small group, to be given executive authority to direct the day-by-day running of the Alliance, and particularly the election campaign, while at the same time maintaining at least the appearance of accountability to the democratic structures of their two parties. Owen, more than Steel, had wanted the group to be even smaller, but Liberals particularly had been worried about its non-accountability. John Pardoe held no office within the party, and Paul Tyler had just ended his term as Chairman. Thus the Insider had been insisted upon by the General Election Committee and the National Executive of the Liberal Party to create a direct line from the Alliance Planning Group for the General Election to the Liberal Party General Election Committee and then on to the National Executive and the Party Council. Conceding this, Owen had added Polly Toynbee from the National Committee of the SDP.

The crucial meeting of the Liberal Policy Committee took place at the House of Commons at six o'clock that Tuesday evening.

Alan Beith, recently-elected Chairman of the Policy Committee, presided, and Steel, Meadowcroft, and Malcolm Bruce were also present from the Parliamentary Party. Jim Wallace had been detained in Scotland. It was a tense meeting, made all the more so by four interruptions while the MPs disappeared for Commons votes. Tim Clement-Jones immediately raised the question of whether the Steel-Wallace proposal was Liberal policy or Alliance policy. Steel said that he hoped it could be an update and revision of Liberal policy. This led to a lengthy discussion, with Meadowcroft and the radical Ian Brodie-Browne and others urging Steel to make it an initiative for Alliance policy. Otherwise it would be seen as attempting to overturn the Eastbourne decision or change Liberal policy, and this would be resisted by a substantial, even if minority, section of the Party, starting up another damaging debate.

The Insider said that Steel was right to want to reassure the public that everyone was 'on board', but while the ideal would be to re-debate Liberal policy and then renogotiate it with the Social Democratic Party, the problem was time. They could not afford to keep defence at the top of the political agenda much longer, and time was running out for the General Election. The only way Liberal policy could be changed was in a fairly leisurely way. Thus a compromise was called for – Steel must be seen to have achieved a success by winning Liberal support for a *Liberal initiative*, but the initiative should be to establish an *Alliance policy* for the General Election and for a five-year administration. After some initial resistance, Steel warmed to the idea and eventually the Policy Committee unanimously endorsed the proposal on these terms.

By the Wednesday evening when the weekly meeting of Party Officers (President, Chairman, Treasurer, and Secretary-General) took place with Steel in his office at the Commons, the Leader was comfortable with the approach and had moved towards accepting that a special assembly was not the best idea.

The Parliamentary Party then met. Jim Wallace introduced the document, and Steel then made a number of points to reassure his colleagues: that there was no reference to Eurobombs, or a third nuclear power; that there was no reference to specific hardware but an emphasis on the strategy because talk of specific hardware made people sound as though we wanted to use it; and that Owen had conceded on four points – the use of the word 'freeze', the spelling out of what was meant by a minimum deterrent, the emphasis on non-nuclear objectives, and the specific reference to a replacement for Polaris possibly not being required.

There was some discussion of the meaning of some words but the document was approved and immediately published at a press conference. Owen released a broad endorsement.

That night the Knowsley by-election day was announced. November 13.

The Insider decided to drive up to Knowsley after a debate with John Biffen at the Cambridge Union on the Friday night. For those who think politics is a glamorous profession, let them be disabused by the Insider's experience the next day.

He woke up in a hotel in Northampton where he had stopped at 1 o'clock in the morning. He was back on the road at 7 a.m., driving up the M1 then the M6, until a couple of miles short of Junction 18 and only a few miles short of the turn-off to Knowsley North. The three lanes of the motorway became one just before some road works, and despite having slowed down to what seemed to be an acceptable speed, he suddenly became aware that the rear of the preceding car was in fact coming towards him at a fair speed. In the split seconds that followed he realised the cars ahead were hitting each other. He braked violently, but there was no way he could stop before crunching into the car in front. This was only a second before a red MG crashed into his rear. There was the sound of tyres squealing and further crashes behind as one car after another joined the pile-up. He tried to open the car door but found that the impact had forced the front part of the car back so that it would not open. To cut a rather lengthy story short, after a lot of disentangling of cars, forcing open of doors, taking of names etc, for no one seemed to have been hurt apart from the cars, he was towed off to the the nearest garage where he spent a couple of hours until he was able to obtain a hire car and continue the journey to Knowsley North.

The by-election headquarters were a shambles. In two corners sat a small number of Liberals folding envelopes while the headquarters were literally being built and decorated around them, it having been a derelict and damp old business premises. In one cold office, a man sat dealing with the postal response to a leaflet that the prospective candidate Rosemary Cooper had put out asking constituents to let her know of any housing or other problems they faced. In another corner Steve Mulholland, the agent for the by-election, and Trevor Jones, over from Liverpool, were busy putting together a leaflet they planned to rush out the following day.

He went out into the streets with Rosemary Cooper. A chill wind was blowing and most of the time it was pouring with rain, but with Channel 4 television following them around, they had no choice but to determinedly plough on. After just over an hour of this, the Insider, committed to being back in Brighton in the evening, had no choice but to climb wearily, cold, and still not having eaten since 6 o'clock the previous night, into the hire car and begin the five-hour journey back to Brighton. At about 8 o'clock, just past Horsham, he ran out of petrol on a lonely country road in the pitch dark. He had to hitch a ride to the nearest garage where they cheerfully informed him that their breakdown charge was £17.50. Fruitlessly he argued that the car was only a mile away, and eventually, outraged, he set off walking. He arrived at the car only to find that he could not get the petrol cap off and spent fifteen minutes wrestling with it in the dark before it finally came loose. Then he found that the petrol can would not fit into the car, and had to empty a soft drink bottle, pour the petrol into the bottle, and from that pour it into the car.

He finally limped home at about 9 o'clock, having spent some thirteen hours travelling, a fair chunk of it on the roadside, having not eaten for twenty-seven hours, and all for one hour of canvassing in Knowsley.

The months November–December

The Alliance dives in the polls ... and unites on defence ... Labour holds Knowsley but the Liberal does well ... plans are laid for an Alliance re-launch ... Thatcher in trouble in Australia ... tragedy on Christmas Eve.

At the end of October, the *Evening Standard* published an appalling opinion poll for the Alliance – it had fallen to 17%, with Labour at 41% and the Conservatives 39%. This represented a drop of 9% in just over a month since the eve of the Liberal Assembly. Steel's personal rating had dropped three points and Owen's six points. This poll, soon supported by others, came as a crushing blow. In previous years the Alliance had always risen in the polls after its two conferences. Whatever their views on the issue itself, everybody in the Alliance now accepted that the defence controversy had been a political disaster. It was now imperative not only to unite on a policy, but to publicly demonstrate that unity.

Some believed there was no alternative but a dramatic special Liberal Party Assembly and a reversal of policy. Others believed an Alliance conference was necessary. The Insider was one of those who argued that once there was unity on a policy it should be endorsed at not one, but a variety of different gatherings, in order to create the impression of a developing solution – a bandwagon effect. The final show of unity could be in January at the Barbican Rally.

All this added urgency to the next of the 'routine meetings' to discuss the initiative – that of the National Executive. The advice from the *Guardian* leader writers was that 'Eastbourne's ghosts ... could only be exorcised by a second, special conference, and the melodrama of minds changed', but the National Executive was not looking for melodrama – especially as it was not convinced that minds *had* been changed. What the *Guardian* and many others did not seem to recognise was that it was relatively straightforward to achieve a Liberal initiative for *Alliance* policy, for Liberals understood that Alliance positions involved a compromise between the policies of the two parties, but that it would be even more difficult now to achieve a convincing show of unity on wholly Liberal policy, for while the pressures may have altered the balance of opinion within the party they had also strengthened the resolve of those who felt particularly strongly on either side of the argument. If the Liberal Party was called upon to reconsider its policy, there would be more than the 'melodrama of minds changed' there would also be the melodrama of an almighty row. Fun for the *Guardian*, and the other parties, but not really helpful to the Alliance.

For these reasons the National Executive endorsed the initiative but rejected a special assembly – officially because it was constitutionally unnecessary, but in reality because it was politically hazardous. It would also not in itself represent re-unification of the Alliance.

On November 20 the Policy Committee met to discuss the forthcoming meeting of the Party Council and the crucial debate on defence. Liberal CND had tabled a resolution for Council underlining that the policy was Alliance and not Liberal policy. The majority of the Policy Committee now set out to persuade a Liberal CND representative that they should withdraw this. At one point the meeting took a dramatic turn when all the lights in the House of Commons went out and William Wallace had to continue to argue his case in pitch darkness. When he finished a number of people tried to intervene. 'How do we catch your eye, Mr Chairman?' someone asked the invisible Alan Beith. But one by one they added to the pressure on the CND representative to withdraw the resolution. Nobody argued with the accuracy of it – it was just that the political crisis called for unqualified endorsement. Finally the Policy Committee elicited a promise that if the advocates of the initiative at Party Council put sufficient emphasis on the fact that it was *Alliance* policy, the Liberal CND resolution would be withdrawn.

The Party Council meeting, attended by more than 200, took place in Bristol on November 22. Michael Meadowcroft cleverly introduced the Policy Committee's report, including the defence initiative, emphasising strongly that it was an Alliance policy, and that it had evolved properly via the proper committees and constitutional forums of the party. The party was, he said, clearly uniting behind this Alliance position. He stressed that with the General Election approaching they were now – 'into Alliance business. It's time to get the defence issue out of the way so that we can make a straight run for the tape.' Meadowcroft wrong-footed Liberal CND by referring to his own membership of CND and then concluding that he was satisfied this was the best that could be achieved for Alliance policy and was an honourable reconciliation of the positions of the two parties.

Liberal CND, accepting Meadowcroft's assurances and, knowing defeat was inevitable, withdrew their resolution and the initiative was endorsed by 200 votes to 3.

One stage remained – final negotiation of the initiative with the Social Democratic Party. Despite the broad public and private endorsement of Owen and John Cartwright at the time the Liberal initiative emerged, there were determined efforts by some within both parties to edge the proposed policy back in their own direction. It all came to a head on December 16 with a meeting of the Joint Policy Committee to finalise *Partnership for Progress*. When the Liberal Policy Committee met just prior to the joint meeting to consider the latest version, two or three Liberals argued that the party had endorsed the defence initiative on the basis that it had already been cleared with the SDP. But now there were changes. Any change at this point would be a betrayal. The Insider replied that if it had been a definitive policy it would not have been called an initiative. What mattered was whether the final wording contained either a serious addition or omission from the Liberal initiative, or whether it fairly reflected its spirit. He felt the latter had been achieved, and William Wallace supported him. Michael Meadowcroft said that the last remaining task always had been to achieve a fuller defence policy in accord with the initiative, and he, too, felt it had been achieved.

There was an agonised discussion. Everybody desperately wanted to end the defence crisis, but there were still uncertainties, above all over whether the revised policy meant that the Alliance would or would not support the introduction of Cruise missiles at Molesworth. It was finally decided that David Penhaligon would raise the issue as a question to Owen at the Joint Policy Committee and that the Liberal team would withdraw to reconsider only if Owen's reply was completely unsatisfactory. When the moment came a number of Liberals were not happy with Owen's interpretation of the key paragraph, and so the Liberal team did withdraw to argue further.

This was an even more unhappy gathering than the earlier one, beginning in a corridor of the Commons and carrying over to a committee room. The group was divided on whether to risk a complete breakdown of the main meeting and wreck the 'signing' of the joint policy programme that evening or whether to accept the wording of the document, as one member, Alan Leaman, despairingly said, 'if only because it is ambiguous'.

Eventually it was decided the existing wording would do. Everybody trooped back into the joint meeting, where after some discussion one or two small last-minute changes were made as a concession to Liberal feelings. The deal was then struck. The Joint Policy Committee endorsed the defence section of *Partnership for Progress* and at last the Alliance defence row was over.

All that remained was for Owen and Steel to announce it publicly the following day. David Steel told a press conference 'this puts the defence debate internally, to bed'. 'Defence accord ends Alliance rift' the *Guardian* reported.

And so it did.

Nearly two months had passed since Eastbourne and the Alliance was at last able to unite and move onto other and hopefully more fruitful political ground.

Not so Labour. Throughout November and December it found its own defence policy bombarded from both sides of the Atlantic. Given the controversial nature of its unilateralism, Labour decided to promote it heavily now in the hope that it would draw the enemy fire well in advance of the election, and also allow the electorate to become accustomed to it and, presumably, begin to see its attractions. Kinnock went to the United States to explain the policy there, arguing that it was the right policy for 'a well developed, well connected medium-sized power'. It was possible for Britain to play a full part in NATO while refusing to have its own deterrent or to host American nuclear weapons. The trip received a bad press.

When he returned to Britain to publish the party's defence document, it was judged by the commentators to be a watering-down of the unilateralist line. There was talk of lengthy and complex discussion with allies before taking action. In answer to questions, Kinnock would not indicate the likely timetable for the removal of American nuclear weapons. But the policy was still described as 'desperately dangerous' by George Younger, the Secretary of State for Defence, and David Owen must have caused a few groans from those Liberals who were unilateralists: 'there is no way that we would give a non-nuclear strategy the time of day'. Norman Tebbit went to New York to assure the Americans that the Conservatives would not abandon its allies. 'Whilst Mr Kinnock says firmly that he is in favour of British membership of NATO, his policies would seem to make that membership impossible,' he said, in a speech really aimed at a British audience.

Just what this would mean at the General Election was unclear. It was hard to believe that the voters would feel as strongly on the subject as the Conservatives appeared to think, but there was much in the view expressed by Peter Jenkins in *The Sunday Times* that 'voters do seem to regard defence as the litmus test of a party's fitness to govern'. Undoubtedly the heavy drubbing the Tories were giving Kinnock on the issue was as much to do with raising doubts about whether he would be a responsible Prime Minister as with defence policy itself.

In the meantime, the Knowsley by-election came and went. Labour held the seat, but Rosemary Cooper achieved a highly respectable second place with a 19.8% increase in the Liberal share of the vote. Once more the Alliance had demonstrated that when people actually voted, its result was far better than its opinion poll rating.

Norman Tebbit launched an attack on the BBC for political bias. While the BBC won the ensuing battle on points, there was an uncomfortable feeling that Tebbit may have had some softening-up effect for the General Election. This caused some concern at the Alliance Planning Group, itself worried not so much about biased BBC opinion as a bias in the quantity of its coverage. Too often Tory or Labour views were reported and the Alliance omitted altogether.

The APG was now meeting regularly. It had evolved a plan. The objective was no less than to recover by January 31 the position in the opinion polls lost after Eastbourne. It would create a fresh Alliance image and then a series of events designed to stress unity. There would be a joint New Year message by the two Leaders; there would be the heralding of the conclusion of negotiations on seat allocations; there would be the naming of the joint Alliance spokesman; there would be the publication of *Partnership for Progress*, the joint policy document; and all this would come to a head at the Barbican Rally. Two of the precious party political broadcasts available to the Alliance in 1987 would be used at the beginning of the year, one just before the Barbican Rally and one after.

The APG was 'going for broke' to recapture lost ground.

The Insider was encouraged by some of the decisions; for instance, to allow John Cleese, who had made a brilliant SDP party political broadcast on proportional representation earlier in the year, to have considerable say in making Alliance PPBS in the New Year. Advertising man David Abbott was appointed to work on a fresh Alliance image, and in early December came to present his first ideas. He proposed gold as the Alliance colour. (This was no easy decision. Only Liberals and Social Democrats would appreciate the loyalties built up within the two parties for their respective colours — day-glow orange for the Liberals, and red, white and blue for the Social Democrats. There would be Liberals who would continue with day-glow orange for the rest of time, come hell or high water, whether David Owen and David Steel went for gold or not. Owen himself was called upon to make an even greater concession — namely the partial loss of his own party's colour, for the Alliance gold was clearly much closer to the Liberal colour.) Abbott proposed *The Time Has Come* as the theme for the Barbican Rally and the accompanying campaign. The Insider would have far preferred it to be *The Alliance. It's Time*, but the others were enthusiastic. Abbott also presented a variety of leaflets and posters on different issues. One was 'Caught between the Devil and the Deep Blue C?' and stressed the Alliance as an alternative to the two old parties. Another emphasised the dividing nation 'The poor north versus the richer south' and one on education was headlined 'More strikes in the schools versus more class in the classroom ... it's time to put children first'.

It was decided that *Partnership for Progress*, the main policy document, should be retitled *The Time Has Come* and that there be a major eight-page leaflet to front the campaign. Paul Tyler and the Insider wrote the leaflet over a bottle of wine in the latter's office one night. (Tyler, a former MP who, after two years as Chairman of the Party, had offered to work as a close aide to David Steel up to and during the Election, was emerging as a key figure, coordinating the activities of the creative people, and the

advance planning for the campaign. Tyler is one of those individuals, Richard Holme and William Wallace being others, who
are happy to work tirelessly behind the scenes for David Steel
and for the Party and who, partly because of their self-effacement,
are much under-valued by many members. If anyone shared
Holme's appetite for all things political, it was Tyler.)

It was decided to encourage Liberals and Social Democrats all
over Britain to organise local campaigns to take advantage of the
publicity likely to be achieved at national level.

While the APG was busy planning its election strategy, the
Government had become embroiled in an absurd court case in
Australia, where it was attempting to persuade the New South
Wales Supreme Court to halt the publication of the memoirs of a
former M15 officer, Peter Wright. It was an affair that was
harming a lot of reputations – that of Sir Robert Armstrong, the
Cabinet Secretary, trapped into admitting in court that he had
been 'economical with the truth'; that of Neil Kinnock, who made
the serious error of telephoning Wright's solicitor on a number of
occasions and thus losing the initiative by opening himself up to
Tory criticisms of disloyalty to Britain; that of Lord Rothschild,
who had to plead with the Prime Minister to clear him of charges
that he was a Russian spy; and that of M15 itself, for it was
becoming clear that the book would show that M15 had far
exceeded its powers, not least in investigating a Prime Minister
(Harold Wilson) while actually in office.

The Insider felt the Wright case contained the beginnings of a
big political row in 1987, but for now it was time for a break. At
last the House of Commons and British politics closed down for
Christmas, the MPS returned to their constituencies, and the
Insider retreated to his home in Brighton to work on his book
and articles and speeches for the New Year. And down in his
beloved Cornwall David Penhaligon rose early on the morning of
December 22 to drive from Truro to St Austell as he did every
year to thank postal workers dealing with the Christmas mail.
His wife Annette – more than his wife, also his fellow worker for
the party cause since they were Young Liberals together – was
busying herself making breakfast for their two children and for
her parents, who had come to stay for Christmas. She heard a
radio report of a road accident on the Truro–St Austell road, and

actually said to the family she hoped David was all right. But he wasn't. On a hill covered with black ice, his car was hit by a van. He was killed at the age of forty-two.

The police called on Annette Penhaligon about an hour later to break the news. The Whip's office in the House of Commons was told, who telephoned David Steel in Scotland, other senior MPs, and the Party President in Brighton. It was a shattering blow. Penhaligon had a special place in the party. Not one of its intellectuals, and, despite some ambitions, probably not destined to become its leader, he was nevertheless a remarkable source of strength, because of his warm nature, humour, commonsense, and a philosophical outlook that often helped the party to achieve a sense of perspective when one problem or another was drifting out of proportion.

He had built up his majority from 464 votes when he was elected in 1974 to more than 10,000 at the last election. He had been an indefatigable fighter for Cornwall, and in particular had waged a remorseless battle on behalf of the declining tin industry.

Liberals needed no telling of their loss, but even his wife Annette was surprised at the impact his death had on the whole country. Liberals everywhere were approached by friends or people they hardly knew, wanting to share their sense of shock and sympathy.

David Penhaligon had preceded the Insider as President of the Party. The latter had doubted whether an MP could also be an effective President but Penhaligon had shown he could. He had only really come to know his predecessor towards the end of his Presidency, but they had come together at Eastbourne and Penhaligon had been exceptionally generous in the way he handed over the office. The Insider would always feel fortunate to witness one of Penhaligon's vintage performances earlier in the year, at the Joint Candidates Conference in Regents Park. Penhaligon had been billed to open the conference, preceding Owen and Steel, but because Owen was late, found himself making a lengthy speech. He revelled in the opportunity, combining humour with passion so that at one moment he had candidates falling about with laughter, and the next cheering him to the echo. Many would recall him waving the draft of *Partnership*

for Progress at his audience and saying 'they say we have no
policies ... we have hundreds of policies, and what's good about
this document is that most of them aren't in it ...' But he spoke
movingly about the need to share power with people. It was a
remarkable performance.

At his funeral service a few days later the minister referred to
David Penhaligon's unassuming modesty, unassailable integrity,
intellectual generosity and infectious gaiety.

On the eve of Christmas in 1986 the Liberal Party had suffered
a devastating blow, but, of course, not comparable to that of the
popular and brave Annette Penhaligon who attached to her
wreath for her husband some words of Shakespeare's: 'When he
shall die, take him out and cut him out in little stars, and he will
make the face of heaven so fine that all the world will be in love
with night'.

The week January 4 to 11

*Two by-elections pending ... 'Cabinet' forming on the Truro
train ... two nations confirmed ... what Norman Tebbit is alleged
to have said ...*

Politics is in at least one respect like show business. The show
must go on. Already in the early days of January talk was turning
to two by-elections, for shortly after the death of David Penhaligon, the Labour MP for Greenwich, Guy Barnett, died. His
majority in 1983 had been only 1,200 votes. Already there was an
Alliance candidate in place there, Rosie Barnes, about whom
much more later. Annette Penhaligon made it clear that she did
not want to fight the Truro seat, although she would have been a
popular successor to her husband, and the word from Cornwall
was that local Liberals were determined to find a local candidate.

David Steel was away on holiday, but the Liberal Party was
turning its mind to the team of Alliance spokesmen due to be
finalised. The party was anxious that the number of Liberals in
the team should be significantly greater than Social Democrats,
to reflect the size of the parties and the greater numbers of
Liberal MPs and local councillors. Parity would be unacceptable.

There were also rumours that David Owen was insisting upon the hard line multilateralist John Cartwright as defence spokesman. This was seen as provocative to Liberals. The party, in view of its strength on local authorities, was also anxious that local government matters should be in the hands of a Liberal. Many in the party saw the resolution of these matters as a test of Steel's ability to deliver in negotiation with the SDP.

Steel arrived back from holiday in time for a four-hour meeting of the APG. Paul Tyler produced a detailed plan for the activities of the two leaders during the General Election. Tyler was determined to keep the two leaders together as much as possible, particularly in the early stage of the campaign, handling the press conferences jointly in London in the morning, and then meeting once more in the early evening for joint regional television appearances and then for the 'Ask the Alliance' question and answer public meetings. The emphasis in the plan was on television coverage. The Leaders were unenthusiastic about the plan to keep them together. They claimed they got bored listening to one another and that this showed. Tyler, however, was determined, and was well supported by the rest of the group. There was overwhelming evidence that their joint appearances were being well-received, they told the Leaders. No one actually voiced their real fear – that if the two Leaders were separated, there could be conflicting messages coming from different parts of the country during the General Election campaign. The Insider sensed that the two Leaders knew this was in the minds of the others but, whatever they felt about this, they were finding it difficult to resist the unanimity of the advice.

The APG approved the first draft of a party political broadcast written by David Abbott. It introduced the 'see-saw' approach that was to be a feature of the Alliance promotional activities for most of the January-February campaign. The see-saw was painted half blue and half red, and the two men at either end, one with a blue rosette, and one with a red rosette, stressed their entirely different attitudes and views, the message being that there was only one way to stop the damage being done by the swings from one set of policies and attitudes to another, and that was to vote Alliance.

After the meeting the Insider and Tyler went with David Steel to watch an interview he had given to Channel 4 news. He began by predicting an autumn election, and when asked who the Alliance would work with afterwards, said it was inconceivable that the Alliance could keep Mrs Thatcher in power. She would have lost the election – lost a substantial majority in the House of Commons. There would be no conceivable way the Alliance could sustain her in those circumstances. He drew a parallel with Heath losing in 1974. He said she wouldn't be the right kind of politician to operate in a coalition.

Afterwards, the Insider and John Pardoe, Tyler and Steel teamed up for dinner at Joe Allen's. It was just the opportunity the Insider had hoped for to discuss the choice of Alliance spokesmen. Steel made it clear that he saw no way of avoiding Cartwright as defence spokesman particularly as the Alliance had worked hard to achieve a place for him on the Select Committee for Defence. Steel hoped that by having a Liberal in charge of Foreign Affairs and thus in the senior of the two positions, Cartwright's post would be more acceptable to Liberals. It was also clear that he was suggesting some radical Liberals for key posts, including Michael Meadowcroft for local government, a choice that would be more than acceptable to the ALC.

The week's newspapers all signalled an election issue for the north-south divide which was confirmed by the publication of the 1986 employment estimates. These showed that people in the South East, East Anglia, the South West had suffered significantly less than people in other parts of the country. More than 90% of jobs lost in Britain since 1979 had been north of the line from the Wash to the Bristol Channel. There was also a 'black and white divide'. Figures revealed that black people were twice as likely, and those of Pakistani or Bangladeshi origin were three times as likely, to be unemployed as whites.

In the *Guardian*, Hugo Young turned his eloquence upon Norman Tebbit and in a passage that was to have considerable consequences he claimed this: 'An argument was raging between Ministers on aspects of public spending. Morality and conscience, it was being suggested by some colleagues, dictated bigger spending in unfashionable "caring" areas. Mr Tebbit was utterly scornful. "Nobody with a conscience votes Conservative anyway" he said.'

On the Saturday, the Insider rose at 4.30 a.m. to drive to London to catch the train to Truro for David Penhaligon's memorial service. Clement Freud had booked an entire first class carriage, and arranged a non-stop service of food and drink for a remarkable gathering. In addition to David Steel and the majority of Liberal MPs, there were David and Debbie Owen, Party Officers, and the tragic, bowed figure of Jeremy Thorpe in his familiar black coat and black homburg hat. Everybody arrived looking cold and sombre, the men wearing black ties and the women black coats or scarves, but breakfast cheered everybody up and by the end of the five-hour rail journey the party was in good heart. The cathedral was packed and there were overflow congregations in nearby churches. The Insider marvelled at the strength and dignity of Annette Penhaligon as she greeted the visitors and he was moved by the number of Liberals he saw in the congregation, people who had travelled from as far as Scotland to queue for a place in the cathedral.

Annette had decided it should be a service of thanksgiving, rather than a memorial, but the combination of the huge impersonal cathedral, the winter chill, and the sense of loss ordained that, despite an informal address highlighting the humanity of David, it was a sad occasion.

The service over, and the tears shed, the party clambered back on the train. His former colleagues and friends were later to say that nobody would have been more amused at the return journey than David Penhaligon. Relaxing after dinner on board, the MPs and Party Officers, and one or two journalists on the train, mingled in the aisles, while Owen and Steel plotted together in the middle of the carriage, trying to finalise their team of spokesmen. One by one MPs would join them to either accept what was on offer, or argue for a better deal. One of the winners was Malcolm Bruce, who refused the first offer and landed the employment post that probably would have been Penhaligon's. The Insider, Pardoe, Dick Newby, the SDP General Secretary, and Debbie Owen formed a group in the next carriage, informing anyone who joined them that this was the 'non-plotting group'.

By the time everybody arrived back in London after more than ten hours on the train, and the few sad hours in Truro, Owen and Steel had almost completed their task. Meadowcroft, Hughes and Kirkwood were planning to go off into the night to plan a last-ditch campaign to achieve a few changes, and the Insider reflected that David Penhaligon's final contribution had been to get the entire Alliance hierarchy together for a day that in its mixture of melancholy and politicking, culminating in the emergence of an Alliance parliamentary team, had probably done more for unity than any event since the SDP had been formed.

January 11–17, 1987

The big freeze ... Tebbit's conscience ... fixing on the election date ... two nations ... Labour in trouble in the opinion polls ... the Alliance names its team ... the north-south divide ... tax and public expenditure ... Owen goes for PR and Steel goes west ... tactical voting

It was beginning to snow as the Insider ended at Brighton his twenty-hour journey to Truro and back. It was to prove the beginning of a blizzard, said to have been swept from Siberia, that would reduce the whole country to a crawl and the east, especially Kent, and parts of Essex and Sussex, to a complete halt. Roads were closed. Trains either could not run or were massively delayed. On one day one of the Insider's friends took seven hours to travel from Victoria to Brighton by train. Cars wouldn't start. Pipes froze, and then later burst. There were stormy scenes of a different kind in the House of Commons as Labour, while unable to actually blame the snow on the Conservatives, condemned them for a hard-hearted response. Mrs Thatcher, motivated either by compassion or the possibility of an election, wasted little time. It was announced that a £5 severe weather payment would be made to up to 1.5 million people. She promised to waive the strict bureaucratic procedures and promised the money within a week.

All of this was to come later in the week, however, for at the beginning the political storm was over the alleged Tebbit remark 'Nobody with a conscience votes Conservative'. On the Saturday Tebbit had a letter published in the *Guardian* condemning it as a 'total fabrication'. He further complained that a letter by his Chief of Staff had been altered. 'You published an invented quotation at best based on unattributed gossip. You deliberately distorted a repudiation of that invention. You compounded and aggravated your libel by repeating it in the front page leading item of your edition of January 9, and encouraged that invention to become part of another anti-Conservative myth...'. He demanded an unconditional apology.

That the alleged remark was having an effect was shown by an *Observer* leader entitled *Mr Tebbit and the New Tory Brutalism*. It stated that: 'In Mr Norman Tebbit she [Mrs Thatcher] has a Party Chairman who is too unsubtle by half. Whether or not Tebbit ever said "Nobody with a conscience votes Conservative", the remarks sounds all too typical of the new brutalism he had brought to the Tory Party'.

The Insider knew that, whether or not Tebbit made the remark, the Tories were justified in their concern. He recalled remarks or alleged remarks that had become a millstone around the necks of politicians before. For instance, the (apparently incorrectly) reported comment by Jim Callaghan when he was Prime Minister, and was returning from a summit meeting to face industrial strife in Britain – 'Crisis? What crisis?' This alleged remark of Tebbit's could turn up from now to the last day of the General Election. (Richard Holme, speaking to Liberal candidates later in the week, was to tell them that if they wanted a Tory equivalent of the Bernie Grants and Derek Hattons to personalise their attacks on the Tories, Tebbit was their man.) It was clearly vital for Tebbit to stamp on the story so forcibly that it would become impossible for the other parties to quote it.

The *Guardian*, however, showed no sign of letting up. James Naughtie reported on Monday that Ministers were concerned that the row would 'tend to draw attention to Mr Tebbit's style, which they believed to be an electoral handicap'. One was reported as saying 'it's the plausibility of the quote that makes it so damaging. He does speak with breath-taking insensitivity. He rather prides himself on the macho image ... the story does not strike me as implausible in the least'.

An unapologetic Hugo Young returned to the issue in his 'Commentary' on Tuesday. He did, however, appear to be suggesting that 'the famous phrase' could have been a coarse way of making a deeper political point. Were not issues of 'conscience' redolent of priorities which a fair number of Conservatives believed to have been responsible for the decline of Britain, for instance a Welfare State which had produced a 'soft nation', uncompetitive in the world, lacking the will to work . . . costing more than the country could afford?

Young's article set the Insider thinking. He could imagine the context for such a remark. A meeting in Smith Square on themes for the election. Someone says 'we have to show we care about the unemployed, the old, the young, the sick . . . that's why I'm worried about a tax-cutting budget. Shouldn't we show that we do care . . . that we have a conscience?' He could almost hear the reply: 'Nobody with a conscience votes Conservative, they vote for us because it makes sense for them – because we've enabled them to own a house and we've enabled them to have a higher quality of living while we've kept taxes down and cut inflation. They'll vote for us because they're better off – not because other people are worse off. Look where our voters are? Are they really likely to vote away what we offer them out of conscience?'

In hard electoral tactical terms it made sense. But who wants the cynicism of a confidential conference on political strategy to be exposed to the voters? It might be acceptable to believe that people would vote Conservative out of self-interest, but it wasn't on to tell them you knew it. The Tories needed to help people to square their consciences; not to tell them they didn't have one. As J. K. Galbraith once wrote: 'The modern conservative is engaged in one of man's oldest exercises in moral philosophy: that is, in the search for a superior moral justification for selfishness.'

Thus Tebbit needed this publicity like a hole in the head. And what was worse for him was that whether or not he made the remark was less the point than that even his friends believed he was more than capable of it.

The week began, too, with a Harris poll that predicted a landslide for Labour, in the Greenwich by-election. (Labour 60%, Conservatives 25%, Alliance 15%.) This would increase the majority of only 1,211 over the Tories to more than 10,000. The credibility of the poll appeared to be strengthened by a comparison with the previous year's local elections, for the boundaries for the Inner London Education Authority were identical to the Parliamentary constituency and Labour had won the seat with 50%, compared with 27% for the Tories and 21% for the Alliance.

Harris had also conducted a poll of marginal seats for the *Weekend World* television programme. If it were to be believed, the Conservatives would win the General Election with a majority of around 100. In the Tory-held seats where Labour were presumed to have the best chance, there had been a swing to Labour of only 1.5%. Of the seats where the Alliance stood the best chance, there had been a dramatic swing back to the Conservatives. Even while Labour's campaign coordinator, Bryan Gould, described the poll as incredible when interviewed on the programme, Neil Kinnock was accepting in a BBC interview that Labour still needed an additional surge in support if it was to win.

Steel and Holme did their best to calm Alliance nerves. Speaking to Liberal candidates, Steel stressed that opinion poll results should be judged on whether they asked a number of questions before the key question – 'who will you vote for?' He argued that Marplan and Gallup were the best indicators of the Alliance's real support because they did this. MORI, on the other hand, consistently showed the Alliance at a lower level, having begun immediately with the 'who will you vote for?' question. Steel argued that as people were still in the habit of thinking first of one of the two older parties, this lack of build-up questions inevitably led to a poorer Alliance figure.

At the same meeting Holme tried to boost the morale of candidates by taking the Gallup figures for one month before each of the 1979 and 1983 elections and comparing them with the result actually achieved. For instance, in 1979, Gallup showed the pre-election Liberal Party with 8% of the popular vote. The actual election result was 14.3%. In 1983, Gallup showed the Alliance a month before the election with 17.5% of the popular vote. The actual result was 26.2%. Holme's message was that the Alliance could count on picking up a substantial number of votes during the campaign itself. He believed there were two reasons for this: first, over the period of the campaign the public became far more aware that there was a genuine third alternative; second, the Alliance received a much fairer share of media coverage during the election than it did in political peace time.

Holme also drew attention to the fact that a month before the 1979 Election the Conservatives had 50% in the Gallup poll, and a month before the 1983 Election 49%. In each case their vote had fallen about 5% during the election campaign. At present the Tories were consistently performing in the mid to late 30's. Thus they were likely to enter the election at a point far below that of either 1979 or 1983 and, on the basis of these elections, their support would fall further during it.

Holme concluded that given that the Alliance had no real expectations of winning the election, but wanted to make a major advance, possibly replace Labour as the main opposition to the Tories, and probably hold the balance of power, the present polls were not as bad as they would seem.

By Monday it was snowing heavily, and the Insider's usual ninety-minute drive to the office (always before or after the daily commuter traffic) became a four-and-a-half hour crawl. He devoted the journey to trying to determine the most likely date for the General Election. The Prime Minister could wait until June 1988. But to delay into 1988 was for the Tories surely the most dangerous option. It was hard to believe that the economy would improve further over the winter and into the spring of 1988, but it could easily worsen. Also the longer the delay, the more the possibility of some unpredictable crisis arising . . . the banana skin syndrome. The Tories had been able to ride out the Westland affair at the beginning of 1986 . . . could they ride out such a crisis if it arose at the beginning of 1988 and they were forced to have an election by June? Also, once the election was delayed until 1988, the opposition parties would know where they stood. No longer would they have to conserve resources, worrying about a possible eighteen-month run-up to the election. If Mrs Thatcher delayed until 1988, she would be cornered.

The Insider was convinced the election would be in 1987. What were the options?

He could not see how Mrs Thatcher could justify an election during the fourth year of a five-year administration, not when she had a huge majority. So it would not be before late May. As it could not possibly be in August, when half the country would be on holiday, or in the weeks before Christmas, her options were late May to mid-July, or mid-September to mid-October. The traditional choices were, of course, May-June or October, and there was little reason to believe that Mrs Thatcher would abandon tradition, unless she chose September to ditch the two Alliance conferences.

Two factors had now to be taken into account. First, which date made the most political sense for the Tories? Second, where would the Prime Minister's own instincts lie?

He decided that if he had been the Prime Minister's adviser, he would have promoted May-June. 'We will have a popular tax-cutting budget in March, and then you will travel to Moscow in the guise of international stateswoman, concerned to achieve peace, but no push-over for the Russians. Apart from that one week of snow in January, we will probably be coming to the end of a mild winter. Above all, the opinion polls show that we will win, albeit with a reduced majority. To balance that, there is no guarantee we will have any positive factors running for us in October, and both the Alliance and Labour will have the opportunity to hold party conferences and put a shine on their image. What it comes down to is this: in my view we *will* win in the early summer, and will probably win in October . . . but why wait if with delay comes uncertainty?'

As for May or June, the case for June was that it was within the fifth year, and also that there would be the local authority elections in May as a final indicator of public opinion. On the other hand, the government would probably do badly in council elections, and a poor result in May, while actually an unreliable indicator of how people would vote in the General Election, could tarnish the government's winning image.

There was, of course, also the question of the by-elections and the effect of any sensational result on public opinion.

The Insider decided that if he was a Tory he would at this point be planning for June. But the Insider was not Mrs Thatcher, and Mrs Thatcher could well think differently. She was dragged kicking and screaming into the last election despite being sixteen points ahead in some opinion polls. She was not a gambler, particularly when the residency of 10 Downing Street was at stake. At no time, despite all the poll predictions, was she *guaranteed* re-election, so there was always some risk. Why take the risk if it could be delayed? Furthermore, if there was a chance she would lose her premiership, why not have another year in office before it happened?

He believed Mrs Thatcher would take a lot of convincing to run in May or June. Her instincts would be to wait until October.

Who would win this argument? The tacticians, of whom Tebbit would be the most influential and who fancied the spring, or the Prime Minister? Clearly the opposition parties had to be ready for an election at any time, but the Insider believed at this point that it would probably be October, but the Alliance must act as if it would be June.

There was, however, one other issue. Election fever was now raging in the media. And had been developing for weeks. If she decided not to run in the spring or summer, would she be forced to say so officially in order to calm the country down? The Insider felt there was some benefit for the Alliance in forcing the issue and he would propose to Steel that at the press conference for the Barbican Rally he should condemn her for 'playing games' and demand that she come clean about her intentions.

While he was coming to this conclusion, the two Leaders were having a press conference at Westminster to announce the team of Alliance spokesmen. (Steel had telephoned him at Brighton the previous evening to tell him that after spending the whole of the Sunday in his office he had concluded the arrangements. He reassured the Insider that there were fifteen Liberals to nine Social Democrats and that while the SDP former Ministers clearly had some senior posts, and Cartwright had defence, a team of radical Liberals were in the key 'people' policy areas of education, health, housing, and employment.)

The following day the Insider shuddered at *The Times* headline: 'SDP leads Alliance election campaign' and the *Independent*: 'SDP secures key jobs on Alliance Front Bench'. Although the *Guardian*'s headline: 'Defence role for Cartwright' was hardly more helpful, it at least commented 'the team itself is something of a victory for Mr Steel who had to overcome hostility from Dr Owen before he accepted the value of joint portfolios, particularly in the election campaign'.

It was clear to him that Steel had made a run for it, believing that the only way to stop endless consultations, accompanied by newspaper speculation, was to settle the team and announce it quickly. He had gambled on the fact that his Liberal team would acquiesce, albeit unenthusiastically, rather than have a public row, and the price for the haste was that a lot of details about how it would actually operate had not been worked out. For instance, on the 'phone Steel told the Insider that this would be a team of election spokesmen, but on Tuesday at a meeting of the Joint Strategy Committee Steel made it clear that the joint spokesmen were in charge of their portfolios 'as from yesterday'.

That JSC meeting was dominated by the Truro and Greenwich by-elections. The Alliance could choose the date of the Truro by-election, and Labour would choose the date of the Greenwich one. John Cartwright reminded everyone of the awful Harris poll and talked pessimistically about Greenwich, saying that while the council was not that much different in its policies from those usually said to represent the 'Loony Left' it had a fairly moderate face. He felt Labour would be difficult to beat. In particular he was anxious that the Truro by-election should take place before Greenwich in order to create a bandwagon effect . . . alternatively it should take place after Greenwich, but not on the same day, because the expected Greenwich defeat would obscure the expected Truro success.

Owen questioned this, wondering whether by having it on the same day the Alliance would be seen to achieve at least one positive result if the Greenwich one was bad.

Andy Ellis said there was a risk that Greenwich would be as early as the last week in February, but as the Truro selection could not take place until February 7 or 14, March 12 looked the most likely by-election date, with March 5 as a possible alternative. He stressed that a lot would depend on the budget date, for it would be a mistake to have a by-election soon after what was likely to be a popular tax-cutting budget.

The subject arose the following day at the meeting of the Parliamentary Liberal Party. There the case for having Truro on the same day as Greenwich was a little more popular, but Steel summed up the mood of the Parliamentary Party: 'Ideally before Greenwich, if not, then on the same day as Greenwich, and otherwise after Greenwich, but not immediately after a budget.'

Given the eventual result, there was at this time a remarkably low level of expectation about the Greenwich by-election, and less than complacency about Truro.

The Insider had wondered whether there would be at the Parliamentary meeting a last ditch protest at the distribution of spokesmanships, but clearly the deal had been accepted by the MPS, and discussion was concentrated on how it would work. Alton tabled a paper on the subject. The Alliance spokesmen would cover all Government statements in their areas of responsibility, and the Whip's office would give only the one name to the Speaker's office in advance of the statement. Any other MP wishing to respond to the statement would simply have to try to catch the Speaker's eye in the normal way. If the Alliance spokesman was not available (i.e. a Peer, or Shirley Williams or Bill Rodgers, or an MP who was absent), the Whip's offices (i.e. Alton and Cartwright) would contact the relevant MPS in both parties to cover. The Alliance spokesmen would be responsible for always attending and tabling questions for Departmental Question Time in their areas.

The lead spokesman in a debate would be the Alliance spokesman. If any other MP wished to speak in a particular debate, the Whip's office would enter their names to the Speaker's office, but it would be made clear that they should be called only after the Alliance spokesman. Any amendments or official motions would be the responsibility of the spokesmen in the given area, but he or she would be expected to consult with a member of the other Party.

The Insider considered that any potential party row over the spokesmanships died with this meeting of the Parliamentary Party. He had been sceptical from the start about the need to 'carry the Party' on the details. He had surmised that the issue was of far greater importance to the MPS and to a few Liberals at the centre than it would be to the Party as a whole who, provided the team looked reasonably sane, and had a majority of Liberals, were not likely to be too concerned about who did what. The face of the Alliance would continue to be mainly Owen and Steel, and it made sound sense for Roy Jenkins and Shirley Williams to be the public face of the Alliance on the economy and home affairs, as it was equally encouraging to have the compassionate Liberals like Meadowcroft and Hughes, Ashdown and Bruce on the issues affecting people in their daily lives. As for Cartwright, there was obviously a danger that he would provoke Liberal CND into occasional outbursts of anger if his presentation of Alliance policy appeared too right-wing, but on the other hand he was probably the safest pair of hands on the issue for the election campaign, given the need for the Alliance to compare favourably with Labour's unilateralist line.

All in all, it was a satisfactory outcome, and Holme set out to remind the political journalists that the achievements of the past month had been those of Steel. Owen had been less enthusiastic than Steel over the need for joint policy (except for the manifesto), but now the parties had united on the policy document (formerly *Partnership for Progress* now *The Time Has Come*) to be published on January 26. Owen had been whole-heartedly opposed to joint open selection but, now that all the seat allocations were complete, many candidates had been or were being chosen by joint open selection. Finally, Owen had been initially opposed to joint spokesmen, but now they were in place. The Holme message was that despite the *Spitting Image* picture of the Owen and Steel partnership, Steel was winning on the big issues.

Holme's hand could be seen in an item in the *New Statesman* that began 'David Owen's insistence that the SDP and Liberal Parties should remain separate has been dealt a blow by the way local Alliance parties have cooperated in selecting candidates to fight the next election. Owen has consistently maintained that the two parties should keep their selection separate, but joint selection meetings have been held in no fewer than 120 constituencies . . .'

Holme's activities were not so much designed to undermine Owen as to boost Steel. Private opinion polls suggested that the *Spitting Image* television programme had done real damage to Steel by its weekly sketches depicting him being bullied by Owen. Owen was also tending to beat Steel to the instant television response. He was, too, being constantly lauded by the Tory press, often at the expense of Steel. Steel, who had always been popular with the media, was for the first time on the receiving end. There was, for instance, a vicious attack on Steel in the *Sunday Telegraph* shortly after the death of David Penhaligon. Written by the once entertaining but increasingly sour Edward Pearce, it described Steel as 'out on his feet' and included a ferocious attack on Steel's wife, Judy. 'It would not be excessive to say that a fervent, sour, dedicated unilateralist without any of Glenys Kinnock's bravado and style, does not make a perfect spouse for a leader of a party . . . Steel, who is physically frail, has not only been battered by the campaign trail, he has limited warmth and support at home. The business of going home from a Liberal quarrel to a *Guardian* wife has imposed a shocking strain upon a Leader whose grasp on power grows ever more marginal.'

Why someone who was a former *Guardian* columnist and counted many journalists on the *Guardian* as personal friends (he attended the wedding of its chief political writer, James Naughtie) should find a *Guardian*-reading wife such a problem, Pearce did not explain . . . in fact the whole absurd article was as inexplicable as it was grossly unfair to Judy Steel. All of this, however, had determined Steel's inner circle to launch a counter attack – not, it needs repeating, on David Owen, but on the image of the Owen-Steel relationship.

The fact was that nearly all of the high-points of the January campaign represented the realisation of Steel's objectives rather than Owen's. Steel's advisers knew, too, that they had one additional card to play; Steel was a much more effective big-occasion speaker than Owen and the Barbican offered the opportunity for this point to be made. They decided to pull out all the stops when the time came to write the speech.

On Friday there was a lift in the big freeze and the Insider drove to Bristol where he found the Alliance Hall, the one he and Shirley Williams had opened last year, packed and excited as it waited for David Steel. The Insider spoke first, kidding the audience that he had only come to ensure they did not tear down his plaque and replace it with the more illustrious name of the Party Leader. Steel's speech began hilariously. Don Foster, the driving force behind Bristol Liberals, had devised a complicated way of introducing Steel as he was about enter the hall. Because of the number of candidates and local Liberals on the platform he had not observed Steel arrive and unobtrusively take a chair just behind him. Foster thus talked on, becoming increasingly desperate as he waited for Steel to appear at the door. Unfortunately no one understood his problem. Finally when Foster had become even more desperate and exasperated, somebody woke up to what was going on. 'He's sitting behind you,' he cried out. Foster turned, saw Steel sitting there looking bemused, and collapsed in a heap amid uproar.

Steel continued the public discussion about a hung Parliament that he had begun when he returned from holiday, but moved from his views on the fate of Mrs Thatcher to the position of Neil Kinnock.

'If people contemplate voting Labour what will they get? They certainly will not get a majority Labour government of the sort Mr Kinnock spends his whole time fantasising about. Every poll sends the same message to the Shadow Cabinet. Labour are losers. To form a majority government, even with the help of an unrepresentative voting system, Labour would not only have to get about 40% of the votes but would also need to drive the Conservatives down to about 34%. They haven't got a snowball's chance in hell of achieving that combination.

'Indeed what extra support Labour has picked up since the last election is precisely where it is not needed for their electoral success. They are getting extra support in seats where they are a poor third. That will melt away when the voters get to the ballot box. They are also getting extra support in their safe seats, Labour's class strongholds. But that support won't help elect a single extra Labour MP. In the Tory/Labour marginals Labour has hardly picked up support at all. The psephological outlook for Labour is bleak.

'Yet instead of coming to terms with electoral reality, Labour continues to hype up its promises and programmes as if Neil Kinnock were going to live at Number Ten, with Roy Hattersley as his next door neighbour. Poor Mr Kinnock has become the Walter Mitty of British politics, dreaming his dreams of being a brain surgeon, or fighter pilot, or Prime Minister . . .

'Mr Kinnock is even out of touch with Labour supporters. Poll after poll shows that, although they fear another Thatcher term, many Labour voters do not believe Labour can win. They want and expect a minority Labour party to talk to other parties rather than trying to go it alone in isolation. That's the sort of attitude they associate with Thatcherism.

'What Mrs Thatcher and Mr Kinnock have in common is a determination to ignore the verdict of the electorate; to pretend that with, say, 35% of the votes and no Commons majority they can claim the divine right to rule as though they *had* a majority in parliament and the country.

'Theirs is a profoundly undemocratic view. What *we* in contrast are saying in the Liberal/SDP Alliance is that we too invite the voters to return us to power, but that if they don't, we will respect their wishes and be willing to help form a government to remove our country's problems.

'I believe profoundly that such a government, having both a parliamentary and a popular majority, could be the strongest government available.'

Steel concluded: 'The sad truth is that the fantasies of the Labour leadership make it more rather than less likely that Mrs Thatcher will continue to be Prime Minister. Mr Kinnock's delusions of total victory for state socialism promote Mrs Thatcher's chances. Her best chance of securing a third term lies in maintaining the myth of two-party adversarial politics.'

Steel and the Insider then moved to the bar upstairs, where the Leader cut a ribbon to declare that newly-completed part of the premises open. The two were soon surrounded by local Liberals. The Insider found himself talking to an elderly couple who recalled canvassing for him in the Hove by-election in 1973. They had also been founder members of their local Shelter group back in the Sixties. They discussed the chances of success at the General Election and the Insider said he felt it could be the mid to late '90s before the Alliance achieved real power. 'Our generation will have done the work but it's the youngsters who will become the MPs.' The older man said gently: 'Yes, and we must be ready to stand aside and let them do it.' The Insider was thus reminded of what he loved about the Liberal Party – the generosity, the self-sacrifice, particularly of the older members.

Then by car to Weston-Super-Mare, where candidates from all over the country were beginning to gather for their annual conference over the weekend. There were only about forty this evening and they gathered in armchairs in the hotel lounge, Steel sitting in their midst. Robert Hutchison, the candidate from Shrewsbury, raised the issue of tactical voting. He reported that Paul Ekins, of the Green Party, and the Socialist writer, Jeremy Seabrook, were about to launch an organisation to urge voters to use the tactical vote to defeat the Conservative candidates in marginal seats. The Ekins-Seabrook point was that the opinion polls showed the Tories clearly opposed by about 60% of the population. In more than 100 seats a tactical vote could unseat the Tory. They wanted a 'one nation' administration, more committed to the poor and disadvantaged (for whom Seabrook was an eloquent campaigner), but above all to remove Mrs Thatcher. This last point had been stressed by Alan Watkins in the *Observer* last Sunday. 'The object of tactical voting is to remove Mrs Thatcher. It is as well to be open about that at the start.'

Watkins argued that tactical voting would work this time where it would not have worked in 1983 because it had been the Alliance's first election. 'Voters now have the framework for decision. The constituencies are virtually the same as they were last time; and the voters know, or can discover, how the Labour and Alliance candidates polled respectively.'

The tactical vote had been given a further boost by the *New Statesman* on the morning of this candidates' conference. In its leading article it stressed that it wanted Labour to win but, if there was a possibility it could not do so, tactical voting should be considered. 'It should be made clear to people that such a plan should be for use only if the polls continue to show the same pattern as at present. It is not a principled position, but a strategic one; one which would rather see a victory through compromise than a glorious defeat. Since it *is* a strategy, it depends on circumstances — but if circumstances do not change it should be looked at with great care. It has obvious flaws; but the most flawed result would be a further Thatcher government.'

Steel's speech in Bristol had, of course, been highly relevant to this, for if the tactical vote movement was to achieve momentum, it would be necessary for Labour to be less dogmatic about its refusal to deal with the Alliance. But Steel had not talked about tactical voting, and now Robert Hutchison and the other candidates wanted to know where he stood. The Party Leader began by saying that he believed the Alliance would be the main beneficiary from tactical voting. Thus there was no reason at all why we should be openly antagonistic. But the only tactical voting that made sense was that based on the elimination of extremism – i.e. the hard Thatcherites and the hard left of the Labour Party. He also rejected the idea of the wasted vote. Every vote for the Alliance, even for a defeated candidate, strengthened the case for a change in the electoral system. Thus he favoured no public support for tactical voting, but no outright opposition either.

Asked by another candidate about the position on dealing with Mrs Thatcher if there was a balance of power – 'What would you do if she refused to go?' – Steel argued once more that she would be forced to go. She would have lost such a substantial majority that she could not stay. Nor was she a coalition politician by nature. If she refused to leave, and the Alliance then refused to countenance supporting a Conservative administration with her in it, it would be the Tories who would tell her her time was up.

The Insider rose early the following morning to take a walk by the beach at Weston-Super-Mare, marvelling that even the sea near the shore had frozen. He considered further the idea of the tactical vote, for he had a feeling that it would need an even more considered response in the coming weeks. There was no question that the opinion polls showed the Conservatives consistently in front and the chance of either Labour or the Alliance emerging from the election with a parliamentary majority looked increasingly unlikely. Yet, as had been pointed out the previous evening, the combined opposition to the Tories in the opinion polls was close to 60:40. If the only aim was to rid Britain of Thatcherism, the case for tactical voting seemed overwhelming. But this begged all sorts of questions.

For a start, Labour would have no part of it. Given the choice between the danger of the Conservatives being returned once more, or acknowledging that they could no longer win a General Election, they preferred the first. They dare not endorse tactical voting. They feared that the Alliance would be most likely to gain. Or that tactical voting would lead to even fewer Labour votes overall, and thus represent both a further blow to its legitimacy as a major party and a further argument for proportional representation. There was also little likelihood that they could keep their constituency parties, and in particular the left, united, once they conceded the need for even an unofficial tactical voting partnership with the man Labour loved to hate – David Owen.

So if tactical voting occurred, it would have to be Alliance-inspired, or voter-inspired. But could the Alliance afford to say to the electorate that its main intention was to defeat the Tories, and that it was therefore encouraging people to vote tactically to create a Labour-Alliance partnership? This would enable Tebbit and company to tell the country 'There you are, we told you so, a vote for the Alliance, is a vote for socialism'. The Alliance had to win Conservative seats as well as Labour seats. This was one of the more damaging anti-Alliance themes that Tebbit could and would adopt. Surely the Alliance could not afford to validate it further?

The Tories and the Tory newspapers were also likely to emphasise the 'moral dimension'. That it was all a bit un-British to behave in this way. That tactical voting was not a direct form of behaviour ... that it was negative.

But there was more to it even than that. John Pardoe had laid it on the line over dinner one evening at Joe Allen's. 'If we are ever to come into power in this country it has to be as the centre and left-of-centre opposition to the Conservatives. Labour can be reduced to a small minority party, but not the Tories. It's Labour we have to replace. And if Labour fail at the next election they've had it. They'll have lost once too often. We have to smash Labour ... even if it returns the Tories to office.'

If you took that view – that it was in the long term cause of the Alliance that Labour was defeated – how could you encourage tactical voting intended to put them into office or to allow them to share office? Once there, they would be in a position to determine the next election date. It would be relatively easy for them to take a few months to introduce some popular policies, win credibility, and then make a run for it, leaving the Alliance behind. Alternatively, if the Labour-led coalition ran into trouble – and a lot of powerful forces would have a vested interest in making that happen – the Tories would be returned, the Alliance going down with Labour.

So, if the only objective was long term power for the Alliance, the best result could be a small Conservative majority with the Alliance advancing, preferably into second place. But what about the country? Could it stand another few years of Thatcherism? Was it not the duty of the Alliance to help rid the country of

Thatcher, Lawson, and the rest, in the cause of fairer economic policies, greater social justice, to save our hospitals and schools, and to create fresh hope for the regions? But, would Labour, even if well-intentioned, not replace one set of problems with another? Perhaps the pragmatic if uncomfortable truth was that the country could stand two or three more years of the Tories if it meant the end of Labour and the arrival of the Alliance, as the main left-of-centre party, and in power by the mid 1990s.

But what if there was no clear majority and the Alliance had to choose to support one or the other? Another implication of the Pardoe thesis was that if Labour had to be 'smashed', then in a balance of power the Alliance could not possibly choose a partnership with Labour. Thus the implications of the Pardoe position was some form of negotiated support for the Conservatives. But minus Thatcher? Would she go? The Insider knew that Steel would have real difficulties working with Thatcher, but found the idea of supporting the Tories under a so-called moderate like Geoffrey Howe much more acceptable.

If this was the way it was going, there were a lot of problems ahead. Could Liberals live with a deal with the Tories? The Insider knew that unless Thatcher went, many could not, and they included MPs such as Kirkwood and Hughes. And what would be the reaction of Labour voters who backed the Alliance 'tactically' only to see it put the Tories back?

The Insider concluded that there probably would be tactical voting, and it would be to the benefit of the Alliance, but that it must be left to others to encourage it. The Alliance must not do so, if only to avoid the justifiable fury of those disenchanted former Labour voters who genuinely believed they were ridding the country of the Tories only to find – possibly – that they were back (albeit – hopefully – without Thatcher).

The Insider also accepted Steel's point that the case for proportional representation rested on the maximum possible Alliance vote.

The position, therefore, had to be 'of course we believe in tactical voting, provided we are clear what the tactic is – the tactic is to vote Alliance'.

The Week January 18–24

Tebbit turns the attack on Hugo Young ... scandals in the City ... another secrecy bungle ... the Tory-run economy and Labour-run local authorities top the agenda.

The Tebbit-Hugo Young row continued. Tebbit announced his decision to sue the *Guardian.* To do this, he had to ask the Prime Minister for permission, and apparently she was persuaded by Neil Kinnock's refusal to stop quoting the now famous remark. If it became a court case it would follow the General Election.

The Insider's week began with a call at home from Duncan Campbell, the egocentric but extraordinarily well-informed *New Statesman* reporter who specialises in uncovering defence information he believes need not be secret. Campbell confided that a row was about to break because the BBC had decided to ban one of his six programmes on secrecy due to be screened in March. He planned to show the programme at the House of Commons the following Monday and asked for support from the Campaign for Freedom of Information.

The Insider was amused, for Campbell was no slouch at achieving publicity and he couldn't imagine what he could do that Campbell couldn't do for himself. This was borne out only a matter of minutes later when the *Observer* arrived and Campbell's story was plastered across the front page. The reporter was up and running and it became the major political story of the week (indeed of the next few weeks).

Campbell's story was about the Zircon project, Britain's first spy satellite, to be put into space above the Soviet Union at a cost of £500 million. Campbell's point was that the satellite's existence and the cost had been kept secret from Parliament despite undertakings in 1982 that the Commons' Public Accounts Committee would be given advance information about expenditure of major defence projects, in particular, those costing more than £250 million. As the week went by ...

● Campbell, with support from the media, kept his indignation at the BBC ban on the front pages.

- The Attorney-General served an injunction on Campbell forbidding him to show the film or publish further details elsewhere, but it was too late for Campbell's extensive article for the *New Statesman* was already published and videos of the film were already in circulation.

- The Speaker ruled that the film could not be shown in the House of Commons, sparking off another row.

- Various MPs saw the film in different places, some Labour MPs at party headquarters, while Neil Kinnock and other senior Labour frontbenchers were given a special briefing by the Foreign Office. In the House of Commons Neil Kinnock surprised many of his backbenchers by supporting Ministers in their attempt to stop the disclosures for national security reasons and, instead, attacking the Government for its laxity on the whole matter.

- The *New Statesman*'s offices were raided by the Special Branch, and the homes of Campbell and two other journalists.

- Letters were sent to all of the editors of national newspapers asking them to ignore the Zircon story. As far as one could tell, not one cooperated.

By the week's end Ministers were in disarray on the issue for it was clear that Whitehall had known for some months that Campbell was making the documentary, and there had even been a four-day delay after the *Observer* article before action was taken to try to stop the film being widely shown.

What was equally clear was that Neil Kinnock had once more bungled an opportunity. This, as we have seen, he had done on the Peter Wright case in Australia before Christmas when he made those 'phonecalls to Wright's solicitor instead of sitting back and let the Prime Minister and Sir Robert Armstrong make fools of themselves. This he had also done at the time of the Westland affair last year, when his speech in the key debate was widely judged to have let the Prime Minister off the hook. Now, with Ministers once more looking foolish, Kinnock had fallen lock-stock-and-barrel for the Foreign Office line when he could have, at the very least, left his options open. Many observers concluded that his behaviour was a result of the self-inflicted damage of the Wright affair and his need to be seen to be as patriotic as Mrs Thatcher.

All this had happened in a week that had begun with the Campaign for Freedom of Information's Awards, presented by Owen, who had made a useful speech in support of freedom of information. The Campaign's position on defence secrets was clear: the fact that the information dealt with defence or national security did not in itself justify secrecy; its disclosure had to *endanger* or *impair* national security.

There was little reason to believe that the plan to put up the Zircon spy satellite need be secret. It would be seen when it was there and the Russians would know what it was for. But was it necessary at all? Should £500 million be spent on a spy satellite? Surely this was a fair subject for debate?

The Campaign also took the view that one of the reasons why it was difficult to maintain secrets when secrecy really mattered was that secrecy had become so indiscriminate. The Official Secrets Act (1911), particularly Section 2, had a catch-all quality that had, when combined with the habit of secrecy that was entrenched in Whitehall, reduced public accountability to a minimum.

Mrs Thatcher, who as her first act in the House of Commons had introduced a Private Members' Bill to force greater disclosure by local authorities, had now become obsessed with secrecy, so much so that she was being berated on the subject by such supporters as the *Sunday Telegraph* and the *Mail On Sunday*. In the former, Edward Pearce had written that Thatcher had been drawn into the Civil Service's 'own passion for self-aggrandising secrecy'. He said: 'Mrs Thatcher finds herself flattered into firing their bullets, defending their honour, being subsumed into their nonsense . . . she is fighting and losing a battle which is neither hers nor ours. All sense demands that she cuts her losses and rejoins the camp of free speech . . .' The *Mail On Sunday* in its leader said 'There can hardly be anyone left who does not agree that our Official Secrets Act and the whole paraphernalia that goes with it is so lunatic in its wide embrace that it is impossible for anyone to take it seriously . . . Mrs Thatcher should call in Sir Robert Armstrong and tell him that we intend to trust the people . . .'

But despite these strictures from her friends and the impressive consensus that the Campaign for Freedom of Information had developed on the issue, she simply did not want to know about freedom of information, and her whole instinct on the Zircon affair was to hold the line, believing, possibly rightly, that the majority of people would not be able to comprehend all the detail of the current case, and would be likely to be sympathetic to her position. The massive headline in the *Mail On Sunday*, 'Search for the Traitor', about the hunt for the mole who had leaked the story to Duncan Campbell, indicated the way it was likely to develop.

In the meantime, all hell had broken loose in the City of London because of disclosures of unethical manoeuvres, and especially insider-dealing. At the centre of it all were revelations of improper conduct during the take-over bid by Guinness of the Distillers Company. In addition to Guinness itself, other top city names were implicated including the merchant bankers, Morgan Grenfell. Hardly a day went by without the resignation of one City name or another, beginning with the chairman of Guinness, Ernest Saunders. The Cabinet were increasingly disconcerted by the affair, not least by the fact that the Secretary of State for Trade and Industry, Paul Channon, was a member of the Guinness family. One Cabinet member was quoted in *The Sunday Times* as saying 'the sooner we get the handcuffs on someone, the better'.

Yet there was little evidence that this scandal was likely to affect the voters. A Harris poll asked 'Has what has happened in the City made you more or less likely to vote Conservative or has it made no difference?' An overwhelming majority, 81%, said it made no difference, 15% said 'less likely' and 2% said 'more likely'.

Norman Tebbit, asked if what was happening in the City would damage the Conservative Party, told the *Independent*: 'It shouldn't be. Because what one sees is a Government which is dealing firmly with the abuses and uncovering them and which has taken power to do so. . . . it was, after all, we who changed the law to make insider-trading a criminal offence . . . we've enacted the Financial Services Act which brings much more effective regulation and the pay off of that is to be seen now with the uncovering of wrong-doing and the pursuit of those who are engaged in it.'

It would clearly be a waste of time to try to persuade Norman Tebbit that what was happening in the City was related to the economic atmosphere created by this Tory regime. Profiteering from money manipulation had thrived in the absence of determined encouragement to people to invest in manufacturing industry.

All of this leads to the economy, and to Roy Jenkins, who had decided to re-launch himself as the Alliance Economic Spokesman with a major speech at the London Business School. Jenkins had over the past few months re-discovered his form. If anybody could claim to have been *the* founder of the SDP it was Jenkins. In the Dimbleby Lecture in 1979, he first made credible the possibility of re-alignment on the left of British politics. A former high-ranking Labour Cabinet Minister who had become President of the European Commission, he, with Shirley Williams, Bill Rodgers and David Owen, was one of the gang of four who launched the Social Democratic Party and became its first leader. But the ill-conceived plan to name him as 'Prime Minister Designate' for the 1983 Alliance election campaign misfired. That he had the courage and the intellect was beyond question, but as an election leader he proved a disaster. Finally, at a meeting at David Steel's home at Ettrick Bridge, painful for everybody present, he was effectively removed from the leadership in all but name. Steel took over. After the election, a dispirited Jenkins immediately made way for David Owen and for some time it looked as if he would fade away all together. Just as Heath remained on the backbenches to taunt Thatcher, Jenkins now only occasionally made sorties into the headlines, usually to gently, yet unambiguously, reprove Owen when he felt him to be out of line with Jenkins' idea of what the Alliance was about.

Then just before the Eastbourne Assembly, Jenkins at the SDP Conference in Harrogate made a brilliant speech, witty, incisive, and loudly cheered. Perhaps no one else in British politics could have made it. After that Jenkins began turning up more at meetings of the Joint Strategy Committee, and it was clear that he was not to be counted out yet. It became inevitable that he would become Alliance Economic Spokesman.

Now, at the London Business School, he outlined the Alliance economic position, its response to the 'deadening danger of low expectations and a sense of nothing to be done about it'.

After arguing that Lawson's prescription for the British economy had proved fundamentally flawed, he turned on Labour who had, he said, offered a false prospect. Labour was committed to increased spending but not buttressed by the policies needed to avoid a wave of inflation and currency instability. Unemployment could only be reduced in a sustained way by higher spending if a firm monetary framework was maintained, if the problem of escalating pay was tackled head-on within the context of an incomes policy, and if industry were given the confidence to invest for the long term.

The Alliance had developed a substantially different policy combination, aimed at achieving a sharp fall in unemployment, but within an essential framework both for monetary policy and for incomes growth. In addition it would place maximum emphasis on developing policies to raise the performance of British industry over the long term. As the benefits from improved performance emerged, with higher output and non-inflationary growth, the short term expedient required to alleviate the unemployment crisis and the incomes policy apparatus required to deal with the problem of excessive pay settlements could gradually be phased out.

The long term objective must be to re-orientate the economy towards export-led growth in order to gain the kind of benefits that had clearly flowed from policies of this type in countries like Germany and Japan.

He advocated joining the exchange rate mechanism of the European Monetary System. This would create the clear monetary framework that was necessary, but had three supporting advantages: first, the target rate would provide a benign focus for speculative activity on the foreign exchange markets, making speculation stabilising rather than de-stabilising; second, with confidence in the stability of the sterling exchange rate, the risk premium associated with the pound would be reduced, and real interest rates in Britain would not have to be maintained at the current record levels; third, if companies were confident that the exchange rate would remain at a competitive level, the response in terms of production and exports would be less tentative and would begin to rise to mitigate the emerging balance of payments deficit.

He then moved on to ask why Britain should not adopt a more expansionary fiscal policy? 'The answer of those who oppose increased public borrowing is that inflation would rise. This notion is excessively simplistic, since the inflationary impact of spending increases or tax reductions will clearly depend on the precise measures taken. In fact, a number of measures could be taken which could make a substantial impact on unemployment with minimal consequences on the rate of inflation. Inflation is domestically generated mainly by rising pay settlements and/or a falling exchange rate. Spending increases will thus have very little effect on inflation if they are targeted on localities or activities where the resources required are in gross excess supply — as in inner city areas and the construction industry.

'The same is true if the expenditure concerned has a low import content. In fact 40% of construction workers are unemployed, and few construction materials are imported.

'Exchange rate stability would be maintained by membership of the EMS. And some fiscal changes, such as cuts in national insurance contributions, would tend to reduce prices.'

He proposed a programme of carefully tailored job-effective measures designed to reduce unemployment by more than a million in around three years. The principle component would be a job guarantee for the long term unemployed to be validated by a series of measures incorporating an inner city building renovation programme, incentives to private employers to recruit from the long term unemployed, enhanced opportunity for direct employment in the health service and the personal social services, and the major extension of job training for the long term unemployed. There would be cuts in employers' national insurance contributions, and an increase in spending on infra-structure. Finally, restraint of excessive pay settlements could on reasonable assumptions additionally result in a reduction in the unemployment level.

'I therefore believe that it is possible to design and implement a wholly responsible and non-inflationary fiscal programme to reduce unemployment by at least a million, financing this improvement by adding around four billion to the public borrowing targets currently planned, beyond the two billion existing scope for fiscal adjustment. This means raising the PSBR from approximately 2% to 3% of the total. This will be no higher than it has been in fifteen of the last twenty-four years.'

Jenkins then turned to the question of incomes policy. The Alliance would introduce a counter-inflation tax, the central notion being to attach tax penalties to excessive pay settlements and companies with over 100 employees. Fair comparability would be the rule for public service pay, where such a tax could not bite. For instance, if the rate of pay settlements consistent with an acceptable inflation performance was judged to be 3% a year, then companies granting pay settlements causing their earnings per man-hour to rise by more than 3% would be subject to a tax on the excess. Genuine profit sharing schemes would be exempt from the tax.

Finally, he stressed the need for policies to improve the competitive performance of industry, particularly in world markets. We needed a 'vision' about the types of activity that offered hope for the economy. The state must ensure that the areas of policy properly within its domain were fully atuned to the requirements of competitive success. Industry must be given what it needed to succeed and the economy must be assisted to adapt to a changing world. Companies must be encouraged to be competitive. There must be aid for the diffusion of new technology, to encourage the flow of capital to industry, and raise the level of education and training. Central industrial policy should be supplemented at regional and local level.

A couple of days later David Owen in his Tawney Society Lecture spelt out his ideas on the integration of the tax and benefit system designed to both attack poverty and encourage enterprise. The aim was to abolish the poverty and unemployment traps that meant many people were worse off by working. It would be done in three ways: first, the new basic benefit would be reduced gradually as other income rose, instead of people suddenly losing all their benefits and at the same time starting to pay income taxes. This would encourage enterprise because it would enable people to combine income from work with income from benefits. Second, employees' national insurance contributions would be merged with income tax. Those who currently paid national insurance would simply pay an integrated tax rate equivalent to current income tax and national insurance. This would be simpler and fairer since the integrated rate would be levied on all income up to a threshold. It would not mean an increase in the tax burden; indeed, many people on low incomes would gain from the reform. Third, the married man's additional tax allowance would be phased out by annual increments over five years. The savings would be used to help those in real need by providing higher benefits, especially for poor pensioners and families with children. The single person's and wife's earned income allowances would be increased so that those who would lose from the eventual disappearance of the married man's allowance would do so very gradually. In fact, the phasing out of the married man's allowance could be done so that there would be no cash losers at all, depending on both the speed of phasing and the rate of inflation.

Owen argued that these tax and benefit changes would not put up taxes. They could apply whether the standard rate of income tax stayed at 29% or was reduced. 'The Alliance does not just talk about redistribution; our actions match our words. Unlike the Labour Party, we voted last year in opposition to the 1% reduction in the standard rate. They abstained. But you do not have to raise the standard rate to achieve a redistribution of resources. While the Conservatives have cut taxes drastically for the rich, people on average earnings are paying more tax and national insurance now than in 1979. Integrating the tax and national insurance systems would significantly reduce the tax burden for the vast majority of tax payers. It would be a fairer, simpler, and more radical change than juggling with the standard rate. What would be difficult to justify would be both to raise the standard rate of tax and simultaneously start to integrate the tax and benefit systems.'

These two major speeches had spelt out in convincing detail the distinctive approach of the Alliance. With *Partnership for Progress* about to be published, the Insider felt that it was becoming increasingly absurd for the other parties to continue the claim – especially made by the Tories – that the Alliance had no policy.

Most of the Alliance campaign committees – including the APG and the Liberal Party General Election Committee – were now meeting regularly to finalise arrangements for the Barbican Rally and afterwards. The Liberal Party's own election planning was well advanced. On the basis of a checklist the Committee had been operating from meeting to meeting, the Party would be fully tuned up for an election by March, with fundraising perhaps the only outstanding problem. The more winnable seats had been identified, and candidates selected for them all. Every area agent was now equipped with a computer and constituency agents were now being placed in the more winnable seats. A campaign guide for all constituencies, and an agent's handbook, were well advanced. A library of campaign artwork material had been compiled. Regular mailings to candidates had begun. Leaflets had been devised to be targeted on specific wards with special problems such as housing, or lack of health or educational facilities. A complete training programme for candidates, agents, and key activists was well underway.

At the week's end the *Evening Standard* published an NOP survey showing that the Conservatives had 42%, Labour 37%, and the Alliance 19%.

Lord Avebury, formally Eric Lubbock, one time Liberal Chief Whip, announced that he intended to leave his remains to Battersea Dogs Home. It made all the newspapers and half the current affairs television programmes. The Insider blanched. About all that could be said for it was that Avebury had not actually announced his plan during the General Election.

The Week, January 25 to 31 . . .

The Time Has Come . . .

Suddenly there really was election fever in the air.

The *Observer* led its front page with a Harris poll that was bad news. The Conservatives were up to 44%, Labour 36%, and the Alliance 18%. The headline said it all: 'Thatcher is poised for a landslide'. It was the first national poll for more than two years to show the Tories holding their General Election share of public support. The Alliance were down eight points from the last General Election, and two from the last Harris poll. Apart from the recent Gallup poll, there was now a consistency about the last few polls that had to be discouraging for both Labour and the Alliance.

More encouraging was the poll evidence of the images of the parties. The Alliance emerged as the least extreme and the least uncaring of the three parties and this confirmed the wisdom of the strategy for the initial advertising campaign, with its emphasis on the moderating effect of the Alliance.

A chart presented to the APG showed the opinion poll trends since 1983. The message was clear: Labour had remained fairly static in the 36–39% range for nearly two years. The Tories and the Alliance began 1986 close to each other and widened to 20% apart after the defence row. There had recently been a small rise in the Alliance percentage, *but* if there were to be an election in May or June the Alliance had only three or four months to rise five or six points and regain the position it achieved during the 1983 General Election, the minimum starting point it needed to make a real breakthrough in this one.

The political editor of *The Sunday Times*, Michael Jones, set the scene of the Alliance's week. He argued that Owen and Steel have 'a more formidable machine behind them than Roy Jenkins and Steel had in 1983, and a much clearer grasp of election strategy. As the Alliance position in the polls is around the same 20% level as it was at the start of the 1983 campaign, the Tories are wise to treat the Alliance relaunch as a serious threat'. He outlined the Alliance strategy of presenting itself as the guarantors of a moderate government. 'As the big guns turn on it, the Alliance will have to fight hard to stick to its game plan. It could just do it.'

The first Tory 'big gun' to be turned on the Alliance was the soft-spoken Sir Geoffrey Howe. He was sent to Cambridge to attack the Alliance on the eve of its press conference. A vote for the Alliance was a vote for a socialist government, he said. A hung parliament, its election ambition, would be 'a dangerous farce'. Such a result would take power from voters and give it to 'party wheeler dealers'. The good government of the nation would be submerged in a welter of sordid party deals pursuing the lowest common denominator.

According to Howe the Alliance offered 'at worst a back door route to power for Labour, and at best a recipe of national inertia'.

It was clear the Tories intended to condemn the Alliance as the enemy of strong government. It was vital, said Howe, that Britain continued to be governed by a party with conviction and vision. 'Weak governments and soft options provide no response to hard questions.'

This, then, was the background as Steel and Owen, Shirley Williams and the Insider entered the room booked at the Central Hall, Westminster, for the press conference on Monday, January 26, 1987. The room was packed with nearly 300 journalists, television crews, and interested parties. At a pre-meeting of the four, Paul Tyler had arrived with two gold ties for the Leaders to wear to match the new Alliance colour. The new slogan 'The Time has Come' stood out in black on a gold banner behind the four. While the photographers took their pictures, the Insider looked across the sea of faces. The press conference had drawn all the leading political commentators.

Steel was in top form, rising as he always does to the media occasion. David Owen, too, appeared to be putting more punch into his presentation. The questioning was tough, and most of it intended to try and demonstrate division between the two. They were having none of it. Both drew on the re-emergence of a coalition from the weekend's West German elections to underline the respectability of a coalition. The Insider noticed that Steel was quick to take two questions that had appeared to be directed to David Owen. One was on the possibility of working with Thatcher after the General Election. Did the SDP Leader share Steel's view that this would be impossible? Steel quickly replied that he felt that her attitude to consensus made working in a coalition impossible, but toned down his position fractionally by saying that you couldn't veto any possibility in politics. The other question was about defence, intended to underline the strains between Owen's clear view that Polaris would have to be replaced and the 'keep options open' nature of the policy as outlined in *Partnership for Progress*. Once more Steel was careful to take the question, saying that it made sense to take the decision nearer the time.

All of this and the new theme tune, Purcell's Trumpet Tune in D, made every television bulletin for the rest of the day and was widely reported in Tuesday's newspapers.

The Alliance had to compete on Monday with the publication of Frank Layfield's report on the Sizewell enquiry. The Insider had led the Friends of the Earth team to the first day of the enquiry back in 1983 and had been chairman of the organisation when it raised well over £100,000 to play its part as an objector at Sizewell. He knew that FOE and the other objectors had felt there was a chance Layfield would turn Sizewell down, or so damn the idea with faint praise, or surround it with reservations, that it would be difficult for Peter Walker, the Minister of Energy, hater of the coal miners and friend of the nuclear industry, to proceed, at least before the General Election. Instead, Layfield was surprisingly positive about Sizewell. It would be safe. There was a case on energy need, and it was cost-effective. The Insider was at least pleased that the Alliance had firmly committed itself to opposition to Sizewell early on, and Bill Rodgers, in his first days as Energy Spokesman, now held the line well.

It was clear that Sizewell would put nuclear power back on the election agenda. Another key factor in the election campaign was likely to be the increasing evidence of the divisions between rich and poor in Britain, identified by some as divisions between north and south. But, as Simon Hughes and Michael Meadowcroft, members for working class constituencies, both stressed at the parliamentary meeting on Wednesday, it wasn't just a question of north and south, but haves and have nots. Hughes rejected one of the new Alliance leaflets, the one that talked about 'the poorer north versus the richer south'. How could he use this in Bermondsey? The point was taken and it was decided to change the leaflet when it ran out of stock.

The statistics 'Social Trends' were published on Thursday and they underlined still further that Britain was becoming more divided with the rich increasing their share of income of the nation's wealth while the poor become ever-poorer. Between 1980 and 1985 the bottom 40% of households had seen their share of income fall from 8.7% in 1981 to 6.4% in 1983, while the top fifth increased their share from 46.4% to 48.6%. While the share of the nation's wealth of the top 10% of the population rose during those two years from 34% to 35%, at the other end of the scale the number of families on or below the supplementary benefit poverty line rose by 1.5 million from 3.9 million in 1979 to 5.5 million in 1983.

Professor J. H. Halsey, Director of Social and Administrative Studies at Oxford, analysing the figures for Social Trends, concluded that 'the process is one of deprived people being left in the urban priority areas as the successful move out to middle Britain ... a pattern has emerged of a more unequal society, as between a majority in secure attachment to a still prosperous country and a minority in marginal economic and social conditions'.

But if this was ammunition to attack the Tories with, there was also ammunition for the Alliance to attack Labour in a report by the Audit Commission on the problems of eight inner London councils. The report found that so-called 'creative accounting measures' by the eight councils amounted to no less than £1,042 per household – a total of some 730 million pounds. The councils were living far beyond their means and faced a management breakdown if there was insufficient money to pay their staff. They had been covering the gap between income and expenditure by drawing on financial reserves, borrowing to meet housing and road costs, and by deferring purchase arrangements. While it acknowledged that some very real problems had been created by central financial decisions, it put most of the blame on the management of the councils concerned. It showed that the councils spent £7 per week per household more than other deprived London Boroughs, took six weeks longer to re-let housing or flats requiring minor repairs, had lower rents but nearly three times higher arrears, spent 20% a year more per household on refuse collection for comparable services, spent more than £5,700 a year more for every child in residential care for a comparable service to other Boroughs, and spent £400 a year more per vehicle on maintenance.

The Zircon controversy raged on, with Tony Benn out-manoeuvring the Prime Minister in the House of Commons by persuading MPs of all parties to refer the Commons ban to the Parliamentary Privileges Committee.

Unfortunately in this week of Alliance unity there was on Wednesday night an embarrassing cock-up. Just as the party political broadcast was being screened Steel and Owen, each accompanied by some of their MPs, opposed each other in a House of Commons vote. It all happened because David Alton was suddenly taken ill. All the Alliance MPs were supposed to oppose a badly-worded Labour motion on City corruption. With Alton out of the chamber being sick, and the SDP Whip, John Cartwright away in Brussels, MPs found themselves heading for the division in some uncertainty. David Steel and five MPs voted for the Labour motion and David Owen and the rest opposed it. Needless to say this 'split' was fully capitalised on by the Opposition the following day. 'Whom God has divided, let no voter put together' John Biffen told the House.

Fortunately viewers of the Party Political Broadcast were not aware of the chaos within the Parliamentary Party, and were telephoning in response at an unprecedented rate. There were more than 5,500 enquiries for literature within the first 48 hours.

The publicity around the Barbican Rally was proving to be extraordinary. Steel appeared on the Wogan programme on Friday evening, and then both he and Owen on *A Week in Politics*. This was to be followed on Sunday by joint apearances on the Frost programme in the early morning and then on BBC's *This Week, Next Week*. Roy Jenkins was to appear on *Weekend World*. And of course there would be all the television news coverage of the Rally itself.

The *This Week, Next Week* team were outside the National Liberal Club on Friday night when the Insider arrived for a Liberal Party meeting to discuss the consultations procedure that would be necessary in the event of a hung parliament. This caused some confusion, for the television team were working on a programme about a possible merger after the election, and had been incorrectly advised that this was the subject of the meeting. Thus, the Insider and others found themselves interviewed on the doorstep while being at complete cross purposes with the interviewer. The resulting programme was confusing to say the least.

The meeting itself was not. Tim Clement-Jones was in the chair, and present were two members of the Scottish Liberal Party, representatives of ALC, four former Presidents (Tordoff, Holme, Watson and Joyce Rose), David Hughes of the Liberal Parliamentary Association, and a number of the National Executive.

Alan Beith opened the meeting by explaining some of the rules of the game. There should be no advance indication of who the Alliance would ally with, unless there had been a specific and publicised pre-election arrangement, 'for if you have a preference for who you would like to work with, you decrease your chances if you publicise it. You drive away those who don't want to see that other party in power, and you reduce your bargaining power in any negotiations'.

He stressed that in a balance of power situation Labour and the Tories could well operate to assist each other. They assisted each other already. Whenever the two-party system came under challenge there was an unspoken understanding that they would each work to prop it up. For instance, in 1974, after the election that saw the defeat of Heath, the Tories would often field less than all their MPs in the lobby to ensure that Labour were not defeated, despite the fact that this could help Labour to become stronger for the next election. Likewise, there were plenty of cases of the two parties working together to thwart the Alliance on local authorities. 'Never underestimate their capacity to delude even themselves into believing that they're assisting the practice of good government by preserving the two-party system,' Beith said. 'They have a considerable incentive to stop us. They know that the prospects of the Alliance would be enhanced by governmental experience and they will do all they can to avoid it. The only way we can combat this is to make it politically less likely for it to happen.'

Beith went on to say that essential to Alliance bargaining power would be its ability to convince its opponents that it could cope with a second election. 'If they think we are not in a position to fight a second election, we weaken our position. It will be assumed by the other parties that we fear – that we can't face – a second election. We must make it clear that if the other parties defy the will of the electorate we are able and willing to go back to the polls.' (The National Executive subsequently decided to pay for insurance for the Party for an early second election and to publicise the fact that it was covered.)

He then went on to talk about the position if negotiations started. We would have the deal with the 'convention of haste'. We would be put under enormous pressure to take immediate decisions, and the media would be calling for the quick formation of a government. The suggestion would be that a few days without a government would be bad. But some delay would be necessary for proper communication within the Party. It could be necessary to spread the negotiations over a week or so.

He talked about the unparalleled press attention and pressure. 'If they're outside the front door now,' he said, referrring to the *This Week, Next Week* team, 'what will it be like in a balance of power?'

He also talked of the party pressures, with concern building up all over the country, and the likelihood of its spilling over into the media. The processes of consultation with the party would need to be known and observed. In particular, the new MPs must understand they could not speak separately to the media, thus creating hostages to fortune and reducing the bargaining position.

Richard Holme followed Beith, saying that there was a tension between the Owen line of promoting coalition and the traditional Liberal line of going for government. The polls showed that people did not like a coalition but they did like the idea of a national government. They liked the idea of the Alliance being part of the next government.

Holme argued that it was unlikely that there would be negotiation. The best planning assumption was another general election quickly. Politically speaking, what was critical was who would be blamed for the second election. 'It's like pass the parcel – everyone will try to leave someone else with the blame. We must be ready and, as Alan has said, we must make it clear that we're willing and able, but if it comes across to the public that we are the cause of that election there will be public rejection.'

(This view was supported a few weeks later by Ken Livingstone, writing in the *London Daily News*. He predicted that if the Tories had the most seats, but not a majority, and Thatcher refused to resign, Labour and the Alliance would vote them down at the first opportunity. Kinnock would then form a minority administration and when the vote was taken on Labour's Queen's Speech, the Alliance would oppose it and the Tories would abstain. Labour would then govern for six to nine months until Kinnock decided to call another election in order to win a working majority.)

But the main discussion centred on the consultation process within the party if negotiations began after the election. The Insider argued that the process must be decided by the party well in advance so that it had authority and full credibility and so that the party's own decision on the process could be used to persuade those who wished to go their own way to keep in line.

It was noted that there was a proposition before the Council meeting planned for February 7 that the Council should be called for the Saturday after the election if no party had a majority. It was felt that this would be catastrophic, because it would be impossible to stop massive media attention on that Council or to educate everybody to the implications of the media attention. The potential for chaos was enormous. It was decided to propose to Council that it should meet within a month of the election.

So, on the Saturday, to the Barbican, where the four-month climb-back to unity from the Eastbourne Assembly was to reach its climax. The huge three-tier concert hall was packed, with many having to settle for watching on television sets in the galleries outside. The day was skillfully compèred by television quiz master, Bamber Gascoigne, whose light touch contrasted well with the fervour of the speeches. There were huge cheers for the brass band playing the Alliance theme, and even bigger cheers for a knock-about opening performance by Cyril Smith, and a nostalgic appearance by Jo Grimond, looking remarkably fit, a striking figure with his white hair, and still full of humour. No other party could persuade two and a half thousand people to pay £7 to hear eighteen speeches, he said. 'It must strike terror into the hearts of our opponents.' There was a reference to the Wednesday chaos in the division lobby. 'At least when we have a cock-up, it's not on party lines.' There was also concern about whether we could achieve any votes from animal lovers 'now they know that the dogs of Battersea may have to eat Eric Lubbock'.

Then came the Alliance team, led by Steel and Owen, with Nancy Seear and Shirley Williams on either side. The whole hall rose and cheered.

David Owen's speech was later to be described as muted, and compared with Steel it was low-key. But it was also compelling. The Insider had sensed beforehand that Owen was surprisingly nervous, and it could be that the SDP Leader now wished that he had a fully written speech instead of a combination of script and rough notes. Nevertheless he was cheered when he said that people did not want tax cuts when they could see millions without work. 'What sort of people do the Tories think we are?' He put a lot of emphasis on changing the system and appeared to have stiffened his resolve on proportional representation.

The hall did not stand when he had finished, partly because Owen is not one for perorations, but he was warmly applauded.

Steel, however, roused his audience. The deliberate decision to produce a slightly tougher Steel, and to accentuate his ability to seize the moment, was now vindicated. Labour were losers and the Conservatives were without compassion or conscience. The coming election would be deeply negative, with fear of Thatcherism and distrust of Labour sweeping the country in two confused tides. The Alliance role was to offer a positive focus for the future, a beacon of hope to penetrate the confusion and gloom. The ideologies of Thatcherism and Socialism must be driven out and the people of the country must be enabled to take power for themselves. He talked of the unemployment and the economic divisions. 'The shot in the arm that Mrs Thatcher promised Britain has turned out to be a shot through the heart.' He demanded that Mrs Thatcher receive no more donations from the City until it had cleaned up its act. 'Year in, year out the City lavishes hundreds of thousands of pounds on the Tories. But how can it possibly be in the interests of democracy and good government that the party which forms an administration is dependent on the handouts of those it is supposed to regulate?

'Just as Labour's relationship with its trade union paymasters has persistently corrupted its legislative programme, so the Tories are bound to be less than whole hearted in cleaning up the City.'

Steel had the audience on its feet. The Insider was warmed by the enthusiasm. He could sense that everyone in the hall wanted, was determined, was desperate to move forward. As he looked round the rows of participants, it struck him that no one could tell who was a Social Democrat or who was a Liberal. Not for the first time he felt that the divisions in the Alliance, in so much as they existed and would exist, were restricted to a relatively small number at the centre. When it came to the rank and file, there was virtually no variation in feelings or objectives at all.

Then came the Alliance team — Nancy Seear, bulldog-like, with her promise that 'the welfare state *will* be safe in our hands ... we, after all, invented it'; Paddy Ashdown promising fresh leadership on education, Charles Kennedy expressing concern for the poor, Simon Hughes arguing for preventative health, and a particularly effective speech late in the morning by Michael Meadowcroft. In the afternoon came Roy Jenkins, receiving a standing ovation when he walked on to the platform, and another when he left. It was a typical Jenkins performance. Heavyweight, but spiced with wit. Given that many SDP Leaders, even Liberal MPs, tend to blame the disunity over defence on Eastbourne, the Insider was happy to hear Jenkins talk about 'our combined foolishness in the summer and the autumn'.

The Insider was much impressed by Ian Wrigglesworth, who made by far the best speech he had heard him make, talking with real passion about unemployment, and creating an impression of considerable competence.

Beith and Cartwright dealt ably with foreign affairs and defence, and finally the two Presidents took up their theme of 'people in power'.

At the end of the day came John Pardoe, who persuaded the hall to rise as one man and one woman and wave their gold folders with the words 'The Time Has Come'. It was just the image of unity the Leaders had dreamed of. All this was accompanied by the third playing of the day of the theme music and as the two Leaders were cheered once more onto the platform the Rally came to a tumultuous end, its exhausted audience spilling out into the streets of the City of London in high spirits.

'The Time Has Come' said the leaflets they clutched in their hands. 'The Time Has Come' ... the words must have still been ringing in their ears, for nearly every speaker had employed them in their closing words.

The Insider was on a high. The time *had* come ... no, the Alliance was not necessarily on course to win, or even to achieve a balance of power, but the defensive battle to recapture lost ground was over. The Alliance was united on defence, united on a joint policy programme, united on who would fight what seats, and united around its spokesmen. The big re-launch week had been a triumph. The APG's plan had worked – better than the Insider had dared hope. There was much enthusiasm as everyone headed back to their constituencies, but also a sense of relief that the nightmare was over. The time had come to move – in more ways than one – from defence onto attack and they were ready. They had made it from Eastbourne to the Barbican. Now onwards to Greenwich and Truro and then to the General Election.

The Alliance
and The Other Parties

From the Barbican to the by-elections

February to March 12, 1987

The Alliance rises in the polls ... The Insider worries abour PR
*... the Leaders differ on the other parties ... the Liberals plan
for a hung Parliament ... and fret about money ... the tactical
voting campaign is launched ... the dirty tricks begin ... by-
elections at Greenwich and Truro.*

The success of the Alliance re-launch was confirmed by the opinion polls. The *Guardian* poll averages for the month of February
(post-Barbican, but prior to the Greenwich by-election) showed
an Alliance increase of three points from 20% to 23%, and also
encouraging was a poll in the *Today* newspaper showing that
43% of electors would vote Alliance if they believed a Liberal or
Social Democrat could win in their constituency.

Labour, who had been stuck between 36% and 39% for nearly
two and a half years, fell in February to the lower end of that
scale, and the Tories averaged 39%, still below the 40%-plus
they needed to face a General Election in the early summer with
any confidence.

But a MORI poll of key constituencies, published in *The Times*,
confirmed the findings of two earlier opinion polls that Tory
voters in marginal seats were more loyal than in the rest of the
country.

In an accompanying article George Brock reminded readers
that marginal constituencies were the front line in the electoral
war. Most general elections were decided by about a tenth of the
electorate living in fewer than 100 of the 650 constituencies.
Thus, this latest poll of seventy-three such constituencies, con-

firming that the swing from the Conservatives to Labour was smaller in marginals than in the country as a whole, suggested a more comfortable Conservative majority — perhaps as many as ninety-four seats — than seemed likely on the basis of the nationwide polls.

This poll was seen as bad news for Labour, but the Insider felt uneasy too. He had always feared that one possible General Election scenario was that the full extent of polarisation in the country would be revealed at the expense of the Alliance. Many people in Conservative constituencies, in work and with earnings increasing at a greater rate than inflation, terrified of what Labour would do, could, whatever their reservations about Thatcher, feel they must vote to preserve the status quo. 'We can't stand Thatcher, but we've too much to lose to rock the boat.' At the other end of the scale, those who were not gaining from the economy would feel so alienated from the Conservatives that they would vote for as extreme an alternative as possible — namely Labour. 'What the hell, we've got nothing to lose.' Thus, with the two nations created by Thatcherism voting in effect in opposition to each other, the Alliance, dedicated to drawing them together, could be in danger of running second to both on their own respective territories. Squeezed!

On the other hand an increased tendency towards tactical voting would benefit the Alliance. This represented a much more attractive scenario. It would involve the first of the two groups deciding that in all conscience they could no longer support Thatcher and that they would be reasonably safe with the Alliance, and many in the second of the two groups deciding that Labour was as much the cause of their problems as the Conservatives, and voting for a complete change – also the Alliance.

At least on the surface, the Alliance looked at the beginning of January to have fewer problems than the other parties. Unlike the others, it was steadily rising in the polls. It had re-established its unity, and, because it had little expectation of winning, had the more achievable target of the three – to win sufficient votes to substantially increase its number of seats and to stop the other two parties achieving a clear majority.

Mrs Thatcher had a number of problems. First she alone must determine the election date, and in this unprecedented three-party situation, whatever she did was risky. Second, she knew that unless her position in the polls improved dramatically, she would enter the election with less support than she had at the outset of the 1983 campaign, and – on the basis of past performance – with little chance of increasing her vote during the General Election itself. Third, she alone had to defend a recent record and confront the 'time for a change factor'.

Kinnock's problem was that no matter what he did, the Labour Party seemed unable to break out of its 38–39 point rating in the polls. Unlike Mrs Thatcher, who had the Budget and the Moscow trip to look forward to, all Kinnock could do was keep his fingers crossed that no one in the Labour Party would rock his already shaky boat.

Kinnock's other problem was that his target was more ambitious than the Alliance one. He desperately wanted a clear majority.

The somewhat negative objective of the Alliance was, of course, forced upon it by the electoral system, for if each party attracted 33% of the vote, Labour would have 291 seats, the Conservatives 263, and the Alliance 71. Not that the injustice of the present electoral system should be news to anyone. At the 1983 General Election, the Conservatives achieved 42.4% of the vote and 61% of the seats – a minority vote producing a majority of 144 seats. In that General Election it took, on average, 32,777 votes to elect a Conservative, 40,482 votes to elect a Labour MP, and no less than 338,089 to elect an Alliance MP. Thus, the Alliance achieved 25.4% of the vote – more than 7.5 million voters – and yet only 3.5% of seats in the House of Commons.

The nature of the injustice was graphically illustrated by one particular statistic: Labour achieved 27.6% of the vote in 1983 and 209 seats; the Alliance 25.4% of the votes and 23 seats.

Could anyone blame Alliance supporters, especially the Liberals who had suffered it longer, for their anger, or for their demands that electoral reform must be a top priority, a non-negotiable precondition of support for either Labour or the Tories, in a balanced Parliament?

In speeches to Liberal regional assemblies around the country, the Insider urged that there should be no compromise on this issue. He had been worried about the fluctuations in the position of the two Leaders. They had both acknowledged that an advance towards PR would be a pre-condition of their support, but Steel had told candidates at Eastbourne that a possibility was PR for local elections and Euro-elections, with reform of the Westminster system to follow later, and Owen, more than once, had suggested a referendum. The Insider felt it would do no harm to apply a little pressure.

At each of the Home Counties, London, and Yorkshire regional assemblies, he was enthusiastically applauded when he said that while the Alliance could not enter any negotiations with a lengthy shopping list, proportional representation should be the exception. There were three reasons why that position had to be made clear to the country, the other parties, and within the Alliance itself:

First, if post-election negotiations with other parties took place and proved difficult, and the Alliance was under enormous pressure to compromise, it would need to be able to count on considerable public sympathy for its demands. The public must know the Alliance was not holding out because proportional representation was helpful to it alone, but because it was essential to enhance British democracy. They must know that this was not an opportunist position, but consistent with all the Alliance had said for many years, as well as in the run-up to the election. This public education had to begin immediately.

Second, this was either an issue of supreme importance to the Alliance, or it was not. If it was, not to seize the first opportunity to achieve the reform would be a failure of duty. If another party emerged with a clear majority at the follow-up General Election, the Alliance would have missed its chance and its case forever after would be weakened. 'Why didn't you do it when you had the chance?' would be a difficult question to answer.

'Third, the commentators and the public will judge our resolve, our strength of character, our will to succeed, on our determination on this issue. Frankly they will think we are mad if we do not take the opportunity while it is there.'

He urged the party to campaign to stress the importance of proportional representation to the electorate generally. More than 50% of voters were women, and yet at the 1983 General Election only twenty-three women were elected, compared with 627 men.

One in twenty-four people in Britain were members of ethnic minorities, and yet there was not one black or brown face in the House of Commons. A single transferable vote system based on multi-member constituencies, would help to change all this. This would require the parties to nominate more than one candidate, and it would be a reckless party that nominated all men, or produced an all-white slate in a mixed community.

If anyone needed convincing of the cynicism of the two old parties it was there to be seen in their enthusiastic acceptance of the electoral status quo irrespective of what it was doing to the democratic process. The Insider expected little better of the Tories, but he was disappointed that some of his more fair-minded acquaintances in the Labour Party would obstinately put selfish (and short-sighted) party interests before their sense of justice. They would talk with passion of 'rights', yet deny 7.5 million of their fellow citizens the right to an electoral system likely to produce a result bearing some resemblance to the way they voted. They talked passionately of 'rights' while denying women an electoral system that would promote their rights of better parliamentary representation. They claimed a concern for the 'rights' of minorities, yet perpetuated an electoral system that reduced their chance of representation in the House of Commons. They talked of 'democratic socialism', but what was democratic about achieving just over 2% more of the popular vote than the Alliance and nearly 1,000% more votes in the House of Commons.

But then, once in power, did not Labour operate the system exactly as the Conservatives? This had been reflected in Kinnock's instinctive support for secrecy over Zircon. Labour had frequently complained about secrecy, but when in power used Section 2 of the Official Secrets Act and refused any advance to freedom of information. Only this February, Labour had helped to obstruct the private members' initiative to produce a Bill of Rights. And at local level, Labour was increasingly using secretive party caucuses to take decisions that were then passed without proper debate in open council. Liberals in Hackney and Sheffield had been forced to raise the money to fight in the courts for their rights to attend relevant committee meetings, or obtain adequate information to represent their constituents.

But the prospect of a hung parliament was concentrating

minds in a variety of ways. For instance, the two Leaders were having to think hard about their attitudes to their rivals. The Insider observed a divergence of view between the two Leaders.

Owen made no attempt to hide an element of respect for the Prime Minister. He was no whole-hearted admirer, but nor would he deny the Prime Minister her achievements, such as the taming of the trade unions, or her conduct during the Falklands war. However the key to his attitude to the two Leaders was defence. On this subject, his attitude to Kinnock was contemptuous. Steel, on the other hand, liked Kinnock and would admit privately that if personal considerations applied and assuming the Labour Leader was prepared to compromise, he would find working with him far preferable to working with Thatcher. Thatcher and Steel disliked each other in equal measure, the former dismissing Steel as weak, and the latter declaring Thatcher's so-called strength to be a combination of autocracy and obstinacy.

In a *New Statesman* article on the eve of the Barbican, Steel had followed up his Bristol speech by warning Kinnock of the dangers of refusing to talk to the Alliance. If Labour achieved the most seats, but not a majority at the General Election, its voters would expect them to talk to other parties. Kinnock would be a true Thatcherite if he refused to come to terms with this. 'The sad truth is that the fantasies of the Labour leadership make it more rather than less likely that Mrs Thatcher will continue to be Prime Minister.'

He attacked Mrs Thatcher once more when he appeared with David Owen on David Frost's early Sunday morning programme. At this point, however, the differences between the two leaders became more public. Steel was emphasising his doubts about forming a coalition with Mrs Thatcher, when Frost asked him if the Alliance would work with her if she insisted on carrying on. Steel said: 'I think it would be almost impossible. I cannot see any circumstance in which it would be possible to work with her in a coalition.'

Owen intervened: 'I think David has gone too far,' he said 'I don't think she is the right person to lead the country and I don't think it will be easy for us to carry on a coalition government with her as head. But once we get into the business of telling other parties who is to be leader, that goes down a dangerous course.'

David Steel, who had a fortnightly meeting, usually early on a Tuesday morning, with his own informal team of advisers, including at this point, Richard Holme, William Wallace, Paul Tyler, and the Insider, discussed with them how to develop his position. Everyone felt that he should not appear to be imposing a leader on another party, but rather to be saying that it was inconceivable that Mrs Thatcher would want to stay on in a hung parliament. She would have lost the confidence of the public. She was philosophically opposed to consensus politics. It was also felt that he should concentrate his attack on Thatcher and Tebbit and their like rather than the Conservative Party. The line should be that a defeat of Thatcher was a defeat for Thatcherism — 'without Thatcher, you can't have Thatcherism'. Working with the Conservatives on an acceptable programme was one matter; working to support Thatcherism another.

In the meantime he and Owen jointly signed a letter to candidates to deal with some of the questions arising from the relaunch. 'There has been some speculation recently about tactical voting. We have undoubtedly benefitted at times from *thoughtful* voting, particularly in by-elections. Now the two-party system has collapsed it is natural that people will want to make their votes as effective as possible. Since we still unhappily have a two-party voting system, that is not always easy. Yet as far as the Alliance is concerned, our advice to voters is simple and straightforward: Vote Alliance. If we win, this is another MP for progress and reform. If not, your vote can be counted as one of millions in favour of a change in the electoral system. Either way you, the voter, win. We are fighting not only to win as many seats as we can, but also to win as many votes as we can. Our negotiation power will depend on both. We want neither the Labour Party nor the Conservative Party to be in a position to govern this country with absolute power on a minority of the vote and the only way to stop that is to be unequivocal in our effort to maximise our vote in each and every constituency.'

They strongly advised candidates not to express a preference between working with Labour or Tory MPs. 'We and you should challenge the other two parties about whether their post-election tactics will include allowing each other to form a minority government, as they have in a number of local authorities.' But it was the electors by their votes who would be demonstrating their preferences between the Conservative and Labour programmes. The Alliance should not express its own. Its stated aim should be a programme reflecting 'as much as is reasonable' of the programme on which it, the Alliance, would have fought the election.

The two Leaders were concerned that candidates would be pressured by the media into committing themselves on what the Alliance should do if there was a hung parliament. 'We think you would be well-advised to avoid filling in questionnaires or being cornered into answering specifically on what shape of coalition you want. Our minimum conditions of electoral reform and economic regeneration will be clearly stated in broad terms before and during the campaign. We will put this forward positively. We will not be pushed into a negative posture on which part of another party's programme we could or could not accept. We should all avoid, therefore, the temptation of creating a detailed shopping-list of demands or sticking points. It is up to both Labour and the Tory parties, and their leadership present and future, to decide whether they are prepared to rise above party and respond.'

They were also anxious to make it plain that they were committed to achieving power at the General Election, whether alone or in cooperation. There would be short shrift for those in either party whose political purity would allow them no room for compromise. 'We are not in the business of protesting, although there is much to protest about, but of changing things on behalf of the decent natural majority of the British people, who are fed up with poor government and industrial failure.

'We are the instrument with which the electorate can finally break the grip of the old two-party cartel which has run Britain, and even Parliament itself, on the basis of a carve-up ... the electors are already sensing this in thinking through the implications of their vote and starting to change the system even in advance of proportional representation.'

Two days later, in a Leicester University lecture, Steel continued his attack on Thatcherism, accusing her of hastening the decline of the British constitution and the values for which it had once stood. Then on Tyne Tees TV's *Face the Press* he faced further questions on working with Thatcher. He only fractionally back-tracked. The Alliance could not retain its self-respect and serve under her unless she introduced proportional representation for a second general election, he said. He described the whole tone of her administration as deeply repugnant and, while refusing to use the word 'never', he said that only a promise to introduce electoral reform would make a deal possible and he believed that 'highly unlikely, almost impossible, inconceivable'.

David Owen, however, continued to concentrate his fire on Neil Kinnock. In an interview with *The Times* the following week, he stated that Neil Kinnock would have to be excluded from decisions affecting Britain's nuclear deterrent if there were any post-general election coalition between Labour and the Alliance. The political command and control of Polaris would instead have to remain in the hands of an inner core of Ministers committed to the principle of nuclear deterrent. Just as Steel had constantly stressed that if Thatcher lost her majority it would be impossible for her to remain, so Owen told *The Times* that 'given Kinnock's pledge to decommission Polaris and his unilateralist views it would be almost impossible for him to be involved in the day to day political control and command of Britain's nuclear deterrent.'

Kinnock would have to be barred from key decisions in the same way that Michael Foot deliberately avoided being involved in nuclear issues when he was Deputy Prime Minister to Callaghan. 'Michael Foot served on the Cabinet's Defence and Overseas Policy Sub-Committee, but because he did not wish to be involved in nuclear questions they were removed and dealt with by Jim Callaghan, Fred Mulley, Denis Healey and myself. We want to ensure that the political command and control of Polaris is vested in people who believe in the deterrent.'

It seemed to the Insider to be an extraordinary position. If the Alliance was supporting Labour in a coalition, then Kinnock would undoubtedly be its Prime Minister, and the suggestion that he should be removed from the decision-making process on the nation's nuclear deterrent was barely credible.

The Insider wondered whether Owen's attacks on Kinnock

were reinforcing the latter's refusal to consider a post-election coalition. In a *Panorama* interview with Robin Day, the Labour Leader said that if he had the most seats in a hung parliament, he would refuse coalition talks with any other party, form an administration, and be confident of success in a second general election. The onus for the collapse of the government in a hung parliament would be on the parties which voted it down. 'To destroy that government would be an immense sin on their heads.'

He confirmed what many in the Alliance feared, that his aim as a Leader of a minority government would be to put the blame on the Alliance for causing a second, unpopular general election.

There was much speculation about the source of an article by Michael Jones, political editor of *The Sunday Times*, stating that Mrs Thatcher would do a deal with the Alliance to stay in power. 'Contrary to speculation she will not, I am authoratively informed, resign in a fit of pique at the nation's unclear verdict or rush to the Palace to inform the Queen that the Thatcher years are over. Instead, she would negotiate with David Owen and David Steel to preserve her seven years of legislation, ensure the permanence of economic revolution and keep out the Socialists. In such an exercise, I am assured, she would be loyally supported by her Cabinet.'

Jones said that 'naturally nothing will be admitted in public' but that such a deal was, 'according to those close to her', her pre-election thinking.

Following the eve-of-Barbican meeting of leading Liberals on post-election arrangements, the Party Council debated the whole question at its February meeting. To the considerable relief of David Steel, it decided not to have a Council meeting on the Saturday after the General Election, should there be a hung parliament, but rather to have a meeting within a month. Council members accepted that it would be able to achieve little on that Saturday when few of the facts were known, but could possibly do a lot of damage; on the other hand it wanted the right to comment fairly quickly on any deal that had been made. It decided on a formula for consultation within the Party. Responsibility for this would lie with the President, President-Elect, Chairman and General Secretary, who would be responsible for taking soundings from the regions, and from recognised organisations within the party, such as the ALC, and others, and for representing the party at the key meetings of the Parliamentary Party.

While the Insider, who was chairing the Council meeting, had no doubt that Council would see the sense of the proposal, he sensed the difficulty that Council members were experiencing. On one hand, they clearly wanted to place confidence in their Leaders, and accepted that in any negotiations the Leaders and the Parliamentary Party would need to have maximum flexibility. On the other hand, many of those present had been involved in detailed negotiations on local authorities where there was no clear majority, and they did not like the idea of Steel and Owen being the only negotiators. They wanted the two Leaders to create a larger negotiating panel. Their experience was that this enabled them to vary their tactics in negotiations and to demonstrate the strength of feeling on controversial issues. It also enabled the Leaders to hold back while others began discussions by establishing those areas of agreement and those areas requiring major negotiations. There was also, they no doubt worried, the danger that the two leaders, operating in a fairly rarified atmosphere at that point, would not be properly in touch with the feelings of the parties. The Insider sympathised with their position but believed it to be unrealistic. He was positive that Owen and Steel were determined to conduct the negotiations alone. He felt, therefore, that the energies of the party would be better concentrated on perfecting channels of communication and consultation so that he, as President, and his senior colleagues would be able to represent the party effectively before any final decisions were taken.

Behind the scenes at the Council meeting, the party chairman Tim Clement-Jones, Andy Ellis, and others were holding an emergency meeting on the party's finances. The party had for years stumbled from one financial crisis to another and with a General Election due, the party once more faced a substantial deficit. Promises from a number of more affluent supporters to guarantee a higher overdraft had not calmed its nerves and the National Executive had insisted that steps be taken to balance the budget. The group decided to make one or two members of staff redundant and to initiate other economies.

The crisis served to underline the unique position of the Liberal Party in British politics. Since the War it has not only fought the major parties under the handicap of the electoral system, but also coped with a colossal disparity in resources. While the big cheques rolled into Conservative Central Office from the City and big business, and into the Labour Party from the coffers of the trade unions, the Liberals had raised their meagre General Election budgets in small donations, and with jumble sales and raffles. Its decentralised structure even put it at a disadvantage compared with the SDP when it came to raising money for national activities. For instance, in 1983, the Conservatives spent at least £3.5 million on their General Election campaign, Labour over £2 million, the SDP about £600,00 and the Liberal Party had only £250,000.

The Insider had been amazed to discover that the Liberal Party, whose objective was no less than to govern Britain, had been coping with a budget half that of Friends of the Earth, of whom he had been chairman, and a third that of Shelter. As he looked back in the files at past budgets, and past financial crises, he marvelled once more at the achievement of the Liberal Party in remaining a major political force in the face of such disadvantage.

The tactical voting campaign by the Green Party's Paul Ekins and friends was now launched. TV'87 boasted a budget of £33,000 and a list of well-known supporters for their campaign to promote tactical voting in key marginal constituencies in order to avoid what one of them described at its press conference as the 'spine-chilling prospect' of the return of Mrs Thatcher. The Group published a list of 100 'prime targets' for tactical voting chosen on the basis of the 1983 General Elections results and subsequent by-election results. It showed the fifty best Labour and fifty best Alliance targets for tactical voting, after eliminating eighteen seats likely to fall to Labour on even a small swing from the Tories and it showed the percentage of 'third party voters' who would have to change their vote to the second party to defeat the Conservative candidate. The smallest percentage was in Richmond and Barnes where only 1% of Labour voters needed to change to the Alliance candidate Alan Watson to defeat the Tories, and in Derbyshire

West where a similar change would also elect an Alliance MP, Chris Walmsley.

The list of supporters was largely made up of mavericks from the arts, journalism, or business. There was one extraordinary contribution at the press conference by Gerald Priestland ('I am not going into politics – theology is vastly more interesting') who said that his objective was to rid the country of Mrs Thatcher. 'I can't think why they call themselves *Conservative*. What have they conserved? They have destroyed whole industries; they have destroyed housing and employment, farms, hospitals and universities; they are trying to destroy the green belt and the BBC. It all reminds me of a painting by the artist Brueghel – you may know it. From a background of desolation, a gaunt woman in an iron breast-plate leads an army of dwarves towards the gates of hell. Scholars say she symbolises avarice and greed. She's called "Die Dulle Griet" – crazy Maggie.'

No prominent members of the Labour Party or the Alliance supported the campaign. Instead, Peter Kellner, political editor of the *New Statesman*, argued that it could do the Labour Party harm. 'Unfortunately this week's offering from TV'87 is seriously flawed. It includes on its list of Alliance target seats a number where Labour would probably be running second to the Tories if an opinion poll were conducted today ... in each of those seats the Alliance's lead over Labour was less than ten points in 1983. In none of them has the Alliance established itself as the natural challenger to the Tories. Not the least of the dangers of the TV'87 campaign to Labour in those seats is that Labour could become established as the third place party – and that would diminish Labour's hopes of ever forming a majority government again'.

Michael Meadowcroft voiced Liberal doubts in an article in *The Times*. 'The inexorable changes in the prevailing ideology of the Labour Party of the past fifteen years or so have widened the fissure between Liberal and Labour into a chasm. Frankly, those who with a rather touching faith persist in believing that, because the two parties share a deep distaste for the Government's divisive and embittering policies there is the potential for an easygoing common approach to defeating the Conservatives, are either closing their eyes to what Labour dominance now means or do not live in big cities controlled by Labour.'

Meadowcroft, too, accepted that the proposition of TV'87 to unite the anti-Thatcher majority was too simple. Precisely because the Alliance was not the Labour Party and could perceive and expose the serious dangers in electing Labour, it could attract a far broader spectrum of electoral support. In any case, the fear of Labour's success could well once more be the Conservatives' best card at the election, in which case, by encouraging the possibility, TV'87 could paradoxically actually help the Conservatives.

Mrs Thatcher showed her bitchy streak by announcing the names of eleven 'working' life peers to strengthen both the Conservative and the Labour Party in the House of Lords, but not one for the Alliance. Both Steel and Owen expressed anger at the snub, but so did many of Mrs Thatcher's own supporters. The *Mail on Sunday* said Mrs Thatcher had weakened the House of Lords and her party's claim to stand for the deep democratic roots that sustained the nation. 'Does Mrs Thatcher really need to be reminded that at the last election the Alliance received over 25% of the vote of this country? Mrs Thatcher has let down herself, her party, and the principle to which she says she adheres.'

The Times said the House of Lords was 'not Mrs Thatcher's poodle' and said that the Prime Minister had simply pursued 'what is now her main strategic purpose – to dish the Alliance and make the point that we live under a two party system and that the two parties are the Conservatives and Labour'. She would, said *The Times*, 'probably have been wise to throw in a couple of Alliance members'.

Her fiercest critic, however, was the maverick and intemperate right-winger Paul Johnson, writing in the *Daily Mail*. He argued that if it was Thatcher's objective to destroy socialism in Britain some party like the Alliance would have to emerge as the main opposition, absorbing the moderate elements within the Labour movement and so displacing it. But at present all Thatcher's short term moves were directed to denigrating and belittling the Alliance, or even ignoring it completely, while confirming Labour's status as the official opposition. The Prime Minister should show the Alliance the constitutional respect it deserved.

If some of the Conservative newspapers joined in the criticism of Mrs Thatcher's list for the Lords, they were soon back gleefully rubbishing Labour over an interview by David Blunkett in *Woman's Own*. He was quoted as saying 'if I had to put my last five pounds on the election, out of evangelical faith I would put it on Labour, but my head tells me I might end up starving'. '*Key Labour leader denies tipping Maggie victory ... storm over Kinnock quote to lose*' was the headline in the *Daily Mail* the following day.

But the Tories were soon on the defensive themselves, firstly because of an extraordinary public relations disaster over their plans for Britain's farmland. Ironically, their actual proposals had a lot to recommend them. Rather than produce embarrassing food surpluses, farmers would be encouraged to come up with environmentally attractive uses for their land, such as forestry, recreational facilities and tourist attractions. There could be a discreet introduction of appropriate industry to the benefit of some of the poorer rural areas. But the farmers did not like what they heard about the plan, and Michael Jopling, Agriculture Minister, panicking at the threat of a censure vote by the National Farmers' Union, so mishandled his disclosure of the policy that he ended up pleasing nobody. Environmentalists, given a false picture of uncontrolled developers running rampant in the countryside, protested, while the National Farmers' Union went on to vote by a substantial majority to demand the Minister's resignation unless he demonstrated he was more committed to their cause. (In doing so, they confirmed the view held by many that farmers saw the Ministry of Agriculture as existing entirely for their benefit.)

Relations between Jopling and some of the DoE Ministers, notably William Waldegrave, had been edgy for some time, for Waldegrave had, with skillful public relations and less real achievement, been building a reputation as a concerned environmentalist, benefitting both himself and also his political mistress who was not impervious to the so-called 'green vote'. Waldegrave had clashed with Jopling before over who dealt with countryside policy (as opposed to agricultural policy). Now some unattributable briefing went on from DoE sources that was highly unflattering to Jopling. As a result what could well have been an attractive and acceptable policy was upstaged by the spectacle of Conservative Ministers shooting themselves in the foot whilst removing the farmers' knives from their backs.

And while all of this was taking place, the affair of Duncan Campbell, and the Zircon project was raging on. In fact, it moved into top gear even while the Alliance was cheering its leaders at the Barbican, for at the same time the Special Branch was taking apart the BBC's offices in Glasgow, removing all six films in Campbell's 'Secret Society' series, together with other material. It was difficult to know whether to laugh or to cry. The farcical side of it was provided by the Special Branch who seemed unable to obtain the correct warrant, and twice had to leave in order to apply for a fresh one. But, of course, the use of Section 2 of the Official Secrets Act for this kind of fishing expedition was no laughing matter. There were debates in the House of Commons, headlines in the newspapers, furious leading articles, and further moments of farce, not least when it was disclosed in the House of Commons that the accident-prone Attorney- General, Sir Michael Havers, had lunched with Duncan Campbell at the Garrick Club and at Covent Garden. One letter from Havers to Campbell included 'look forward to seeing you on Thursday, Yours ever, Michael'. Norris McWhirter and his Freedom Association attempted to obtain injunctions to stop further showings of the Zircon film, now being seen all over the country. Campbell derided this: 'It is encouraging that opposition has apparently moved from Ministers to marginalised right-wing loonies.' McWhirter's bid failed. Scotland Yard's bid to find the mole who had leaked the information to Duncan Campbell also failed, as did attempts to stop newspapers and magazines from discussing the Zircon project.

The longer the Zircon controversy continued, the less it appeared that the project need ever have been secret. At a time when money was desperately needed for a whole variety of social reasons, and was being denied because the country 'could not afford it', it was planned to spend £500 million of public money without any parliamentary debate or public approval of any sort. And for what? An expensive project that Britain really could not afford and that, more than likely, was not necessary. Was the secrecy to protect the spy satellite, or to protect the Prime Minister and her colleagues from justifying it? Hardly the former, for there would be no hiding a spy satellite once it was up there, above the Soviet Union, for all to see. In fact there was no possibility of keeping it a secret even before it was put into space. Nor any particular need to. And, once the details were disclosed, what possible benefit could there be for the Government in the clumsy use of the Special Branch to obtain revenge?

As the Insider suspected when Duncan Campbell first telephoned him, the journalist was more than up to the political challenge and out-manoeuvred the Whitehall machine at every turn.

If the Insider does not devote more attention to this issue, it is because, as with the City scandals, there was no evidence that in itself it would have any effect on the General Election. What was possible, however, was that the Zircon affair, coupled with the Wright affair, added to the earlier Westland affair and a whole list of excessive and insensitive abuses of power, were beginning to add up to a broad impression of at best, incompetence, or, worse, an elective dictatorship out of control. This could yet have electoral effect.

With the crucial pre-election Budget due on March 17, all parties now turned their attention to economic policy. It was becoming increasingly clear that the Chancellor of the Exchequer, Nigel Lawson, would have a lot of money to spend; the question was: what on? The Tories were in no doubt. They would spend it on winning the Election, above all by cutting taxes and introducing measures to encourage a drop in interest rates, hopefully including mortgage rates. Labour's Shadow Chancellor, Roy Hattersley, speaking to local councillors in Leeds, made clear Labour's alternative. They would reverse any tax cuts and spend the money on a job creation programme. Roy Jenkins told the Alliance parliamentary party that he would be producing a 'shadow budget' for publication the week before Lawson's, but that his inclination was that the Alliance should vote in opposition to any tax cuts, whilst not necessarily being committed to reversing them. He argued that decisions about the level of tax could only be taken at the appropriate time, and a promise to automatically reverse the cuts was a nonsense.

There was increasing evidence that the pending General Election was likely to involve unprecedented personality attacks by the Conservative media. There had always been a fear that this would be a dirty General Election, particularly with Norman Tebbit in charge of the Tory campaign, and there was little question that the main target would be Neil Kinnock. But it was not going to be left just to the media. On February 18 the Speaker had to step in to stop three motions being tabled in the House of Commons by Tory backbenchers, led by Marcus Fox, ferociously attacking Neil Kinnock for incompetence, inexperience, and 'inability to exercise self-control'. After the Speaker's intervention, the two Chief Whips, John Wakeham for the Conservatives, and Derek Foster for Labour, issued a joint pledge to do their best to 'restrain such behaviour'. They said 'personal abuse and attacks on the integrity of individuals has reached an unacceptable level damaging to parliament.'

The Fox initiative followed closely on an extraordinary attack on the Labour Leader's wife, Glenys Kinnock, by Edwina Currie who implied that Mrs Kinnock was the real leader of the Labour Party.

Kinnock was not, of course, beyond attacking his opponents — he had the previous year described John Wakeham, Lord Whitelaw, and the Prime Minister as 'the top trio, the Chief Whip, the Chief Drip, and the Chief Lip of the Tory Party'. He said that when he had last seen them on *Spitting Image*, the television puppet show, he had assumed he was watching a documentary. But there was a difference between the witty invective of Kinnock and the sustained assault being mounted to humble the Labour Leader, particularly by the Conservative papers with whom he seemed to have little chance of achieving any just treatment whatsoever. While there was evidence from opinion polls that voters did not automatically accept the verdicts of opposing politicians about each other, for it had to be said that Mrs Thatcher herself had been subjected to sustained invective from the left over the years, and the polls also showed voters seemed to be able to distinguish between the positive and negative characteristics of the different leaders, it did seem likely that this sustained assault on Kinnock would in the end have some effect.

The dirty tricks brigade weren't just content with attacking Kinnock at national level; they also were set loose on the Labour candidate in the Greenwich by-election, Deirdre Wood, who was deservedly an issue in the campaign because of her position on the hard left of the Labour Party (albeit modified during the campaign), but who found herself vilified in newspapers such as the *News of the World* for apparently taking a year or two off her age and because of family problems that were totally irrelevant either to her current life or to the by-election. In the face of unpleasant pressure from the *News of the World* she broke down at a press conference, winning the sympathy of many (including her Alliance opponents) who witnessed the scene on television. This wrong-footed the newspaper concerned, and probably neutralised the effect of the attacks.

The Insider sympathised. When he fought the Hove by-election for the Liberals in 1973, he had himself become a campaign issue as he threatened the Tory seat and manoeuvred Labour towards its lost deposit. He was smeared by canvassers on the doorsteps. Answers he had given during an interview for a job three years earlier were taken out of context and circulated by the Labour Party. An article he had written for the *Guardian* in the late '60s sceptical about liberals with a small 'l' was reprinted on a Tory leaflet, but with a capital 'L' to make it appear as if he had been attacking his own party. The Insider had urged his supporters not to retaliate, convinced that in the end the dirty tricks helped rather than hindered his campaign. He preferred to contrast himself as the clean new-style community politician fighting the discreditable techniques of the old-style parties. But he could still remember how unpleasant it was to stand up before audiences who were clutching in their hands leaflets distributed by the Tories outside the hall attacking him in personal terms.

He knew, too, that there had been one or two lapses in taste by Liberals during by-election campaigns. One that had been disowned by the candidate, Richard Livsey, was a leaflet in the Brecon and Radnor by-election stressing that he was the only candidate leading a happy 'family' life. The Labour Party had waxed lyrical about the so-called dirty tricks of the Alliance in the Newcastle-under-Lyme by-election, but the Insider believed these charges were not justified. On that occasion, it had been the Alliance tactic to raise questions over the way the retiring MP, John Golding, had manoeuvred his wife into the candidature. Golding was a wheeler-dealer politician in the Mayor Daley class and it seemed to the Insider that the Goldings had been fair game. Obviously the voters had felt the same, for the Alliance candidate had nearly pulled off a sensational win.

As we have seen, by-elections had developed an importance far beyond that of electing an MP for a particular locality and with full time professional teams moving in behind each candidate, were being fought with enormous determination and energy. It was becoming increasingly difficult at any of them to keep the debate concentrated on the issues. However, this is what the Alliance did at Greenwich, assisted by an extraordinary candidate. David Owen could hardly believe the SDP's good fortune when he first saw Rosie Barnes in action. Had the party spent years perfecting the ideal by-election candidate, and kept her ready for such an hour, it could not have done better. She was local, married to a Greenwich SDP councillor, and a parent-governor of her children's two local schools. She was able and self-confident, attractive and friendly, brave and determined. She spoke in public with aplomb and handled the media like a veteran. When the Insider met her at one of the morning press conferences he could hardly believe his eyes and ears. It was usually the role of outside personalities to lend some heavyweight support to a vulnerable by-election candidate. But this was no nervous candidate in need of protection. This was somebody so in command that the Insider had to do little except watch in admiration. Likewise, at the main by-election rally with David Owen and David Steel, she insisted on taking all the questions personally. Above all, she was determined to succeed. 'I intend to win this by-election,' she said from the start and by sheer force of personality, backed up by probably the best by-election organisation the Alliance had so far achieved, she set about trying to do so.

Clearly the choice of the leftist Deirdre Wood as the Labour candidate helped, but it was never going to be easy. Rosie Barnes had to build from that early opinion poll showing Labour with 60% support, and private polling and early canvassing confirmed that Labour were ahead. At the beginning of February a BBC TV *Newsnight* poll put Labour at 48%, up 10% on their 1983 General Election result, the Conservatives at 26%, and Rosie Barnes at 24%. Yet the Liberal by-election veterans, Peter Chegwin (the party's expert at the production of targetted leaflets) and Chris Rennard (who was the agent for the West Derbyshire campaign), were unimpressed by the polls. Both put money on Rosie Barnes with the local bookmaker. Andy Ellis was also predicting fairly early on that it was winnable.

In charge of the campaign was Alex McGivan, the SDP national organiser, who by the last Saturday had well over a thousand volunteers canvassing on the streets. McGivan backed up by John Cartwright, the SDP MP for neighbouring Woolwich, decided on a strategy from the start – they would take a positive line on policy, stressing the theme 'our heart's in the right place, but so is our head. We care but we are realistic too.' Second, they would promote Rosie Barnes herself, emphasising the local contact – 'Rosie Barnes live here'. Third, they would bid for the tactical vote. The Conservative candidate, a youthful merchant banker, did not stand a chance, and so the message would be that a vote for the Alliance, unlike the Tories, was not a wasted vote, and that if voters wanted to avoid a Labour left winger, it was to Rosie Barnes they must turn.

Letters were individualised, and mailings directed at specific groups, including opinion-formers such as doctors, publicans, priests. The combination of intensive, targetted leafletting, and the outstanding media coverage that Rosie Barnes was able to achieve, began to have its effect. Within a week of its first poll, BBC's *Newsnight* was showing that Labour's lead had been nearly halved from 22% over the Tories to 12% over the Alliance. For the first time newspapers began to talk about the possibility of a shock result. So rattled were the Conservatives that Angela Rumbold, the Minister of State for Education, became involved in a press conference row with *Newsnight's* Vincent Hanna, she claiming the poll was 'dodgy' and Hanna threatening to sue her for slander.

The Insider last went to Greenwich on the Friday before polling day. An NOP poll in the *Evening Standard* that day put Labour at 40%, the Alliance at 35% and the Tories at 22% – almost exactly the picture Alex McGiven wanted. By then he, Andy Ellis, and the others were all confident that Rosie would win. It was more than possible to pick up those last few percentage points over the final days, and the small deficit at this point would undoubtedly inspire the helpers they wanted over the weekend.

By the Monday Andy Ellis was saying to the Insider 'we're going to win Greenwich'. The Insider replied 'you're really definite about that?' Ellis said: 'I've just spent £3,500 on a post-by-election appeal to be posted on Friday morning – I'm that confident.'

So to polling day, and when *Newsnight* came on the air, Vincent Hanna, the programme's veteran by-election pundit, announced that an exit poll suggested a Rosie Barnes win by nearly 5,000 votes. The Insider, remembering how John Cartwright had been so concerned to reduce the impact of an inevitable Greenwich defeat when the by-election had first been discussed by the Joint Strategy Committee, was amused to hear him telling Robin Day that 'we have done a good deal better than many of us expected at the beginning of the campaign'.

At last the result came. There had been a 68.4% turnout, up on the General Election, and for Rosie Barnes it was a triumph – a majority over Labour of 6,611. Labour, the main opposition party, had lost a by-election in a seat it had held since the Second World War. The Conservatives, who achieved 3,852 votes, were witnessing their worst result since Sutton and Cheam in 1972. The Alliance fight-back from Eastbourne, initially intended to reach its climax at the Barbican, had continued to even greater levels at Greenwich.

What had been the reason? Apart from the superbly professional campaign, and the quality of the candidate, the initial reaction was that it had been a classic case of tactical voting, with Conservatives determined to keep out the Labour candidate of the left. But a special opinion poll commissioned by the *Independent*, involving interviews with 1,160 people as they left the polling stations, suggested there was more to it than that. The newspaper reported that if the 16% of those questioned who identified a tactical vote as their primary or secondary reason for voting Alliance were redistributed between their initial choice of parties, Rosie Barnes would still have won with a 1% lead over Labour.

The poll showed that the issues that affected voters were health, education, unemployment, crime and violence, and housing, all areas where the Conservatives were vulnerable and where

Labour had, at least in Greenwich, failed to persuade the voters they had the answer.

Norman Tebbit, who had seen the way it was going, had kept a card up his sleeve. A founder member of the SDP, John Horam, previously a Labour MP, announced at the weekend his resignation from the SDP. This, said Tebbit disingenuously, was far more noteworthy than the Greenwich by-election. Within the Alliance it hardly caused an eyebrow to be raised. (It wasn't even referred to at the APG meeting the following week.)

David Steel seized the opportunity to spell out the meaning of Greenwich in an *Observer* article. 'Britain now has three-party politics. The evidence is incontrovertible; in the result of the last General Election; in the result of the country and district local election in the past years; and, of course, in local and parliamentary elections. In the fifteen by-elections of this parliament, the Alliance leads the three-party race, with 37% of all votes cast, with 30% to the Conservatives, and 30% for Labour.' He pointed out that Kinnock should be deeply depressed by one statistic: in those fifteen by-elections, the Labour share of all the votes cast had already fallen by 1% from the already deeply depressed levels of Michael Foot's 1983 General Election. Labour, he said, were losers.

Labour, as always in defeat, started to turn on each other. Michael Cocks, the former Chief Whip of the Labour Party, wrote an article for *The Sunday Times* describing the by-election as a 'shattering blow to Labour's prospects of winning the General Election'. The hard-left Labour Party had done damage to the Labour movement throughout the country with its obsession with minority interests. 'What can one say on the doorstep to people who say they are doing their best to bring up a family but all the Labour Party seems interested in are gays and lesbians?'

There was other evidence of Labour's capacity for self-inflicted wounds. On the night of the by-election, Vincent Hanna, who had been at Greenwich for the duration, reported that the 'smears on Deirdre Wood' had largely been planted by Labour Party members at the time when they were choosing their candidate. Likewise Francis Beckett, a Labour Party journalist, writing in the *Spectator*, said 'the Alliance didn't smear her, anymore than they smeared Mrs Golding (the Newcastle-under-Lyme candidate). The stories about her were in place before the by-election started, they were part of the fight for the nomination . . . it's all the legacy of the years between 1979 and 1983, when the left laid about with its ideological scouring brush. Sometimes Labour seemed less like a party than a loose federation of groups . . . many people, from former Cabinet Ministers to local ward secretaries, were driven out of politics by constant personal abuse, often for the smallest divergences from approved doctrine . . . those who remained still bear the scars — and the thirst for revenge.'

As Labour's nightmare continued beyond Greenwich (the Alliance hardly bothered to fight a Euro-election in the West Midlands on March 7, and yet Labour saw its majority of nearly 20,000 fall to just over 4,000, with the Alliance taking almost all of its votes), Kinnock told his press secretary, Patricia Hewitt, to organise a meeting of leading London Labour Party members to try to counteract the 'loony left' problem. Whether deliberately or not, her letter addressed to Frank Dobson, chairman of the London Labour MPs, was leaked. It stated 'it's obvious from our own polling, as well as from the doorstep, that the "London effect" is now very noticeable. The "loony Labour left" is taking its toll; the gays and lesbians issue is costing us dear amongst the pensioners; and fear of extremism and higher taxes/rates is particularly prominent in the GLC area . . . private and public polling is now showing very clearly that, whereas London at the height of the GLC campaign was pulling Labour's national average support up, London today is pulling Labour down. I think there are many in the London Party who still fondly believe they are doing well — they need to be disabused'.

As if all this was not bad enough, a former Labour Prime Minister, James Callaghan, now precipitated a further public relations disaster. In the midst of the 1983 campaign, Callaghan had made a speech disassociating himself from Michael Foot's unilateralist defence policy, and now, in a Commons debate, he did similar damage to Neil Kinnock. This provoked Labour's employment spokesman, John Prescott, to confront Callaghan before disbelieving Tory MPs in the Commons tearoom. 'You've done it again,' he was reported to have said. 'Two elections in a row. You have snookered us again.' This made front page head-lines the following day.

Richard Heller, an adviser to Labour's Shadow Home Secretary, Gerald Kaufman, was forced to resign within a matter of hours after writing an article for *The Times* supporting the Callaghan view. Labour's defence policy required the British people to 'believe six impossible things before breakfast'. Dr John Gilbert, who had been a thorn in the side of Mrs Thatcher over the Westland affair, added his view that Labour's defence policy was 'an albatross and a burden'.

While Labour was busy holding inquests, Andy Ellis was in Truro working with the local campaign organiser, Malcolm Brown, to achieve a respectable result for Matthew Taylor in the Truro by-election. Ellis had set his heart on around 60% of the vote in order to be able to demonstrate a sustained Alliance momentum. The Insider travelled to Truro to spend a day there with David Steel, first at the press conference with the cool and confident twenty-four year old candidate, and then on the streets of Truro itself. If Taylor was destined to be the baby of the Commons, his youth was clearly not worrying the voters. As with Rosie Barnes at Greenwich, the Insider was impressed with the candidate's determination. Whatever his inner fears, they were kept well hidden. In fact, the Insider judged, there *was* little to fear. The response was nearly always the same — 'if you're half as good as David Penhaligon, you'll do for me'. At least one constituent, albeit a non-voter, did not share the prevailing enthusiasm for the Liberal. While Matthew Taylor and the Insider were talking to fishermen on their boat in one of Cornwall's picturesque harbours, a seagull deposited its own vote upon the candidate's head in full view of the television cameras!

The seagull's was a lonely verdict, for this remarkable ten weeks for the Alliance was now to reach its climax. When the votes were counted, Taylor had lifted the 10,480 majority of David Penhaligon to an astonishing 14,617.

The Insider had no doubt that loyalty to David Penhaligon had been a factor. As one local Liberal had said to him, 'you'll be surprised by the number of people who now remember voting for David Penhaligon who could not have done at the time ... otherwise his majority would have been double.' But life was hard in Cornwall these days; an entire constituency was not likely to cast its votes out of sentimentality alone. Matthew Taylor was entitled to say, as he now did on his day of triumph, that it was not only a vote of confidence in Penhaligon, but also a vote for a Liberal to fight for Cornwall.

But if it had been a triumphant few weeks for the Alliance, what had it been for the others? For the Conservatives, probably bewildering. Yet the Tories were keeping reasonably calm. 'We have seen Liberal by-election victories before,' Tebbit kept saying. Greenwich was put down to tactical voting and Truro to the Penhaligon factor. It would all be different when the General Election came.

Labour could look for no such consolation. It really was beginning to look even to the most optimistic of the Labour leadership as if disaster was staring them in the face.

And what lay ahead? A popular budget? A Thatcher television spectacular from Moscow? A possible further Alliance advance at the expense of Labour in the local authority elections in May? Where was the cheer for Neil Kinnock?

The Alliance, The Other Parties and The Voters

From by-elections to General Election

March 15 to April 6

A tax-cutting Budget ... focus on social issues ... Tebbit attacks the Alliance ... the Alliance regains control in Merseyside ... and rises in popularity in Scotland ... Kinnock goes to Washington and Thatcher to Moscow ... Owen predicts May 7 ... but the Alliance is geared up for June ...

Hardly a day went by without speculation about the date of the General Election. Every opinion poll and every word spoken by the Prime Minister or Norman Tebbit was closely examined. Would it be May 7? Would it be June? Or would it be the autumn? It was generally accepted that two events could swing it one way or the other – the Budget on March 17 and the Thatcher visit to Moscow at the end of the month.

The Alliance parliamentary party met to hear from Roy Jenkins what he would say in an 'alternative budget' to be published on March 10 and how he proposed the Alliance should respond to the official Budget the following week. He recommended the Alliance should not oppose an increase in allowances, but should oppose any cut in the standard rate of tax on the grounds that tax-payers would benefit more from sensible public expenditure to tackle unemployment and to improve the health service, education, and housing.

There was considerable discussion about what to do if the Chancellor increased the ceiling on mortage tax relief from £30,000 to £35,000. The Alliance's established position was that mortage tax relief should be restricted to the standard rate, and now Jenkins said additionally that he himself was unsympathetic to an increase in the ceiling. He said the system of mortage tax relief was irrational, but it would be difficult to abolish; only time and inflation could reduce its negative economic and social effects. This would not happen if the ceiling was continually increased. On the other hand, he said, many candidates in constituencies in the south of England, where house prices had risen, felt that it would be almost suicidal to oppose an increase in the ceiling, particularly because Tebbit would distort this into evidence that the Alliance would eventually eliminate mortgage tax relief altogether.

It was typical of the choice politicians often have to make between what they know in their hearts to be right and what they believe to politically possible, yet the Insider found it disturbing. He had already argued to Owen and Steel at an APG meeting that an increase in the ceiling would help nobody. It may appear to be helping those buying increasingly expensive houses with big mortgages, but the tax relief was part of the reason for the high prices. The effect would be to push them up still further, reducing the mobility of home owners and dashing the home-ownership hopes of those who had no existing house to trade. It also meant public subsidy was increasingly loaded in favour of the better-off. He had also spoken and written to Roy Jenkins on the subject. But the Insider was a home owner. He knew all about the burden of mortgages and the value of tax relief. Jenkins was right – the system should wither on the vine; it could not be completely eliminated without severe damage to the finances of a vast number of people, and this would, of course, be political madness. But the MPS were not discussing eliminating it; they were discussing whether they should oppose an extension of it. If an opposition party did not oppose this, who would? And if it did not oppose it in opposition, what chance would there be that it would act rightly when in office?

The debate was overshadowed by the activities of Norman Tebbit who had been publishing leaflets suggesting that the Alliance would abolish mortgage tax relief altogether. Simon Hughes's criticisms of it were widely quoted by the Tories. David Steel had tackled the chairman of the Conservative Party on it, accusing him of lying about Alliance policy. But Tebbit would seize on any Alliance opposition to an increase in the ceiling to strengthen his case that the Alliance was anti-occupier. In the end, it was decided to abstain on the issue. David Steel was honest: 'It's not a particularly honourable position, but we know what we'll do in the long term, and in the short term it will be difficult to counter what Tebbit would say if we actually opposed it.' (As it turned out, even the Conservatives saw the lack of logic in a further increase in the ceiling. It stayed at an already excessive £30,000.)

In a crowded room at the Central Hall, Westminster, on March 10, Roy Jenkins, together with Ian Wrigglesworth and Malcolm Bruce, published the Alliance 'alternative budget', called *More jobs in a fairer Britain*. Jenkins began by saying the Alliance would oppose any tax cuts. This did not mean it would necessarily re-introduce the present level of taxation – there was little point in committing itself to this until it was in a position to look at the books. He said that a higher balance of payments deficit was inevitable and acceptable. The Alliance differed from the Tories by its determination to reduce unemployment and differed from the Labour Party in its belief that unemployment could only be reduced within the framework of anti-inflation discipline – i.e. an incomes strategy. The promise was to reduce unemployment by a million over three years.

The performance of Nigel Lawson the following week was low-key, and compared with the predictions, the Budget itself was less than sensational. Predictions of a tax cut of 4p on the standard rate proved exaggerated; he cut it by 2p to 27%. Personal allowances went up in line with inflation. The duty on drink and tobacco remained unchanged. *The Times* summed it up fairly: 'It was a budget clearly designed to keep down prices, drive down interest rates, and make it difficult for the opposition to claim that it represented an irresponsible pre-election give away.' In this respect it was a clever Budget. The hyping-up of the possible give-aways in advance had enabled Lawson to introduce a Budget attractive to traditional Conservative supporters while at the same time creating the impression of a Chancellor putting what was right for the economy ahead of what was right for his party.

Followed as it was by a fall in the unemployment figures, a predictable fall in interest rates and mortgage interest, and figures to show that inflation had steadied over the past month, the Budget was seen by press and politicians as a political success for the Tories. The momentum behind a June election began to build.

But had the Budget really impressed the voters? To hospitals, to schools, to beleaguered local authorities, all desperate for money to maintain services, it was no help, and one of the more encouraging findings of opinion polls over the past two or three years had been acceptance by voters that their standard of living did not only relate to their income and immediate material circumstances, but also to the condition of the communities and cities and country they lived in. Asked directly whether they would prefer more money spent on schools, hospitals, housing, and other social provision, rather than on tax cuts, a majority had always voted for the former.

On Budget day itself Home Office figures showed that the number of crimes in England and Wales had risen by 7% in the past year, higher than the annual 6% between 1980 and 1985. Shirley Williams was able to say that the Tories' claim to be the party of law and order had been shattered by the upsurge of crime and the fall in the clear-up rate. 'Crime on the streets has its echo in high places in the frauds and insider dealings which are coming to light,' she added.

Parents all over Britain were being infuriated by the prospect of another teachers' strike, ultimately caused not by their dispute over pay, but by the decision of the Secretary of State for Education, Kenneth Baker, to withdraw local negotiating rights and impose a settlement centrally. Paddy Ashdown made his first major speech as Alliance education spokesman in the Mole Valley constituency of Baker himself, spelling out the facts on Conservative education performance. Since 1980, 1,791 schools had been closed; 5,000 teachers, mostly the best ones, had quit for better paid jobs; 12 million lessons had been lost because of disruption; 141 schools had been forced to drop special subjects for the less able and handicapped children; and the physical condition of schools had reached the point where two in every three were in need of substantial repair. After eight years of the Tories we had slum schools, a widening gulf of opportunity for children, a growing chasm between what industry needed and education provided, and a demoralised teaching force.

The National Housing Forum organised a 'Housing Week' to draw attention to the increasing numbers of homeless, now over 100,000, the deteriorating quality of housing, and the acute scarcity leading to unbelievable prices in the places where people had to live in order to work.

The chairman of the Health Education Council made desperate attempts to squash a report he acknowledged was 'political dynamite' showing inequities in health provision. The President of the Royal College of Nursing announced that 'the national health service is in danger of breaking down because of increased pressure on overworked nurses'. The British Medical Association was also embarrassed by the leaking of an internal document, *Deprivation and Ill-Health*, arguing that increased illness caused by deprivation could only be tackled by increasing resources for housing, job creation, income support, education, health and social services.

The challenge to both opposition parties was clear – to focus public debate on these problems so that voters would conclude that the price for the Tory tax cuts was too high.

The challenge, too, was to create a picture in their minds of the two nations that could emerge from another term of Thatcherism. One, centred almost entirely on the South-East, would be affluent and elitist. An increasing number of couples would inherit houses, the mortgages of which had been paid off by their parents, and thus would be receiving substantial sums of unearned income to add to salaries which were themselves running ahead of inflation. Working for them would be a new servant class, unable to afford the decent housing, unable, because of unemployment, to wield any negotiating muscle, destined all their lives to be inferiors, and to pass the inferiority on to their children. As more and more of the affluent opted out of the state health service, and out of state education, so the new servant class would be catered for by public services increasingly deprived of adequate resources and thus bereft of the best professional skills, aids and facilities, and would have few articulate voices to defend them. There would be bitterness and this would lead to crime and probably to more riots, and the response would be tougher policing, particularly of the affluent areas. In the meantime, in other parts of the country, especially the North and West, unemployment would grow, poverty would grow, and the quality of life would be so inadequate compared with the South-East that Disraeli's prophecy of two nations would finally be fulfilled.

All of this would be sustained by North Sea Oil, used to pay the unemployed and to deal with social problems just enough to take the edge off the anger and to foster apathy.

But back to the present, and particularly encouraging for the Alliance was a Marplan poll for the *Week in Politics* TV programme. It showed increasing confidence in the Alliance to tackle social problems, particularly education. Peter Kellner, presenting the results, said 'this confirms what Marplan found for us last month when they tested party images: that voters were now beginning to turn to the Alliance for positive reasons, and not solely as a protest at the other two parties'. The APG decided to accelerate two Alliance campaigns, one on health, and one education, and launch them both in early April.

Tory vulnerability in this area was reinforced by a Harris poll in the *Observer* the following Sunday, March 22, showing them still below that critical 40% mark – Conservatives 39, Labour 33, and Alliance 26. The poll had been carried out after the Budget and showed no improvement in the Tory position; in fact, there was a 1% fall in approval of their economic policies. Noteworthy was still further evidence that voters would have preferred to see more spending on public services than tax cuts. Asked, 'some people say that the next government should put income taxes back to the level they were at before this week's Budget and use the money instead to increase public spending, do you agree or disagree with this view?', a majority, 52% agreed, and only 38% disagreed. The *Observer* reported that support for reversing the tax cuts was spread evenly throughout all age groups and social classes and even one in three Tory supporters believed that Lawson's priorities were faulty.

The following week a Marplan poll in the *Today* newspaper showed that while the Tories were on 36%, the Alliance had achieved the same level as Labour – 31%. In other words, no overall parliamentary majority for any party. *The Times* reported that 'the prospects for a June election receded sharply'. Then a Gallup poll put the Alliance in second place – Conservatives 37.5%, the Alliance 31.5%, and Labour 29.5%. All this was too much for Norman Tebbit, who loaded both barrels and turned them on the Alliance. At a stage-managed Conservative Party conference in Torquay he raised a spectre of a Lib–Lab pact, giving Kinnock the ladder to climb into Downing Street by the backdoor. The Alliance, according to Tebbit, 'is playing a dirty game; what makes the Alliance game dirty is its cynical objectives. The aim is quite simply to smile and say nothing'.

He accused the Liberal Party of 'downright deceit, the selling tactics that would land a doorstep encyclopaedia salesmen in gaol'. The Prime Minister took a lead from him at the same conference the following day. The Liberal Party, she said, had always put Labour into power. 'They did it in 1924, in 1929, in 1974 and in 1977. And given half the chance they'd do it again.' All of this totally ignored the fact that the Alliance's best prospect of power ultimately lay in replacing the Labour Party as the main opposition to the Tories.

Tebbit was now constantly referring to the Alliance as 'a socialist party'. Virtually out of control, he devoted Central Office funds to a special party to mark the tenth anniversary of the Lib-Lab pact. At this he tried to blame the Liberal Party for the 'Winter of Discontent' in 1978–79 (the pact had, in fact, been concluded some months earlier) and warned that any post-election coalition between Labour and the Alliance would lead to the implementation of socialist policies and to a reversal of the economic and social gains over the last eight years. But it all backfired. The media responded with scepticism. And the Insider, chairing the launch of the Alliance local election campaign that same morning, was able to appear on all the television news bulletins, revelling in the evidence of the fear the Alliance was engendering in Tebbit. The widespread view was that the Tory chairman had gone over the top, publicising the Alliance to its advantage rather than his own. In his column in the *Independent* Peter Jenkins began: 'It is going to require some genius for the Conservatives to lose the coming election but they may have found their man in Norman Tebbit.' Instead of the Alliance being on the defensive, Tebbit was now having to appear on television programmes and explain away his campaign.

Geoffrey Smith, the conservative columnist in *The Times*, suggested that every time the voters heard 'a savage attack on the Alliance, it confirms what offends them most about the Conservatives'. Sir Geoffrey Howe and Norman Tebbit had attacked the Alliance from a similar viewpoint, he said, but 'when they both make the same point Mr Tebbit manages to sound like a political assassin, while Sir Geoffrey gives the impression of having been forced to his conclusion by careful analysis. That is the tone that is most likely to impress the voters . . .'

Liberals met for their Scottish Assembly at St Andrews in jubilant mood. They cheered Roy Jenkins when he suggested the target should be total power. And they cheered David Steel when he told them the Labour vote was collapsing and that the potential for the Alliance was unlimited. In a telling attack on the Tories he said any perceptive elector could tell from the values and characters of Mrs Thatcher, Mr Tebbit, Mr Lawson and their colleagues, the sort of policies they were likely to get. The perceptive elector could see the kind of Tories who have been dropped from the Cabinet.

'I do not claim, and I never will, that the Alliance is always right about everything – but I do believe that at root our attitudes and aspirations are closer to those of the British people than the hard greediness of Thatcherism.

'We stand for fairness, for personal freedom and positive partnership. Thatcherism stands for grabbing what you can get and setting each family against its neighbour.'

The polls showed the Alliance moving ahead of the Tories in Scotland, with an increase in support of nearly a third since November. There was a possibility of doubling the number of Alliance MPs from Scotland. Taken together with Labour's healthy position in Scotland, this held out the prospect of what Scots had come to call the 'domesday scenario' – namely, the Conservatives in control at Westminister, based on their strength in the south of England, but with virtually no Scottish MPs and thus ruling Scotland with hardly a pretence of a Scottish mandate. Even in 1983 they only reached 27% of the popular vote in Scotland and they were showing well below that figure now.

Alliance MPs in Scotland were reluctant to stress this point, for it sounded defeatist and also there was a danger that it would lead to another explosion of Scottish nationalism with the Scots Nats winning votes that would otherwise come to the Alliance. Not that the Alliance was ill-equipped policy-wise to take advantage of the position; it had consistently argued for a Scottish Assembly and devolved powers, while Labour had not taken any of its past opportunities to legislate in these areas.

There were also mixed feelings within the Alliance when the Law Lords finally disqualified forty-seven Labour and Militant councillors from holding office in Liverpool, projecting Sir Trevor Jones and his Liberal-led Alliance back into power in a city facing a massive financial crisis. In effect Labour had indulged in a spending spree without money in the bank and left the Alliance to pay the bills. David Alton raised the question at a parliamentary party meeting and it was decided that David Steel should confront the Prime Minister in the House of Commons the following day with a request to her to meet a community-based deputation of all parties and also of religious and business leaders to hear at first hand of the city's special problems. In the event she refused, saying 'those democratically-elected must learn to take responsibility for their actions'. Labour claimed that it would recapture control in the May elections, but an early by-election in the St Mary's ward of the city showed the Alliance had a real chance of confirming its control. The Liberal candidate turned a Labour majority of 410 into an Alliance majority of 490 after what was for a council by-election a substantial turn-out — more than 50%.

The Insider had considerable confidence in Trevor Jones, David Alton and their Alliance colleagues in Liverpool to hold their own in a battle with Labour and with Militant, but he shared the concern spreading from the Liberal leadership in London to the ALC and throughout the party over the problems of the Liberal-council in Tower Hamlets. Under intolerable spending controls imposed from Whitehall, and confronted with acute housing problems, they were drawing fire for two decisions. The first was to cut back on the funding of a number of voluntary organisations, notably in the arts, and was a row largely contained within the area. The other, more controversial, and beginning to achieve national publicity, was the refusal of emergency help under the Housing and Homeless Persons Act to some Bangladeshi families because they had made themselves 'intentionally homeless' in the terms of the Act.

The council's position was desperate. It had some of the worst social and economic conditions in the country. It had been run by Labour until May 1986, and rate-capped by the Conservatives on the basis of the Labour Party's last budget. The Alliance had won control in May 1986 and complied with the rate-capping legislation. Despite the controls, it had increased spending on the homeless from the last Labour budget figure of £4.5 million to £18 million. Just the same, the rate-capping limited how much it could spend overall to £124 million whereas Alliance councillors believed they needed a minimum of £159 million. Despite these problems, their budget for the homeless was 15% of council spending, more than any other local authority in London.

In the first year in office, it had accepted over 1,000 extra families as being homeless. About 80% of these were of Bangladeshi origin. During that year sixty families who said they were homeless were provided with accomodation by the council, pending consideration of their cases, and subsequently not accepted because under the rules of the legislation they were believed to have made themselves intentionally homeless.

Thus it was trying to cope with a national problem with limited local resources. Yet, inevitably, when those affected by policies are from a racial minority, councillors opened themselves up to charges by their opponents of being both heartless and racist. This was nonsense, but unfortunately the public relations had been appalling. Instead of replying to criticisms with calm explanations, they replied truculently or not at all. The more pressure was applied from outside, the more some council leaders developed a siege mentality.

Consultations took place between David Steel, Michael Meadowcroft, the Alliance spokesman for housing, Simon Hughes who, as a neighbouring MP was in danger of suffering some of the political flac, and the ALC. It was decided that some experienced ALC councillors should travel to Tower Hamlets to help solve the problems, while Meadowcroft and Shirley Williams, the Alliance home affairs spokesman, would jointly write to Ministers demanding that they meet a deputation to discuss how Tower Hamlets could be helped. The Tories made no attempt to respond quickly for they and the socialists were equally enjoying the Alliance embarrassment.

It would not be exaggerating to say that the Liberal leadership was holding its breath and hoping that the ALC, and in particular the experienced Andrew Stunnell, could help to find a solution.

The time had now come for Margaret Thatcher to play her second electoral card. The Budget having so far failed to boost her in the polls, she now prepared to set off for Moscow. In response Kinnock, hoping to make his own international mark, and despite poor media coverage of his last attempt, flew to Washington, this time to have a meeting with the President himself.

The Kinnock trip was an even bigger disaster than its predecessor, although, apart from the decision to travel there in the first place, it was not Kinnock's fault. He was received courteously by the President, relative positions were outlined, and he left at least having explained Labour's defence policy face to face with Britain's main international ally. Unfortunately, while Kinnock was offering a fairly up-beat account of the meeting to journalists, the President's press secretary, Marlon Fitzwater, was declaring at his daily White House conference that in a meeting lasting 'approximately twenty minutes' Reagan had, in effect, read Kinnock a lecture. This was all the Tory press needed. The headlines were based on the Fitzwater version: 'Angry Reagan slays Kinnock' said the *Daily Express*. 'The revenge of Reagan' said the *Daily Mail*. 'Reagan rebuff for Kinnock over defence' said *The Times*.

There was little question that Kinnock had been 'stitched up' by the Reagan administration. In fact, it was almost too effective a demolition job ... almost counter-productive, in that the Kinnock and Denis Healey version sounded more credible than Reagan's and it led to a number of follow-up investigative pieces that tended to confirm the Kinnock rather then the White House account.

Even David Owen commented to the Joint Strategy Committee that he believed Kinnock had been outrageously treated.

Margaret Thatcher, on the other hand, was given the full red carpet treatment by the Russians, a suitable television spectacular being staged for British voters and the word coming forth from both the Russian and British public relations machines that she and Gorbachov had established a highly effective working relationship.

The Thatcher trip to Moscow had always been intended to achieve this, but the Kinnock fiasco was a bonus. The message to voters was clear – Thatcher was the experienced international elder statesman; Kinnock the naive and incompetent pretender.

The two forays overseas were followed by a series of opinion polls. At one point three out of four showed Labour in third place. A Gallup 2,000 poll for BBC's *Newsnight* on April 3 showed the Conservatives with 36.7%, the Alliance with 31.8%, and Labour with 29.1%. It was very close to polls in the *Daily Telegraph* and *Today*, although the *Today* one had the Alliance and Labour equal on 31%. The most devastating news for Labour was a poll in the *Observer* showing the Conservatives with 39%, Alliance with 33% and Labour with 26%.

Then on April 5 *The Sunday Times* published a MORI poll showing the Tories 12 points ahead of both the Alliance and Labour, each on 29. With Labour planning to counteract this with a major speech on policy by Roy Hattersley and a *Weekend World* television appearance by Neil Kinnock, David Owen spectacularly stole the headlines by all but announcing an election for May 7. The SDP leader had been convinced for some time that the election would be on May 7, and his adrenalin was flowing. The way he saw it, if he was right, then he would put the Alliance on full alert, if he wasn't, it didn't really matter. Either way, it would catch the headlines. Such was election fever at this point that he did exactly that. But if the media were influenced by Owen, the Prime Minister was not. No election was called.

April 6 to May 7

Alliance planning moves into top gear ... bright ideas for the manifesto ... Tory MPs in trouble ... Owen questioned on a hung Parliament ... more on tactical voting ... Peter Wright re-

emerges ... defence issue neutralised? ... the Election is called ...

The week of April 6 was one of intense Alliance activity and meetings. Acting on instruction from the National Executive, the President and Chairman of the Liberal Party met with Shirley Williams and Bill Rodgers, President and Vice-President of the SDP, to discuss how the parties would consult with their members should there be a hung parliament and negotiations with either the Tories or Labour.

The Insider reminded the Social Democrats of the 1974 fiasco when Edward Heath failed to win a majority in the House of Commons and summoned Jeremy Thorpe for talks. This had not been anticipated by Liberals and as a result there had been chaos within the party over that weekend. It was vital to learn from that and set up a proper consultation process.

The Insider outlined the Party Council decisions and said that the process was based on the assumption that the two Leaders would slow down any negotiation process and that there was little likelihood of decisions being taken over the weekend following the General Election. Rodgers was sceptical. He said that no matter what the Leaders may intend to do, that come a call by either Mrs Thatcher or Neil Kinnock to negotiations, they would be under enormous pressure to make a deal quickly. 'We have two Leaders who scent power – when the crunch comes, they'll be moved by the sheer momentum. In any case, if we're not careful we will be forced into a position where we are seen to be dithering.' Shirley Williams shared his view, adding that if in the last week of the General Election campaign it looked as if the Tories would not achieve a clear majority, there could be a run on the pound; the Alliance would be under heavy pressure to play its part in establishing stability as quickly as possible.

The Insider replied that if this was so, and there would be little opportunity for consultation with the parties after the General Election, some should take place in advance. He expressed his concern that the party had not been properly informed of the range of options and of what was at stake.

The two SDP leaders were sufficiently concerned by the issues raised to urge a meeting with Owen and Steel, and the Insider and

Shirley Williams undertook to approach their respective Leaders.

The Insider wrote to Steel: 'It was clear at the Party Council meeting and it is clear to me that the Liberal Party understands that any decisions will be taken by the parliamentary party, guided by the two leaders. That is established. But it must be equally clear to you that in the extraordinary circumstances that may prevail, and with the likelihood of a further election, when our fate may partly be determined by the way the two parties handle the difficult position of a hung parliament, support from the two parties in the country and a show of discipline and unity is crucial. That cannot be achieved unless (a) they feel they have at least been fully consulted, and (b) they understand the reasons behind any decisions that are taken – and that they understand the reasons at the time, rather than being helped to understand them later.

'That is why we have been anxious to set up, with your support, a consultation procedure.

'First, will there really be time for that consultation procedure to work properly?

'Second, will people be sufficiently educated about the factors involved to be able to respond properly?

'On the first question, I know it is the intention of yourself and David Owen to slow the process of decision-making, to conduct negotiations at your pace, rather than have a pace imposed upon you. But both Bill Rodgers and Shirley Williams were doubtful about whether, when the time comes, that will really be possible. Their view is that a combination of circumstances, not least the response of the City to any sign of instability, could be such that you will be under enormous pressure to move quickly. In those circumstances, there is a serious danger of consultation being jettisoned for what will then seem the best possible reasons. However, they will not be the best possible reasons if such a position has been anticipated as I am now doing, and if it has not been acted upon.'

The following day, Richard Holme raised at the Joint Strategy Committee his concern at the lack of 'hung parliament' scenario-planning. Others quickly took advantage of his words to express their own concern. The Insider spelt out his worries about the parties not being adequately educated. Owen and Steel both responded constructively, and David Steel then replied to the

Insider's letter: 'Thank you very much for your thoughtful letter about consultation with the party in the event of a hung parliament. I do see and understand the points you make, and if we can find time in the first week after Easter, we can certainly have a meeting with Tim, Shirley, Bill and David Owen.'

The Insider now met his successor, the President-Elect, Adrian Slade, to discuss how they would operate during the consultation process. They decided that whoever was President would be the senior member and spokesman of the group of four – the others being Clement-Jones and Ellis – and that they would insist on being represented at all major meetings that took place within the Alliance during any negotiating process.

They worked out how they would consult with the party, and also decided they would not consult on the detail of negotiation, but rather seek answers to a small number of broad questions. The aim of the exercise would be two-fold: (a) to enable them to reflect accurately to the Leaders what the party could support; (b) to demonstrate clearly to the party that its views had been taken into account.

The Insider then drafted a letter to go to all of those who would be part of the consultation process, advising them of these arrangements, and concluding as follows: 'I would like to make a few broad points: first, we must all understand that any decision that is taken will be the decision of the parliamentary party. It will be our responsibility to convey to the parliamentary party what we believe the party in the country can accept and support. But it is their decision.

'Second, there will be enormous media pressure on all of us to find out what our views are. This must be resisted. This is not in order to impose some kind of centralised control for the benefit of the Leaders, but because publication of differing views will create an appalling public impression and could be of immense value to those with whom the Leaders are negotiating.

'Third, for reasons of confidentiality, but also because we believe it is the best way to proceed, we will not be consulting on every detail of the negotiations, but rather seeking a response to broad questions. Some of them you can imagine.

'Fourth, you should be yourself working out who you are going to consult, in order to guarantee the view you convey genuinely represents the group for whom you are responsible and it will be necessary for you to pass the importance of confidentiality on to all whom you consult.

'Fifth, there will be immense media speculation at the time. You should encourage everybody not to assume that it is accurate. Otherwise we will all end up not only having to deal with opinions on the real issues, but a whole variety of imaginary or media-created ones.'

He also warned that if the two Leaders were asked to meet the leader of the party with the most seats on the Friday evening, they would have to do so. No one should panic and assume they were being bounced; such a meeting to establish the others' opening position could only be helpful to the parliamentary party meeting on the Saturday.

It is worth emphasising that all of this work was undertaken despite the fact that the Insider, and most of the others involved, knew the percentage chances were that negotiations would never take place. But, it was vital, should a hung parliament be the result, that the Alliance handled it well, and that was why these discussions within the Alliance were both necessary and urgent.

In the meantime there was still the problem of the General Election itself, and at the Joint Strategy Committee on April 7 there was a lengthy discussion on the state of the polls. Alliance support had risen 4.6% from February to March in the seven main monthly polls, while Labour had fallen 4.3%. But the Conservatives had opened a majority-producing lead over the now evenly divided opposition. The five polls since March 19 showed the Conservatives averaging 38.6%, the Alliance 30.6% and Labour 29.6%.

On the day of the Joint Strategy Committee meeting *The Times* had published the second of its MORI opinion polls in marginal constituencies. It continued to show a surge to the Alliance at Labour's expense but indicated a possible Conservative majority of ninety-two seats if the election was held immediately. Also that morning, TV AM broadcast a Harris poll showing the Conservatives with a 13 point lead over Labour – Conservatives 43, Labour 30, and the Alliance back in third place on 26.

Looking at the polls generally, the JSC noted that only one elector in every five or six expected the Alliance to win, even in the seats where the Alliance came closest in 1983. Some felt the Alliance should now start talking up its chances of winning, and talking less about a coalition or hung parliament. In particular, there was a danger that Owen's publicly-stated belief that a hung parliament was the only realistic objective would become a self-fulfilling prophecy. Could he be indirectly telling people that the Alliance couldn't win and thus fostering the wasted vote syndrome?

The Insider, convinced that people would not be motivated to vote for second place or for a hung parliament, suggested that the Alliance needed to be much more positive. Candidates on the doorstep needed to be able to convince people they could win, and a more up-beat message needed to be projected nationally.

Richard Holme argued that 2 or 3% of the vote at the last General Election had been effectively tactical in the sense that people would have liked to vote for the Alliance, but believed their vote to be a wasted vote, and so voted for their second choice. This was tactical voting, and it had worked for the other parties. 'If we are to talk up our chances we could pick up that two or three per cent. I think some upping of our sights is needed. If we are going to talk about a balance of power, let's at least talk positively about becoming part of government.'

Others said it was not credible to suggest the Alliance could win. No-one would believe it.

Both Owen and Steel took the view that the emphasis must be on attacking Labour, stressing that they could not win and did not deserve to win. The Alliance must not let Labour recover. Steel talked about achieving the position of being the popular opposition in the country.

It was clear that the Alliance would have to improve in the polls before there would be any encouragement from the two Leaders to people to talk about 'winning'.

With many of the details of the General Election campaign now well-advanced, the Alliance Planning Group later that week turned its mind to the party manifesto. This was being drafted by Alan Beith, in consultation with seven representatives of each of the two parties' Policy Committees. But the APG had undertaken the task of coming up with one or two special ideas to be major selling points during the General Election. Some initial work had been done by the Insider and Polly Toynbee, who had each come up with a variety of proposals.

Polly Tonynbee was concentrating on education and health, and the Insider on the elderly and on housing. Both Polly and the Insider had come up with a similar idea to help solve the emergency housing problem, and the Insider had now developed it to the point where a decision was called for. With more than a hundred thousand families now being accepted as homeless by the authorities, the aim was to create an incentive to more than a million owner-occupiers and half a million council tenants who had spare rooms in their homes to let them, no doubt mainly to single people, particularly the young, and those moving in order to get work. The proposal was that they should be able to let up to a maximum of two rooms in their own home, free of income tax up to a maximum income of, say, £60 a week. There would be measures to guarantee they could end any tenancy arrangement on a fortnight's notice. Clauses in mortgage contracts or in local authority letting contracts forbidding sublettings would be invalidated.

They believed that the chance to let rooms without financial penalty and provided they could be regained easily and quickly would be enormously attractive to many owner-occupiers, either young people just buying a home, or elderly people, and could lead to a near-solution to the problems of single young people, young couples, or people needing to move around the country to find work.

The APG was suitably enthusiastic and it was decided to process the idea further, dotting the i's and crossing the t's, and then include it in the manifesto, probably publicising it separately in advance.

Polly Toynbee and the Insider were asked to develop this and other ideas fairly quickly in consultation with the Alliance spokesman and other policy advisors.

That evening the first meeting of the headquarters team for the General Election took place with John Pardoe in the chair. Roles were defined, and practical problems discussed and resolved. The Insider had succeeded in receiving APG approval for his twenty-four-hours-a-day plan, namely a day team and a night team, the latter to be coordinated by himself.

The Night Team would come on at about 10 o'clock and be responsible for monitoring media coverage, and undertaking overnight analysis, and preparing material for possible use at the morning press conference and in press releases and speeches the following day. He had recruited Hilary Muggridge and Tessa Horton to do the monitoring. Hilary, who worked at the Constitutional Reform Centre with Richard Holme, had done this before, and Tessa Horton had been David Steel's secretary until becoming a trade union parliamentary lobbyist. Alan Leaman would be the writer of press releases, speech material, etc, and Andrew Cooper of the SDP and Kieran Sensle from the Liberal Whip's Office would help with policy research. Laura Thomas would come from the Insider's office to act as overnight administrator.

During the day, Pardoe and Harris would be the chief decision-makers, with Polly Toynbee and Simon Bryceson of LPO organising the press conferences, Jim Dumsday the national news media operation, Simon Lewis the radio and television current affairs and discussion programmes. Paul Tyler, and David Owen's PA, Maggie Smart, would be responsible for the Leader's tours, and Penny Moon, who had organised the Barbican Rally, would be responsible for setting up the 'ask the Alliance rallies'. Andy Ellis and Dick Newby would run their respective party's local election campaigns and Geoff Tordoff would be responsible for commissioning articles, speech drafts, and back-up material. Paul Tyler described the Leader's programme. Assuming an election was called on the Monday or Tuesday of a week, the Leaders would from the Thursday to Saturday travel around the country launching regional campaigns and providing media briefing. A meeting of the Campaign Committee would take place on the Sunday. And then from the following Monday the campaign would be underway. A typical day for the Leaders would be the first Thursday of the campaign, when David Steel and David Owen would do the press conference in the morning, and then Steel would fly off to connect up with his 'battle bus' to tour Hereford, Shrewsbury, Montgomery, and Brecon, and then travel by helicopter to Liverpool. David Owen would use his bus to cover inner London and then fly north to visit Bolton, before linking up with Steel in Liverpool for a joint Granada television interview, followed by an 'ask the Alliance rally'. They would then both fly back to London.

Saturdays they would spend in their own constituencies and Sundays in London for meetings with the Campaign Committee.

On the Sunday April 12 the question of what the Alliance would do in a hung parliament was raised in a notable interview given by David Owen to *Weekend World*.

Owen was confronted with the suggestion that not to offer the country a prospectus of what it would do in a hung parliament was to ask people to vote for a 'pig in a poke'. He replied that the Alliance would have shown the country how it would wish to govern, and it was obvious that it would want as much of its own agenda as it would be reasonable to ask for.

He confirmed that if the Alliance was not involved in discussions about its contents, it would vote down a Queen's Speech introduced by one of the other parties. It was only interested in supporting a negotiated programme for a fixed term.

Pressed on whether he favoured a coalition, Owen indicated that, subject to the number of votes achieved at the General Election, this would be his preference. Asked about Cabinet posts, he repeated that the first need would be to negotiate a fixed term, probably not less than two years, and then a legislative programme for that time. 'People are not interested in demands for offices and big cars – they want to know what you're going to do.'

On PR, he said that constitutional reform, which should include a Bill of Rights and freedom of information as well as PR, would probably have to be spread over two or three sessions, and the introduction of PR might begin with the Euro-elections which were imminent, and then be extended to local authorities, to reduce extremism in local government, and then apply to the legislative parliament the Alliance wanted introduced for Scotland and to a Northern Ireland Assembly. There would also be a need for 'progress' towards PR for Westminster. He acknowledged that a referendum for Westminster was a distinct possibility, but it should be a post-legislative referendum.

Charged with lacking resolution on this issue, he replied that he was being realistic; it was extremely difficult to get constitutional reforms past the House of Commons – 'I would like to get changes on the statute book that will last.'

On the economy, he stressed that there was a lot more to the Conservatives than Thatcher and Lawson and that there were many Conservatives who would welcome the Alliance approach of greater public expenditure and borrowing to reduce unemployment. It would be necessary to show to the country that a coalition involving the Alliance and the Conservatives was not just pursuing Tory policies – that there was major investment.

He agreed that the Alliance could not support repeal of Conservative trade union legislation which he described as 'necessary and proven to work'. But he felt that otherwise there would be little difficulty tackling employment in coalition with Labour.

On defence, he stressed that the Alliance would keep Polaris for its full life, and if Kinnock insisted on unilaterally disarming, there could be no deal. Likewise, it would be difficult to deal with the Conservatives if they refused to look at alternatives to Trident as minimum deterrent.

At the conclusion, his interviewer tried to press Owen to acknowledge that he sounded more likely to make a deal with the Conservatives, but Owen repeatedly interrupted to suggest a more even-handed approach.

The programme ended: 'I put it to you that you are more likely to do a deal with the Conservatives than Labour.'

'That's up to Mr Kinnock.'

The Insider had been pleased and impressed with Owen's performance. He had taken considerable care to cater to Liberal sensitivities, he had not allowed his interviewer to demonstrate he could deal only with the Conservatives, and he had, in the Insider's view, established a credible General Election position.

He was, therefore, astounded to see a headline in the *Guardian* the following morning: 'SDP Leader pours cold water on postelection deal with Labour' and an article by John Carvel stating that Owen had come 'as near as he dared to admitting that he could do a deal with the Conservatives after the next election but not with Labour'.

Bryan Gould, the increasingly impressive Labour campaign manager, was quick to seize the opportunity to create a distorted impression of the interview. He was quoted as saying, 'Dr Owen came out in his true colours. He almost revealed his ready-packaged terms for a post-election deal with Mrs Thatcher.' With a dig at the advocates of tactical voting, Gould continued: 'Anyone who thinks a vote for the Alliance is a means of getting rid of Mrs Thatcher will discover that in Dr Owen's hands their vote will simply keep her in Downing Street.'

The Insider read a transcript of the interview. It confirmed his earlier impression. Every effort had been made to tempt Owen to say he preferred to work with the Conservatives, and Owen had resisted the temptation. For instance:

Interviewer: Now, so far as the economy was concerned you did see scope for some kind of a deal with a large part of the Conservative party which you felt was moving, or could be moved towards the Alliance's ideas . . .

Owen: And the Labour party.

There was another moment:

Interviewer: You've said that you don't see Neil Kinnock as fit to be Prime Minister of this country . . .

Owen: You didn't give the full quote . . .

Interviewer: . . . or of Labour to take key decisions.

Owen: I said that of Mr Kinnock while he pursued these policies of unilateral nuclear disarmament and kicking the US out of their nuclear bases and challenging NATO, I isolated him . . .

Interviewer: But you don't seriously expect him to . . .

Owen: He's got to change his views on the nuclear policy and defence, there's no question of that. So has Mrs Thatcher got to change her views on unemployment. There's no question about that either.

There were other instances where Owen was being led in one direction, and refused to follow.

But credit to Gould. He had spotted the opportunity. How many people actually watched *Weekend World*? If he could talk it up in the way he did, many Labour supporters, tempted to vote Alliance tactically, would accept the newspaper versions of the interview and act accordingly. More critically, many Liberals (and some Social Democrats as well) would be concerned and there was a chance of a break in the ranks.

The Insider decided to write to the *Guardian* to counter-balance the effect of Carvel's front page article. He believed that many Liberals who had not seen the programme would accept his version of it. The letter duly appeared that Wednesday: 'John Carvel correctly reports that Dr Owen was accused of being "a man who is more likely to be able to do a deal with the current Conservative Party than with the current Labour Party"; and that he replied: "well, that is up to Mr Kinnock."

'Surely that is the case. At present, Mr Kinnock is adamant that he will deal with no one. If he has the most MPs but a minority of the Commons, based on a minority of votes in the country, Mr Kinnock's intention is to pretend otherwise; to pretend he really has been democratically elected to govern.

'So, of course it is "up to Mr Kinnock"; if he won't even consider the power-sharing approach the electorate will have produced, it will be he who settles the issue in favour of the Conservatives (assuming, of course, they are ready to be more "reasonable" and of course, to repudiate much their leader has stood for). This is what David Steel meant when he said earlier this year: "The sad truth is that it is the fantasies of the Labour leadership that will make it more rather than less likely that Mrs Thatcher will continue as Prime Minister."

'Then, of course, Labour also will need to moderate some of its extreme policies. That, too, is "up to Mr Kinnock" and the rest of the Labour Party leadership. But it is also up to the Conservatives whether they will moderate their policies, for Dr Owen – as David Steel has often done – made it equally clear that we could not possibly endorse Thatcherism as the way ahead, all the more so because the electorate would clearly have rejected it.

'I believe that both Liberals and Social Democrats who saw the programme would share the view that rather than "pour cold water" on a post-election deal with Labour, Dr Owen laid down a challenge to both the other parties; it is a challenge we have no doubt the electorate will endorse whenever it has the opportunity.'

Still there were Liberals who remained unhappy with the interview, and the Insider, brooding over it on yet another journey from Brighton to London, concluded there were two different reasons for the unease. The first was their suspicion of the SDP

Leader, and the second was that many had not worked out what the likely post-election scenarios were.

Of course many of Owen's problems with the Liberal Party were self-made. He had at times in the past barely concealed his view of many Liberals as naive, woolly, lacking in appetite for power and responsibility. The Insider doubted if even Owen would pretend that in any circumstances he was an easy man to work with. He was abrasive and impatient. He could be devastatingly dismissive of others' opinions, arrogant, and moody. These characteristics did not endear him to many in his own party, let alone Liberals. Of course this was only one part of the Owen personality, but few got close enough to see the more attractive qualities. For instance, he would listen; even if he did initially attempt to brush it aside, if the advocate of a particular case had the strength to pursue it and it made sense, Owen was never too proud to be seen to change his mind. He also knew that the higher the stakes, the more you had to gamble, and he was always ready to take a risk or try a new approach. At first acquaintance, and even at the beginning of meetings with people he knew well, he could sometimes be abrupt and cold; when he relaxed, he demonstrated a surprising warmth. The point about Owen was that he was uncompromising. There was little light and shade. This was reflected in his speeches. He made little attempt to ingratiate himself with audiences, or end with a flourish to spark off a standing ovation.

The Insider believed that if the Alliance had been a commercial company, Steel, the listener, more interested in the broad principles and the overall objective than the detail, would have been chairman of the board; Owen, with his incredible energy, desire to be involved, and driving personality, would have been the managing director. Steel's inclination was to steer his party in the right direction; Owen's to drive it there. Owen's attention to organisational and policy detail was staggering; and there appeared to be no aspect of the SDP or the Alliance he did not like to be involved in. Their conflicting personalities and approach to leadership were, however, complementary.

The Labour Party, aware of Liberal sensitivities, continually accused Owen of being right-wing. But it was an absurd analysis of Owen's politics. He was, in fact, a genuine radical, contemptuous of the establishment, and committed to wholesale constitutional reform. When the APG looked at the variety of ideas being devised for the manifesto, he told it 'the Tories are for the rich – the big men ... we have to be for the ordinary man, those who need help', and, even when Dick Taverne mishandled the presentation of the proposed tax and benefit scheme in the autumn of 1986 Owen made clear his support for the principles and never ducked the electoral dangers of a radical scheme calculated to concentrate public resources on those in real need. Those who accused him of being a dictator in his own party were underestimating his colleagues. It was not Owen's strength which caused Cartwright and Wrigglesworth and the others to risk their political careers by leaving the Labour Party ... it was their own strength, more than sufficient to hold their own in any internal party debate.

Why, then, was Owen mistrusted so much?

First, because he appeared to have no need to be liked, and such an individual is inevitably hard to like. To get on with Owen you had to come to terms with this uncompromising aspect of his personality, and have the strength to hold your line.

Second, he was a man of action. He was not by nature anti-democratic (why should he be? He had been elected an MP, become a Cabinet Minister, and then become Leader of his own party via the democratic process), but he chaffed at the delays. And it showed.

But the main problem was his obsession with defence. It is arguable that if David Owen had never been Foreign Secretary he would have been a much more effective and popular leader of his own party and of the Alliance. But he *had* been Foreign Secretary and a member of the Cabinet. These were his credentials, and it is human to make your personal power base the area where you have unchallengeable authority and experience. The more Owen was asked to do radio and television interviews as a former Foreign Secretary, and write articles on major world issues, the more that base was strengthened. It is equally human to be most affronted when challenged by others in that area of authority and experience, and Owen barely disguised his view that he knew what he was talking about and that ninety per cent of Liberals (and probably ninety per cent of the rest of the population) did not. Furthermore, as we noted at Eastbourne, his pleasure in talking about the subject with which he felt most secure could at times make him sound far more hawkish than he intended. The problem was that it distorted his presentation of himself and the Alliance, so that the genuine radical, and the man with an instinctive feel for the deprived, was obscured from view.

On many occasions the Insider longed to say to him 'for heaven's sake, could you not talk about defence for three months, and make speeches about the need to shake up the system, about the potential of the tax and benefit scheme to tackle poverty and need, about the problems of the young ... about the future of your own children ... and how the threats have to be anticipated and overcome'. Owen's anger and impatience harnessed to those causes, and they were causes he genuinely shared, could have transformed his image.

Steel and Owen shared in common a lack of desire to be loved, and in consequence they were not. This is no criticism; probably it is to their credit. On the other hand, Steel understood the importance of being liked — of popularity. Owen was probably more concerned to be respected. Alliance campaign organisers found this a useful mix — 'the tough guy and the nice guy'.

The Leaders both shared a dislike of making speeches; they both found it a strain. They both knew it was not their outstanding skill. And they both preferred a more conversational approach, Steel because it fitted more naturally with his easy-going conversational style, and Owen because he liked to talk to people, to argue a position, convinced that if he could just spell it out, explain, the audience would follow. This is why they both preferred the 'ask the Alliance' question and answer meetings, to big election rallies.

To say that Steel was to the left of Owen, or Owen to the right of Steel was to over-simplify their differences. And those differences were relatively few. They were also mainly of emphasis. For instance, Steel's earlier years in Africa meant that he tended to see foreign affairs more in terms of the struggles to relieve Third World poverty, and overcome racism, whereas Owen would see foreign affairs more in terms of defence, and relationships between power blocs. Owen, as a doctor and a former health minister, would on the domestic front talk most interestedly on health and social services, while Steel, a former chairman of Shelter in Scotland, would talk first of housing.

The Insider was convinced that if the two Leaders had an instinct to work with one or other of the Conservatives or Labour, it came down as much to personality as it did to policies. Owen, the 'let's look at the facts', 'let's get on with it', 'managing director of politics', probably felt that if you could make a deal with the Tories, you could make it stick and get on with changing things. He had spent too many years in the Labour Party to believe it was possible with them. In any case, could you really be serious about working with Kinnock? Kinnock the unilateralist. Kinnock, the man who said that on no account would he even consider working with the Alliance? At least Thatcher had appeared to indicate she would deal; why waste time with someone who didn't understand the facts of electoral life and was leading his own party to destruction? Steel, on the other hand, used to the more relaxed Liberal pace, affable, the 'chairman of the Board', happy to make a less formal deal and play it as it came, instinctively reacted unsympathetically to the cynicism, the ill-disguised self-interest of the Tories. The uncompromising and shrill Margaret Thatcher could not have been more unattractive to David Steel; Kinnock's affability and obvious decency were much more to his liking.

The Insider also worried about the implications for the Liberal Party of a hung parliament. The more he considered it, the more the outcome was clear. The Tories would have the most seats, Mrs Thatcher would ask the two Leaders to call on her, and they would have no choice but to at least open up negotiations. They could not tell her to go. And thus within a matter of hours of the election many Liberals would have to come to terms with the fact that their Leaders were talking with the dreaded Thatcher. Of course the probability was that they would not reach accord. But what if she offered just enough – if not 100% PR, a major step towards it? And economic changes? And an end to Trident? It sounded impossible – but what if ...? Were the two Leaders to turn down a deal with Thatcher on those terms?

And what if they did? Kinnock would be called to the Palace, he would introduce a Queen's Speech, and it is possible that the

Conservatives would either abstain, or arrange for a small number of MPs to be absent so that it was passed. Labour, introducing some popular policies, obtaining all of the added credibility of office, would then be set to crush Alliance ambitions at the following general election. Or, the Tories would combine with the Alliance to defeat the Labour Queen's Speech, and there would be another general election. This time, however, Mrs Thatcher could say 'there, we offered to make a deal and we were reasonable, and the Alliance did not want to know ... we told you this would happen if there were three parties ... if you want stability, you've got to ignore these people'.

The problem the Insider could not solve was how Liberals could be assisted to recognise in advance the probabilities when, for obvious reasons, the scenarios could not be properly and openly debated.

He was convinced, too, that the real problem was the Prime Minister. A recent opinion poll had shown that more Alliance supporters would prefer a deal with the Tories than with Labour. Alliance activists would probably vote differently but given the experience that many were having with Labour at local level, there was no guarantee of that. It was not the idea of working with the Conservatives that was the problem although some were most unappealing. It was Thatcherism. Liberals had responded positively to David Steel's attacks on Thatcher earlier in the year, assuming that he was working towards eliminating her from any deal with the Conservatives. But most, including Steel, had grudgingly come to the conclusion that Owen was right – it could be no part of a deal with the Conservatives to insist that she went. Or to insist that the Alliance would only negotiate with another Conservative leader. The talks would have to begin with Thatcher and the probability is that they would end with Thatcher, one way or the other.

The question of what the Alliance would do in a hung parliament inter-related with tactical voting, and as the Insider had anticipated at Weston-Super-Mare, tactical voting had now emerged as one of the major issues in the run up to the election.

It was now clear that it would take a miracle for Labour to win. It was equally clear that with opposition divided between Labour and the Alliance, the Conservatives would be almost unstoppable. The anti-Thatcher forces were now divided on the tactical voting question into two new groups: those who put their own long-term party considerations first, who saw Labour or the Alliance respectively as the party that had to be crushed; or those who were concerned, above all, to remove Thatcher and believed it was the duty of Labour and the Alliance to do it, possibly working together.

The *Guardian* fell into the second category, and now launched a sustained campaign of leading articles promoting the concept. It argued that the horrors of another few years of Thatcherism could be avoided if all non-Tory voters rallied behind Labour or behind the Alliance, but this appeared unlikely to happen. 'The two competitors for the anti-Tory vote will cancel each other out while their common enemy marches to a third majority term and who knows what else on the basis of a third successive (and decreasing) minority vote. Yet there is a third way of avoiding these consequences – tactical voting. Tactical voting now appears not just as one way of defeating the Conservatives at the coming election – but the only way.'

The *Guardian* concluded that 'the political reality of Britain in 1987 is that a divided opposition is minimising its own chances and propping up an incumbent government at the same time. The opposition parties ought to be co-operating. But if they won't do it, then maybe the opposition voters must do it for them.'

In the *Observer*, columnist Neil Acherson wrote in support. He too accepted that the opposition parties could not offer a lead. 'The electorate will have to make the tactical-voting decision alone, while its political leaders gibber angrily from the wings. But I see the tactical voters as midwives restraining Britannia – struggling, protesting "elderly prima gravida" – so that she can give birth. There are twins here, and they will out. The first is the anti-Tory political block which is already impatient to leave the womb ... the second of Britannia's unwanted twins, which tactical voting can help to deliver, is a reform of what passes for a British constitution.'

Eric Hobsbawm, socialist intellectual, writing in *Marxism Today*, furthered the call. 'The Thatcher government could not have been elected but for the divisions among the opposition i.e. between Labour and the Alliance, and if Thatcher had any chance of being re-elected it is entirely due to the continuance of these divisions.' There was only one logical conclusion: to vote for the candidate who offered the best chance of beating the Tories.

'None of the leaders of the parties of opposition will tell us to do so. In fact all will tell us the opposite, following the electoral mythology which holds that politicians, like boxers before the big fight, must on no account admit that they could not knock the other fellow out of the ring.'

He was supported by the editor of *New Socialist*, Stuart Weir, who stated that only a Mr Magoo could now ignore the Alliance, and yet Labour's strategy, publicly at least, remained essentially unchanged. The almost certain result of their strategy was that Mrs Thatcher would once more profit from the division of her enemies.

Weir acknowledged the problems for Labour in tactical voting; that the principal beneficiaries were likely to be the Alliance ('the Alliance-Labour traffic is asymmetric: the Alliance get twice as many votes from Labour as Labour does from them'); second, that in the feverish atmosphere of an election campaign, tactical voting would give an added impetus to the band wagon effect which the Alliance was adept at conjuring forth. He determined, however, that tactical voting was here to stay. Thus, Labour had to develop a strategy to neutralise the Alliance's hype and to take advantage of tactical voting itself. Tactical voting offered the only real possibility of stopping Mrs Thatcher. 'It could of course fail, but its failure would hardly leave Labour any worse off, and could even leave Labour better off.' (Weir was forced to resign; so much for freedom of expression within the Labour Party.')

With the polls now beginning to show the Tories pulling away – an NOP poll on April 23 showed them with a 15 point lead, and a Harris poll on April 26 showed them 11 points ahead of Labour (Conservatives 42%, Labour 31%, Alliance 25%) – Kinnock was being given a chance, both by the radical newspapers, and by some influential supporters, to change his position and seize the moment. He did not – probably could not – take it. Instead at a 'red rose' rally that was hyped up as the launch of the Labour election campaign, he made a furious attack on the Alliance and its talk of coalition. It was 'fruit machine politics'. It could be just possible to dislodge a few Tory MPs by voting Liberal, SDP, Nationalist, or whatever, he told the Rally, 'but I ask people: are you really willing to make such a gamble, take such a risk, go for such a flutter . . . are you really willing to play fruit machine politics just hoping that enough people and enough places will spontaneously, coincidentally, and in the secret of the ballot booth, vote together to turn the Tories out?'

He said 'People can object to Toryism by voting for just about anyone. They can only eject Toryism by voting Labour.'

At that moment, the chance of any encouragement to voters from the Labour party to use their vote tactically, if it had ever been possible, disappeared. Labour had decided to take on Mrs Thatcher – and the Alliance – alone.

Meanwhile, whatever life was like under the Conservatives, life *for* the Conservatives was getting better. Not only were they rising in the polls while their opponents were divided, but there were signs that the much-manipulated employment figures would take them below three million by June 18, and this was now being projected as a possible election date. It would also allow Mrs Thatcher to be seen once more on the international stage virtually on election eve, by making at least a flying visit to the Venice economic summit, due to start on June 8.

The Tories were also revelling in Labour's other problems. The disruption in schools, caused by the teachers' campaign to keep local negotiating rights, and industrial action by civil servants enabled the Tories to start talking about a 'summer of discontent' with its reminder of the 'winter of discontent' and its link between Labour and industrial problems. Even at such a critical time Labour seemed unable to stop fighting with itself; the row this time being over the determination of its national executive to block any recognition of a 'black section'.

Tory morale rose even higher when the Cabinet took a matter of minutes to approve a 9.5% pay rise for the country's nurses.

For the Alliance there was some good news too: the campaign by David Owen and David Steel to persuade the BBC and ITV to allow the Alliance to have parity with the other parties, so that each would have five party political broadcasts, succeeded, and with it came the opportunity of equal coverage on radio and television generally.

The meeting of the two Leaders, the two Presidents, together with Bill Rodgers and Tim Clement-Jones, to discuss consultations in the event of a hung parliament, duly took place. Steel and Owen re-affirmed the plan: if whoever led the party winning the most seats in the General Election asked them to a meeting on the Friday evening, they would probably accept the invitation; in fact, they would have little choice, for they would have to be seen to be responding positively to pressures for an early return to stability. In any case the sooner they knew the other's opening position the better. There would then be a meeting of the newly-elected Alliance MPs on the Saturday morning, followed by consultation with the party in the country during the remainder of the day. For the Insider, and for Shirley Williams, the critical question was the right of the senior party officers to attend those meetings, both to represent the views of their parties and to be able to carry out their consultation duties effectively. The two leaders were concerned that any historic decision to enter into an arrangement with another party should appear to be constitutionally correct, and should be taken only by the parliamentary parties. A satisfactory compromise was achieved; that the party officers would attend all the meetings of the parliamentary party up to the moment of decision; they would then have a final opportunity to make any submission, and answer any questions, and then would leave the parliamentary party for its final discussion and its vote.

British politics had now entered an extraordinary 'phoney war' stage. Even senior Conservatives were doing little to discourage predictions of an election in June. Labour, showing admirable self-possession despite bad news in the opinion polls and ongoing problems with the black sections, was skilfully presenting fresh policy packages, almost on a daily basis, and imaginatively published a spoof on the Tory Party manifesto, printed in identical style to the 1983 manifesto, and suggesting a hidden agenda for a third Tory administration, including increases in VAT. But Neil Kinnock must have been infuriated by the problems caused by his black militants; at a meeting in Birmingham the candidate for Nottingham East, Sharon Atkin, went completely over the top and described the party as racist, and said that given a choice between fighting for the needs of blacks, and the Labour Party, the latter came a bad second. This was the last straw. The National Executive suspended the candidate and replaced her with another.

The APG was busy completing its detailed planning and its consideration of the new ideas for the manifesto. Polly Toynbee had been particularly energetic, and a number of proposals were being sympathetically considered, including replacement of the annual Christmas bonus for pensioners with a more generous doubling of the pension at that time; a scheme to help elderly people realise the capital in their houses so that they would have more money while they were alive to spend it; and proposals to tackle crime more effectively. The Insider was promoting the 'lifeline' project to help the elderly living alone to be more safe and secure, by allowing them to have telephones installed free, and by providing security locks, and free installation.

At this edgy time Peter Wright, the former M15 officer, made a spectacular re-entry into British politics via the *Independent*. It had received and decided to publish substantial extracts from Wright's book alleging that senior staff of M15 had been involved in a treasonable plot to force Harold Wilson out of office as Prime Minister. Its extracts were widely reported in other newspapers, Mrs Thatcher, who when confronted with bad news usually reacts by shooting the messenger, turned the now almost comical figure of Sir Michael Havers onto them with threats of injunctions and prosecution. She refused all requests for an enquiry, but when the newly-knighted former Prime Minister James Callaghan asked for one in the House of Commons, she revealed that an internal enquiry by the new head of M15 had been carried out and the charges proved to have no foundation. This satisfied no one. Even those who believed that she may be justified on the facts, felt that politically she was unwise.

On Thursday, May 7, the day after the Botha regime received a fresh mandate from the small minority of South Africans permitted to vote, and on the day Gary Hart, the frontrunner for the Democratic nomination for President of the United States, was forced to withdraw from the race, his career ruined by revelations of marital infidelity, the weather in Britain was bright and sunny and this, together with the almost obsessive media concentration on politics and the likelihood of a general election, led to a re-

markably high turnout – around 60% in some areas – of voters
to elect some 12,000 councillors on district councils in England
and Wales. Whatever was at stake locally, everyone knew what
this day was really about, for the Prime Minister planned to meet
her senior colleagues at Chequers the following Sunday to
finalise plans for the General Election. Only a catastrophe on
May 7 would now block a June election.

The Insider had kept the day free, because he was to appear
on BBC television's *Question Time* that evening, and needed to
relax and to prepare. Perhaps because it was a similar day to
that sunny Sunday when the Liberal Assembly began in Eastbourne back in September, he found himself reflecting as he
drove from Brighton to London on the changes that had taken
place over the nearly nine months since that event. The swings in
the fortunes of three parties had been remarkable. He recalled
the words of Harold Wilson – 'A week is a long time in politics.'
The nine months had been an eternity. This was probably the
reason that he felt Owen and Steel had been surprisingly
untouched by one or two depressing polls recently, such as the
MORI poll in *The Sunday Times* the previous Sunday showing
the Conservatives 13 points ahead of Labour and 21 points ahead
of the Alliance. He felt their mood was buoyant and he knew too
that they were both impatient for the battle. If the Prime Minister
decided at this point to postpone the election it would be a
terrific let-down.

Then there was the issue that nearly destroyed the Alliance
last year – that of defence. Who would have believed at Eastbourne that by May 1987 the two superpowers would be engaged,
as they now were, in negotiations to not merely halt but substantially reverse the nuclear arms race. With what appeared to the
Insider to be remarkable patience and resilience the Soviet Leader
Mikhail Gorbachov had responded to every American rebuff and
to every setback by making fresh proposals and maintaining the
pressure on the Americans to respond positively. There was now
a real possibility of a nuclear-free Europe (in the words of the
'notorious' Eastbourne amendment).

One effect of the superpower negotiations had been to take
some of the electoral potency out of the issue. As had been the
case after the Reykjavik talks all three parties were able to claim

vindication for their position. For the Tories, it was proof that a tough stance had forced the Russians to the negotiating table. For Labour, it was proof that a non-nuclear world was not quite the fantasy its opponents had claimed. For the Alliance it was proof that its flexible policy, and refusal to be forced into an early decision about the replacement of Polaris, was justified.

Yet that evening he was reminded of the price the Alliance had paid for its row over defence, when Peter Walker, the Tory Minister appearing with him on *Question Time*, made fun of what he claimed were divisions within the Alliance over defence. It was clear that no matter how much Alliance spokesmen protested, both the Conservatives and Labour would continue to hammer home the same message — 'Whose defence policy? Owen's or Steel's or the Liberal Party's?' — until it stuck in the minds and memories of voters, and it would be used not so much to raise a question mark over Alliance defence policy as over Alliance unity.

After the programme, he drove to the SDP headquarters in Cowley Street, where the Alliance had chosen to house its election night service. The second floor had been cleared, and was now brightly illuminated by television lights, for the BBC were broadcasting reports live from there until about 3 a.m. On one side of the room there was a huge scoreboard, with columns for gains and losses, and beside there were maps with stickers indicating Alliance councils held or gained, and parliamentary seats that on the basis of these results would be won by the Alliance.

In nearby rooms the telephones rang constantly as results were telephoned in by Alliance workers around the country. There was a special hotline to ALC in Hebden Bridge, who were recording all Alliance gains. These were being fed to Andy Ellis and Dick Newby who, in turn, announced them to the crowded room and altered the scoreboard accordingly. In one corner David Steel was being briefed on the significance of the results so far, in order to be able to comment authoritatively on them in a television interview. In another corner, David Owen was eagerly awaiting the last result from Plymouth, where in his own constituency the Alliance was hoping to gain the balance of power (it missed by one seat). Most of the Alliance Planning Group were there.

It was an evening of changing moods. While Andy Ellis kept reassuring everybody that the Alliance was on target for its predicted 400 gains, they came agonisingly slowly (many were not due until the following day). At the same time it was clear that the Conservatives were doing well and Labour was performing badly.

When the count was over, however, it was the Alliance's night. Its eventual gain was over 450, compared with a net gain of 75 by the Conservatives and a loss by Labour. (Labour had been winning council elections and by-elections since 1983 consistent with 37% in a general election; on this result it would achieve around 30%, and for an opposition party in these circumstances this must have been a devastating blow.)

It had been the tenth successive year that the Alliance parties had increased their influence on local authorities; since 1983 the Alliance had improved from 1,941 councillors to nearly 3,500. It had won control of six more local councils – Tony Greaves and his colleagues had triumphed in Pendle, there had been a surprise win in the previously Labour stronghold of Blyth Valley, and there was encouraging news for Paddy Ashdown – South Somerset had been won, and this was largely in his constituency. The Alliance had also won Three Rivers, West Lindsey, and Eastleigh. It had held Hereford, Eastbourne, Adur and Chelmsford, where Stuart Mole, David Steel's former PA, stood a real chance of winning the parliamentary seat. There had been one disconcerting result – the loss of a council on the Isle of Wight, where Stephen Ross was retiring as the Liberal MP and Michael Young was hoping to take his place.

But the headlines were unanimous – a General Election on June 11. The Chequers meeting duly took place, the Cabinet met the following Monday, Mrs Thatcher went to the Palace, and June 11 it was.

All over Britain Liberals and Social Democrats told their employers they were taking a few weeks' holiday, cleared their desks, and headed for meetings with their agents and local supporters. Village and town halls were booked for meetings. Election addresses were finalised. And canvassing began. At the House of Commons Liberal MPs met for the last time, taking their opportunity to comment on the draft manifesto, and then having a buffet dinner together at a wine bar in Victoria to say farewell to Richard Wainwright and Stephen Ross who were retiring from the Commons. Andy Ellis and Dick Newby began the re-organisation of Cowley Street to accommodate the campaign team.

The Insider cancelled his engagements, dealt with the remaining correspondence on his desk, and then, as leader of the headquarters team from 10 p.m. until the following morning, he literally disappeared into the night.

The Campaign

The 1987 General Election –
The Insider's Diary

Week One

Sunday, May 17 (P-25 ... Polling Day – 25 days)

At last we're under way. Last week's 'phoney war' campaign was so effective that by Friday the commentators were suggesting we had peaked too soon! Wednesday's press conference in the Jubilee Room of the House of Commons to launch the 'Great Reform Charter' – a list of our constitutional reforms – was packed and chaotic, but a success. It led both the BBC and ITV news bulletins at lunchtime and received wide publicity the following morning. Hugo Young's article in the *Guardian* was particularly sympathetic: 'The constitutional package, pressed with the seriousness and conviction it now enjoys among all Alliance politicians, is what best makes good their claim to be a radical party rather than a group swilling around in the diluted centre ... a fair amount of professional criticism could be heard yesterday, saying that the Alliance had gone too early and too heavy. I disagree. The effect, one must hope, will be to remove the oddity present alongside these distinctive policies ever since they were invented. This oddity is that they have not been challenged with anything like the intensity applied to their formulation. The Alliance has spent a great deal of time working out an information policy, a devolution policy, and the basic beginning of a written constitution. These have mostly been opposed by silence or hot air, brought out so prominently and so soon, they now stand as a rebuke to both Labour and the Conservatives.'

That evening I assembled my Night Team for a 'dress rehearsal'. It was a shambles. An engineer was still trying to sort out the telephones. Bells were ringing all over the building, and telephone lights were flashing on and off, but when you picked the receiver up there was no one there. David Steel was cut off twice before he finally got me at about midnight. The photocopier broke down, the typewriters weren't right, and the team of seven was inadequate for the task. I decided to recruit at least one more helper, and otherwise hoped that a bad 'dress rehearsal' would make for a good first night.

Morale rose with the opinion polls, especially Gallup showing us ahead of Labour (Conservatives 39, Alliance 30, Labour 28). We had the headlines we wanted – 'Alliance keep Labour in third place' (*Daily Telegraph*), 'Blow for Labour as polls show Alliance support increasing' (*Financial Times*), and 'Joy for the Davids as Kinnock slumps into third place' across the front page of *Today*.

On Thursday the Leaders made their whirlwind plane journey to Cardiff, Belfast, Glasgow, and then Newcastle, before David Steel appeared on a rather disappointing *Question Time* (although David himself came over well, especially when expressing anger that the Tories were celebrating a fall in unemployment to just over three million – 'who got it up from one million in the first place?' said Steel to loud applause). The dramatic trip, with television crews in the plane with them, guaranteed more extensive coverage.

There will be at least fifty opinion polls between now and June 11. Two more appeared on Friday morning, and unfortunately they suggest the Gallup poll was a 'rogue'. Marplan in the *Daily Express* had the Tories on 41, Labour 30, and the Alliance 26, and MORI in *The Times* the Conservatives 41, Labour 33, and the Alliance 24. The MORI poll was the regular one conducted in key marginals and on the basis of it *The Times* claims the Tories are still on target for a big win – perhaps by the 140 seats they achieved last time.

Prize for the first major gaff of the campaign goes to Denis Healey who on a brief trip to Moscow intended to take some of the lustre off the Thatcher visit and declared the Russians were 'praying for a Labour victory'. Even if this was so – and he was quickly forced to admit he had 'perhaps exaggerated' – it was hardly helpful to Labour. As David Steel said in the Commons 'given Labour's defence policies, this is not surprising. I am surprised that he should be so eager to announce it . . . The people willing an Alliance victory are to be found nearer home.'

The blunder was matched by Margaret Thatcher. In several interviews she denied that if she was re-elected she would stay in Downing Street for only two or three years. She had every intention of going 'on and on'. She talked about a fourth term. There was even a reference to the turn of the century. As *The Times* columnist Geoffrey Smith commented, 'That was disturbing not only because it seemed arrogant, nor even because it is in dubious taste to be asking for a fourth term before the voters have offered a third. It was disturbing because it used to be one of the pleasing aspects of Conservatism that it had a broad approach to the governing of the country, recognising that it would be neither possible nor desirable for one party to rule forever.'

David Steel was also quick to capitalise on this during the last PM's Questions before the House closed down: 'Does the Prime Minister recall the number of leaders of other countries who in recent years have proclaimed themselves leaders for life? Since she is now aiming for the end of the century, is this what the leader of the House (John Biffen) had in mind when he warned on Sunday about the arrogance that comes with power? Does she agree with him, or are his days now numbered as well?'

———————————

It was too good to last. Friday was a bad day for us, and especially for David S. While we knew that Kinnock and Thatcher were due to make their first major campaign speeches, we hadn't really taken on board that this was not a day when we could expect much publicity. We should have launched 'Rent a Room' another day. Furthermore, the Leaders did not stick to the game plan; having launched 'Rent a Room' in Leeds, they talked about other issues elsewhere. The effect nationally was to undermine the impact of the launch of 'Rent a Room' and the rest of the housing package. In fact, the BBC TV News concentrated on Owen talking about loony left councils, and on pictures of the plane trip itself — the housing ideas were not even mentioned.

In the meantime, Kinnock and Thatcher stole the headlines. If anyone was in any doubt that the years of consensus politics were past, their opening exchange should have convinced them.

The Labour leader pulled no punches in his attack on Thatcher and the Tories. Speaking on home ground in Wales he said the Tories wanted to re-create a Britain 'rotten with injustice and misery and division'. He talked of 'that job-destroying, justice-trampling, oil-wasting, truth-twisting, service-smashing, nation-splitting bunch of twisters under a one-person government'.

Thatcher, he said, lectured the nation on the 19th century and spoke of continuing to the 21st, but had missed out on the 20th century — 'the one we are living in'. Under her, everybody could either stand on their own feet or live on their knees.

He defined Toryism as strength without care — 'savage and brutal and selfish, and socialism as an alternative to the strength of the jungle. We cooperate, we collect together, we coordinate so that everyone can contribute and everyone can benefit. Everyone has responsibilities like everyone enjoys rights. That is how we put care into action. That is how we make the weak strong, that is how we lift the needy. It is called collective strength, collective care. And its whole purpose is individual freedom.'

He talked movingly of youngsters who asked him pitifully if they would ever work, a fifty-five-year-old woman waiting to go to hospital, her whole life clouded by pain, and young married couples living in their parents' front rooms. All were living in a free country but did not feel free. He spoke of old couples spending months of the winter afraid to turn up the heating, who stayed at home because they were afraid to go out after dark, whose life was turned into crisis by the need to buy a pair of shoes. 'They live in a free country — they fought for a free country — but they do not feel free.'

He said Thatcher had talked about new ideas ... like privatising schools, de-controlling rents, paying for health care. But anyone attracted by these new ideas had better ask themselves why every single one of them had been abandoned fifty and more years ago. The reason was simple: 'The system that existed before that – the system that Margaret Thatcher wants to return to – was wrong and wretched, it was squalid and brutal. It was rotten with injustice and misery and division. That is why it was discarded.'

Kinnock had stepped impressively and movingly onto the moral high ground, only to find that Margaret Thatcher was claiming it too – her aim, she told Scottish Tories later that evening, was to replace the prehistoric vision of socialism with a moral crusade for popular capitalism.

For most of the century socialism had advanced and conservatism had been in retreat, she said. Even a few Conservatives had begun to fear that socialism would triumph, that the future would be of nationalised industries, central economic planning, municipal housing, and the gradual disappearance of the entrepreneur, and of almost anyone who did not either work for or depend upon the Leviathan state. But now Conservatism was advancing, not because it was being imposed on people, but because people were finding that what the Tories stood for was in tune with their own hopes and dreams. It didn't strike them as political dogma but simple common sense that people should want to buy their own homes, save for their old age, have shares in companies they worked for, and do the best for their children. Of course there would be people who in the name of morality sneered at this and called it materialism.

But morality lay in improving living standards, saving and having the means to support the charities people believed in. There could be no morality without freedom of choice – that's why there was a strong moral case for reducing taxation.

The Conservative emphasis on family values tapped the strongest and best motives in human nature. 'To work against that grain is to stand morality on its head, it is the very reverse of a moral crusade.'

While these high-flying sentiments were being expressed from the platform, things had reached a low level in the Tory conference bars, where a malicious and totally false rumour had been sparked off involving David Steel's private life. Before the day was out David had been telephoned by the *Star* and the *Sun* and it was made clear that if he didn't wish to deny the allegations they would be published with a 'David Steel refused to comment . . .' line. Jim Dumsday, the party's press officer, duly issued a denial, and the stories appeared in both newspapers on the 'Steel denies allegations . . .' theme. It ruined David's weekend. Lawyers had to be consulted and further denials drafted, but they didn't stop the *News of the World* publishing a particularly appalling 'Allegations denied . . .' story and putting beside it an even nastier article about the private life of one of Neil Kinnock's aides.

Still, tonight the media is in retreat. ITN apologised for broadcasting the allegation and the story generally has become 'Smear on Steel'. Nevertheless, it has clearly upset David, and I felt some of his earlier buoyancy had at least temporarily gone when he attended this evening's meeting of the Campaign Committee.

———————

The two Leaders, but in particular David O., came to the campaign committee meeting convinced we should start by attacking the Tories. We should talk Labour down, dismiss them as irrelevant, stress they cannot win, and tell the country that only the Alliance stands between it and another dose of undiluted Thatcherism.

While no one said it, underlying the discussion was a difference in objectives; Owen's heart was set on the balance of power, and this could not be achieved unless the Tories were reduced below 40%. Others, believing the Alliance would be the longterm losers from a balance of power and determined to replace Labour as the main opposition party, were more concerned to see Labour knocked out early in the fight. It was argued, however, that only by attacking the Tories could we attract a bigger share of the anti-Thatcher majority; crucial tactical voters would not respond positively to attacks on Labour, but they would if we were seen to *lead* the attack on the Tories.

We'll be accused of arrogance for writing off Labour in this way, but let's look at the bright side and call it self-confidence. We won't capture the imagination of voters if we don't believe in ourselves. Anyway, the Tories are defending the citadel; if we are to be credible as potential rulers, we have to be seen to lead the assault on the citadel, and not to be engaged in a skirmish with

Labour on the other side of the moat. It's worth asking what the Tories would prefer? The Alliance and Labour knocking each other out, or the Alliance and Labour both attacking the Tories? Surely it would be the former; surely this argues for the latter. In any case, we can count on the Tories to attack Labour. And hopefully we can even count on Labour to self-destruct.

There is another argument for attacking the government of the day; in challenging its record and its policies we are best able to communicate our own approach and values.

For all these reasons, I too believe that if we have to attack one or the other, it should initially be the Tories, and there is for me a conclusive factor: David Owen is, rightly or wrongly, widely believed to prefer coalition with the Tories; if he is seen to be personally leading a broad assault on them in the early part of the campaign it will help to put those fears to rest, and this too will help those candidates hoping to seduce tactical voters away from Labour.

So I supported the Leaders, as did the majority of those present, although I did wonder afterwards whether we should have considered in more depth an attack on them both on the lines of my Eastbourne speech – as the two parties that have shared power, the 'unholy alliance of the past'.

We had arranged that after the campaign meeting the Liberals would have a relaxed dinner together in a Chinese restaurant near Victoria, but it proved an edgy affair with an understandably irritable and tired David Steel having to spend the time talking to Paul Tyler about his travel plans for the next few days. From there, I went to Cowley Street for the first full-scale overnight operation. The brief for the morning meeting is in the form of two A3-size scrapbooks, the first being 'the overnight report' on the polls, the main issues, and campaign strategy, and the second comprising all the day's press clippings.

The first editions of the *Independent* and the *Daily Express* have picked up on comments by Ian Wrigglesworth on the TV programme *This Week Next Week* that our policy is to oppose privatisation of public monopolies such as water where there is

no competitive element, but not to halt privatisation already
under way, or where the prospectus has been issued. As Ian
said, any further proposals will be judged case by case and 'the
criteria by which we judge these matters is whether there
is going to be competition. It's only the political dinosaurs of
the past who carry on this great battle over the ownership of
industry.' However there is likely to be some controversy over
his refusal to rule out privatisation of steel. We have drafted
answers to the questions we can expect at the morning press
conference.

The first editions for Monday have promoted the Steel story
to front page headlines, but now they are all positive: 'Steel
attacks smears, lies and slanders'; 'Steel lashes lies as rivals
plead: Keep battle clean'; 'Steel takes libel action over lies and
smears'; etc. There are a number of leading articles that are
sympathetic.

Monday, May 18 (P-24)

> 'The Labour Party is unelectable, but that cannot
> mean that the Conservatives are irreplaceable.'
> David Owen

By launching the manifesto today we've maintained the impression of being ahead of the other parties, more ready for the
battle, and we've capitalised on the decision of both the Tories
and Labour to launch theirs tomorrow; we've had undivided
attention while they now have to share their coverage.

At the press conference David O. described the manifesto as
the most radical and reforming programme from a political party
for decades. David Steel emphasised we are 'the pace-setters',
first to launch our campaign, first to launch our manifesto, and
the only party with forward-looking policies. In answer to
questions on funding, David O. said that the programmes have
been costed, that we don't expect to have to increase taxes to pay
for them, but that our public sector borrowing will be higher.
Both leaders confirmed that electoral reform and unemployment
are the only non-negotiable factors in coalition discussions. It

was a press conference dominated by David O., partly because it was on the detail of policy, and he is better equipped to deal with that, and partly because David S. had no opportunity to prepare for it, having been diverted into dealing with the smear campaign over the weekend. But the imbalance was noticed; we'll have to watch this.

On his battle bus, David Steel left journalists in no doubt about the strategy, referring to the 'callous vocabulary of Thatcherism' and saying 'we don't see any reason to pay much attention to Labour. What's the point of going on and on about what a Labour government might do when there is not going to be one?'

At Labour's press conference Bryan Gould actually made a small concession to the idea of negotiating with a third party by saying that any electoral pact designed to drive Thatcher from Downing Street would be 'worth looking at'. But, he said, a vote for the Alliance would not achieve that. 'Voters would wake up on the morning after polling day and find that David Owen had gratefully pocketed their votes, had claimed the seats which he had gained as his own, and would use them, as he had made clear he would do, to sustain Mrs Thatcher in office.'

Norman Tebbit also spoke today on the question of a hung parliament: 'I don't think the largest party should negotiate. Obviously you set your Queen's Speech and you carry on and govern, and if people bring you down, they bring you down. But I don't think that situation is going to arise.' Owen later retorted 'he is not the Prime Minister and he is usurping the role of the Prime Minister'.

This evening I drove out to Twickenham to address the assembled populace on behalf of John Waller who on paper stands some chance of winning. The assembled populace consisted of about a dozen people, and increased during the evening to perhaps twenty. This must have been as discouraging for John as it was disconcerting for me. We found ourselves having to deal with two persistent questioners, one an Irishman chipping away at proportional representation on the basis of the Irish experience (I told him the problems in Ireland would be exactly the same whether they had PR or not), and a man in the front row who turned himself into a kind of Robin Day, asking repeated questions and even summarising the result of the ensuing discussion – not in a particularly flattering way.

It was all a bit deflating. Maybe the meeting was just too early in the Election campaign.

Tuesday, May 19 (P-23)

> *'This is a foul smear . . . I put my political career*
> *on the line to fight unilateralism, and to try to give*
> *the impression that our defence policy would put at*
> *risk the defence of this country is a travesty of the*
> *truth.'*

David Owen
(on the Conservative Party manifesto)

The newspaper editorials on our manifesto are predictable.

The *Express* headlines it 'A Cynical Manifesto' and says that if there was a vote for 'having your fudge and eating it' the Alliance would capture it. Alleged inconsistencies were blamed on the fact that 'the Alliance is no alliance. It is a cynical marriage of convenience between two parties united only by their lust for power.'

The *Daily Mail* says that under the Alliance 'the land will flow with the milk of government generosity and the honey of national consensus'. The appeal of the manifesto was that of 'the plastic key to a boundless togetherness where the waiting is taken out of wanting'. It would be good to see the Alliance establish itself as the most popular party in opposition, but for the present it was too soft an option to be entrusted with the burden of government.

The *Times* states that 'the Alliance have never lacked for theme tunes. What they have lacked is a theme.' It notes that 'Britain

United' is a theme of sorts, but the manifesto still lacks a philosophical base. '"Britain United – The Time Has Come" suggests that Mr Steel and Dr Owen see the lack of unity in Britain as the major plank on which they are to fight the government. In essence it is a message to those who have prospered in Mrs Thatcher's Britain to feel guilty about their success. It hopes to persuade such people, of whom there are many, that Tory economic benefits can be harnessed for the good of a greater number of citizens; that Britain will be more united if Britain's wealth is more evenly spread . . .; that mechanical changes in government can provide the motor power for this better application of social justice. This is a potentially powerful message. But it is also a recipe for confusion about how such a society goes about creating the prosperity in the first place.'

The *Financial Times* says that 'Britain United' passes all the conventional tests. It is serious, comprehensive, and costed, and where it is good 'it is very, very good. Best of all, however, is the section on constitutional reform . . . however the Alliance fares in the election it will have done well to put this subject on the agenda.'

The *Guardian* says 'the Alliance can fairly claim to be a party of the reforming centre-left', but goes on to challenge us to come off the fence and say with whom we want to work after the election.

The only newspaper that appears to be openly supporting us from the start is *Today*, (what a pity it has such a small circulation). Describing the manifesto as 'an attractive package', it says that no longer can the Alliance be accused of having no policies.

———

The Tories have called their manifesto 'The Next Move Forward' and it is in two volumes, one looking back on their 'record', and the other looking forward. They say they'll continue to privatise state-owned industry, starting with electricity and water. They will introduce further trade union reforms to enable members to stop the union from calling a strike without holding a secret ballot, and to protect those who refuse to strike from being disciplined. They will force union leaders to submit themselves to a secret ballot every five years. Their more radical schemes include the abolition of domestic rates and its replacement with a community charge. However, the real controversy is likely to centre on education and housing. There will be a new national core curriculum and state schools will be allowed to opt out of local authority control if the parents decide. London Boroughs will be allowed to opt out of the Inner London Education Authority. They intend to give tenants of council housing the right to break up estates and turn them into cooperatives, or transfer individual homes to non-council landlords such as housing associations.

Labour's manifesto is called 'Britain will win' and their theme is 'the country is crying out for change'. It's cautious, even bland. If they have any genuinely socialist plans, they're holding back until they're elected. Thatcher has been saying that the Labour Party as presented to the electorate is like an iceberg; only the tip is open to view, and the real menace is under the surface. There's a lot of potential in that line of attack.

I have been infuriated by the Tories' theme 'Power to the People'. How can they have the nerve? I've dictated some notes for David Steel in the hope that he will incorporate them in his Cheltenham speech tomorrow evening:

I ask her: what power? What people?

It is clear that she has no concept of what the majority of people mean when they talk about issues of power and individual freedom. When she talks of power, she means *economic* power. There is no suggestion anywhere in her manifesto, as there is no thought in her head, of allowing people *political* power.

Her attitude is straightforward: 'I'll give you the power to meet your own needs, if you are capable, and to suffer if you are not; all political power will reside with me.'

Thus, Thatcher power is the power of the rich to opt out of the community while poverty and unemployment reach record levels; the power to buy and capitalise on vital public utilities such as electricity and water; the power to make a fortune out of property while the number of homeless rises above 100,000; the power to get rich quick in the city, without any proper regulation or control, while our prisons are bursting with people convicted of minor crimes, much of it caused by the strains of urban life and unemployment.

Thatcher power is the power to exploit and manipulate; the power to rise by trampling on the hopes and aspirations of those less privileged.

By contrast, Thatcher's power has been increased by a savage attack on the rights and responsibilities of democratically-elected local authorities, by terrorising the BBC, by the use of the security forces to intimidate legitimate dissenters, by banning trade union rights for some workers altogether, by curtailing age-old rights to public demonstration, and generally creating an atmosphere where it is understood, as she has herself said, that you are either for her or against her.

I then spell out what real people power means – a fair electoral system, freedom of information, protection of human rights, decentralisation, making the House of Lords and the House of Commons democratic and effective. All of these real steps towards real power for real people the Alliance is committed to. Yet the Prime Minister refuses them all. How dare she talk about 'power to the people'? No Prime Minister in post-War history has taken power so much to herself and shown such arrogant contempt for the rights of people to have power over their own lives.

I hope David will use it.

The television pictures of the press conferences staged by the other two parties are instructive. The Tories appear to have bungled theirs. They packed the journalists into a hot over-crowded room after making them arrive early and sit around waiting (apparently for security reasons), and then crowded Ministers on the platform around Thatcher like a pack of in-gratiating schoolboys pressing close to the headmistress, who either patronised them when she allowed them to speak, or put them down. Kinnock and Hattersley, on the other hand, marched up the aisle of a huge convention centre to a fanfare, joining colleagues on the platform, and then standing together at a lectern. It looked, commented one newspaper, like a gay wedding! It may have been over the top, but it was a not unimpressive indication of the new professionalism behind the Labour campaign.

David O. has taken umbridge at the suggestion in the Tory Party manifesto that the Alliance defence policy is unilateralism by default. There is a reference to 'fellow travellers'. This, together with a Tory Party political broadcast on television tonight, full of union jacks and patriotic sentiments, and implying that only the Tories are genuine patriots, have been too much for the Doctor. He has denounced it all as a 'foul smear' and demanded a retraction. I'm afraid it has been a red rag to a bull and is likely to put defence on top of the agenda – not exactly where we want it.

Wednesday, May 20 (P–22)

> 'It sticks in my gullet that there is this
> extraordinary belief that the Union Jack belongs to
> the Tory Party.'
>
> David Owen

David O. and Thatcher have exchanged letters on the 'fellow traveller' charge, David demanding a retraction, and Thatcher replying by adding insult to injury. It's all making the headlines – but are they the kind of headlines we need?

I watched the Tory Chief Whip John Wakeham make a catastrophic appearance on Robin Day's *Election Call* programme this morning. Wakeham, who has hardly been called upon to say a word in the Commons for years, has clearly forgotten, if he ever knew, how to deal with the public or with direct questions. He began the programme looking complacent and at ease, and ended it a broken man. At one point a railway worker's wife took him apart, asking what was in the manifesto for her and her husband who earn £95 a week basic. Wakeham replied that an efficiency drive in British Rail would improve his job security. She said he had not answered the question. Of the £95, £27 went on rent, £15 on gas, and £10 on electricity, they hadn't had a holiday for eight years. Wakeham, now defensive, said that a lot of people were now better off than when the Tories came to power but he didn't pretend it was easy for everybody. The woman told him, 'I have never heard so much rubbish in my life. Never. I only hope all Labour voters get together and get you out. If they don't, God help us and millions like us. You are living in another world. You have no idea what it's like.' Wakeham couldn't answer, but you could almost see on his face the making of a private resolution that if he escaped the studio in one piece it would be his last television appearance ever.

———

If there's a feel to this campaign so far, it is that Labour are doing well. The shambles of the Michael Foot campaign of 1983 has been replaced by an impressively smooth operation and Kinnock is looking good. Tonight they produced the best party political broadcast I've ever seen. It was simply called 'Kinnock' and was a glossy ten-minute television commercial directed by Hugh Hudson (who made *Chariots of Fire*). It succeeded in conveying the likeability, the youth, but also the tough side of the man. There was a powerful sequence from his speech attacking Militant a couple of years back. I don't know about the Tories, but it shook us!

The Tories obviously want a short campaign. They're playing the first week low key. Thatcher's first press conference, apart from the launch of the manifesto, will not take place until Friday. It's possible this has helped Labour to a flying start. And it's all the more maddening that we have ourselves made defence the issue when we could be promoting our positive policies before the Tories enter the ring.

———

David Steel used most of my words on Thatcher power in his Cheltenham speech. It was well covered on television.

Thursday, May 21 (P–21)

> *'Who cares what Mr Tebbit says, or what Mr Bryan*
> *Gould says Mr Tebbit says, or what Mr Tebbit*
> *thinks of Mr Bryan Gould, or what Mr Gould thinks*
> *of Mr Tebbit?'*
>
> David Steel

Bad news in the *Daily Telegraph*. Last week's Gallup poll showing us ahead of Labour was obviously a maverick for this morning's has the Conservatives at 42, Labour 33, and the Alliance 23, an apparent, damaging, yet almost certainly illusory slump of seven points in our support. The headlines are as bad as last week's headlines were good; 'Gallup shows Alliance dive to third place' was the *Telegraph*'s front page lead. 'Alliance face poll disaster' said the *Express*. Damn Gallup!

At the morning meeting Andy Ellis was asked if he could explain the polls. He suggested, firstly, that the Gallup of the previous week had been 'a rogue' (Gallup had made some changes in their approach) and that the latest one was broadly in line with our position in the polls generally. Also when an election was called people tended to return initially to their old party allegiances. It was a classic by-election feature and the reason why the Alliance usually began by-elections behind in the polls. As the campaign developed people whose support for one of the others was 'soft' would begin to waver, and when added to the undecided could easily create a surge to the Alliance. He produced a graph to show that our drift in the polls over the last couple of weeks has been identical to that in 1979 and 1983, except that we are operating at a much higher level of support than we were then.

I had been worried overnight by John Cartwright's press release for this morning's conference. It appeared to go beyond 'The

Time Has Come' and beyond the manifesto in suggesting a prefer-red option for replacing Polaris. Up to now we've simply stated that we would consider all of the alternatives at the appropriate time, a perfectly tenable position, but John now argued at the morning meeting that we would look weak if we couldn't de-monstrate we had an answer to the question 'what will you replace Polaris with?' We decided on a form of words that holds the party line but also demonstrates we understand the options available, and we told John that he should feel free to enlarge on any of them in answer to questions. In fact, he performed brilliantly at the press conference and it went by without diffi-culty.

While David O. and Margaret Thatcher have been busy correspond-ing on defence, a headline-catching row has broken out between Labour's Bryan Gould and Norman Tebbit over Labour ads quoting Norman Tebbit as saying in 1983 that if unemployment had not fallen below three million in four years he would not deserve to be re-elected. Tebbit replied by saying that if Labour could prove he actually said it he would pay £500 to a charity of Labour's choice, but if not, he expected Kinnock to pay £500 to a charity of Tebbit's choice. This morning Labour produced at their press conference a tape recording of the interview. As a result both sides have claimed victory. Tebbit was right to claim that he never said 'if employment is not below three million in five years, then I'm not worth re-electing'. Asked whether he thought that in four or five years time unemployment would be below three million, he had in fact said 'if I did not think we could do that I don't think we would be in a position to win the next election'.

At her adoption meeting in Finchley tonight, Margaret Thatcher returned to defence, arguing that the policies of both Labour and the Alliance would leave Britain without an effective deterrent.

Late in the evening we had a panic on the issue. The two Davids appeared on *This Week* and after it the Press Association issued a report saying 'in what would appear to be a sudden shift of policy Dr Owen said Alliance leaders would take advice from senior military figures about keeping a ballistic system such as Trident'. Then on the BBC's *Nine O'Clock News*, David Dimbleby said: 'Tonight Dr Owen appears to have modified his position somewhat. He said he is prepared to take advice from senior military figures about keeping a ballistic missile system such as Trident.'

In fact David had never used the words 'such as Trident'.

Our immediate concern was that Liberals who had not seen *This Week* would be infuriated by the alleged change of course. We made contact with the two Leaders who authorised an immediate statement: 'An Alliance government would cancel Trident. In the case of a balanced parliament we would not negotiate over the proper defence of Britain so we would reject unilateralism. But we would be ready to listen to advice on systems from the chief of staff as we made clear in the statement on defence published in November and in "The Time has Come" published in January. That remains the position.'

We contacted BBC TV *Newsnight* who responded favourably to a request that one of the Davids should appear live on the programme to deal with the issue. The two Davids were driving in separate cars from London airport and at one point pulled up at a red light, wound down their respective car windows, and in a shouted conversation decided that David Steel should do *Newsnight* and David Owen appear on BBC Radio 4's *Today* programme the following morning. They then sped off into the night, Steel duly appearing at the end of *Newsnight* to say that he and David Owen had been amazed at the reports . . . the latter had never used the words 'such as Trident'. David then read the key section from *The Time Has Come* and said this remained the policy: 'We will cancel Trident.'

We will now have no alternative but to deal with the issue at tomorrow's press conference, and that means we're stuck with defence for another day. I don't like it. We will not make an advance in this election on defence; we *must* move onto more positive ground.

Friday, May 22 (P–20)

*'I flicked from channel to channel on television and
found politics on three sides. Then on the fourth I
found King Lear – and that's full of politics. The
public will go round the bend by the end of the
campaign.'*

John Pardoe

I don't know what effect Trident will have on the Russians if it's
ever used, but it can wreak havoc on a general election campaign!
None of the later editions took up the two Davids' correction of
the PA story, and all the Alliance spokesmen on early morning
radio and television were having to fend off questions on the
issue.

One reporter after another tried to persuade David O. to say
unconditionally that he would cancel Trident. David replied that
if the Alliance came to power it *would* cancel Trident, but if it
was the junior member of a coalition, or involved in some other
power-sharing arrangement, it would obviously be a matter of
negotiation. David S. reinforced this, emphasising that the only
two non-negotiable issues were unemployment and electoral
reform. David Dimbleby pressed Owen: if the advice of Chief of
Staffs, if the economic advice, if all the information at his dis-
posal, supported the Trident system, would he still reject it?
Others pressed him similarly. Owen's reply was that the advice
and information he received would be required to relate to the
overall defence policy – not the other way round. The Chief of
Staffs would be advised of the deterrent capacity that an Alliance
administration would require, and that capacity would not
necessitate the use of Trident.

He ended the press conference cleverly by reminding journalists that he had now dealt with the question and that every
word spoken at two press conferences on the subject had demonstrated the Alliance determination to defend the country, to
maintain a nuclear deterrent, and to reject the unilateralist
approach of Labour. His audience should now turn their attention
to Labour's appalling defence policy.

At the APG at 10.15 we discussed whether we would accept a
BBC TV News request for a debate tonight between the Secretary

of State, George Younger, Labour's defence spokesman, Denzil Davies, and John Cartwright. John Harris said we had little choice; if we refused it would appear we were afraid. Despite wishing we had never been drawn into it, I reluctantly accepted that we should now let the debate continue in the hope that by covering the ground fully on every conceivable TV programme we would exhaust the subject early in the campaign – at least as far as *Alliance* policy is concerned.

———————

Shirley Williams opened the press conference on law and order, climaxing her presentation by producing some frightening weapons allegedly available on the streets of London. At one point she produced a flick knife but could not trigger the blade. 'I don't know that I can make it work,' she said, and then suddenly turned to David Owen and said, 'David, you take it – you'll know how to do it.' The assembled journalists rocked with laughter.

———————

There was a lengthy discussion at the 10.15 meeting about the state of the campaign after five days, and how the two Johns should brief Sunday newspaper political writers. Andy Ellis said they should demonstrate that our 'temporary' dip in the polls was consistent with past history. He repeated his earlier points: the calling of an election often triggered old party loyalties and it always took time for the Alliance to draw in the undecided and then pick off voters from the softer edges of the other parties. John Pardoe asked Andy and Dick Newby what they had picked up from the constituencies. Dick reported that candidates were more worried by the national polls than by what they were seeing in their own canvass returns or hearing on the doorstep. Andy shared this view, although he sensed some rising concern about the strength of Labour support. John was advised to stress to journalists that the feel on the ground was good, that the 'Ask the Alliance' rallies had been packed, that we were having to reprint the manifesto, despite a first run of 150,000, and that one opinion poll that morning had shown that a majority believed the Alliance was running the best campaign. The message was 'no cause for concern ... we're on course'.

But this was what we were telling the newspapers; in the privacy of our meeting we were more concerned. Any dreams we had that by the end of the first week we would be neck and neck, or even have overtaken Labour, have been shattered. Instead, Labour has made the running. The public writing-off of Labour at the beginning of the week has made our position worse, for we have publicly failed to achieve a publicly-stated objective. And, despite some lively press conferences, we have not really established a positive image, partly because of the focus on defence, and the Trident controversy. We have let the first week slip away. John Pardoe asked what we should be discussing at the Sunday campaign meeting and I proposed that we should prioritise the issues. 'We have to face the fact that our campaign is not being effective in getting our ideas across. We should choose a number of issues, and organise mini-campaigns, ensuring that if we have a press conference on crime, or housing, or whatever, that the two Leaders are seen to follow it up during the day and evening, and that there are corresponding press conferences in the regions, and other activity. We should insist that all our opportunities on radio and television are devoted to that topic. We should force the topic onto the agenda, and force the other parties to respond to our position. And we must stop talking about defence.' It was decided as a first step to try to reinforce the press conference on the elderly on Bank Holiday Monday with pictures of the Leaders with old folk in the afternoon, and – hopefully – a follow up speech in the evening.

Our mole at the Conservative press conference returned to report that Thatcher had run into trouble over education. She had been questioned on the proposal that schools could opt out of the local education authority and operate independently, funded by trusts financed by the state. Two questions arose: first, what would the selection procedure be? (If it was on the basis of academic ability, would it lead to a return of a kind of eleven-plus? If not, would 'opt-out schools' become havens for middle class and professional people, attracting the best teachers, and possibly able to afford the best equipment, creating two tiers of education?) Second, would the schools be able to raise additional funds?

She hoped the funding of the schools from the Exchequer would be sufficient, but added 'so far we have not thought to preclude those schools from raising extra sums of money and I think it would be wrong to do so. We should of course look very closely if there was any imposition of a fee upon children because clearly those schools are meant to be schools where children receive a different form of education paid for and supplied by the state.'

But how would pupils be selected? Thatcher replied that heads and governing bodies would establish their own admission policies. 'The matter is for the school to choose, as it has always been for direct grant and for some voluntary aided schools to choose the pupils who are admitted to them. If the school goes independent and becomes a direct grant school then in fact it is up to the school to pursue its own admissions policies.' Under pressure about this approach to selection, she attacked one questioner: 'the idea that there is any selection by ability or aptitude is to you horrific. It is not horrific.'

By the evening the Tories were doing their best to correct the damaging impression given. Tebbit, at his adoption meeting in Chingford, went out of his way to say 'we do not, and will not, charge admission fees at state schools'. The Prime Minister's own aides had to publish a correction: 'The Prime Minister referred to the ability of schools to raise funds, extra to the government per capita grant. This is not new, there are many examples of local education authority schools supported by charitable trusts. This would continue. We do not and will not charge admission fees for state schools.'

It is vital that we move the General Election debate onto such issues as education and health, and it begins to look as if there will be plenty of scope to do so. This 'opt-out scheme' for schools is vulnerable to attack. So is the Tory record on the national health service. There's a letter in *The Times* this morning from a number of junior doctors saying they feel compelled to write and correct the Prime Minister's misrepresentation of its record. 'In the last eight years, to achieve financial savings, wards have been kept empty whilst waiting lists have grown. Catering and domestic staff levels have been drastically reduced, resulting in poor quality food and filthy hospitals. Low salaries make it impossible to recruit vital staff . . . the existing staff are therefore stretched to breaking point attempting to maintain standards of patient care. Hospitals and subsidised accommodation have been sold for short term financial gain . . . how can all this be equated with claims of increased spending and patient throughput?' They charge the Conservatives with asset-stripping the NHS by subterfuge. This is dynamite. I have a feeling the Tories are more vulnerable on the health service than education or even unemployment. It may be a little unfair, for there has been some necessary rationalisation, and they have achieved some results, yet there's no denying the waiting lists and there's no denying that for all Thatcher's protests that 'the health service is safe in our hands', people just don't believe it – they just don't believe the Tories are committed to it. It doesn't help that when the Prime Minister, or senior colleagues, are ill, they themselves opt for private care.

The APG and the headquarters team are working remarkably well together. John Pardoe has turned out to be a tower of strength. For all his larger-than-life personality, he has no sense of self-importance and combines being suitably decisive with a capacity to encourage other opinions. He is amusing, realistic and apparently indestructable, and he is performing brilliantly on radio and television. Given the occasional counter-productive performances by Tebbit, Labour had an early advantage with Bryan Gould as their all-purpose spokesman, but John has now emerged as a worthy rival. I can't think of anybody else in the Alliance who could have fulfilled the role better.

The two Davids made a big mistake in not encouraging John to play a more conspicuous role. He should be chairing the press conferences, where his charisma and cavalier style would have complemented their more serious approach and given our platform more punch and even more substance.

It is also rewarding working with Polly Toynbee; she is always direct, talks sense, does what she says she will do, works incredibly hard, and is proving a real heavyweight organising the press conferences and some of the follow-up activity. Paul Tyler and Maggie Smart are working tirelessly and with endless patience coordinating the Leaders' activities, Andy Ellis and Dick Newby get on marvellously and make a calm and sensible team overseeing the campaign in the regions and also the running of headquarters.

The structure of my day is now established: I take over with the Night Team at about 10 p.m. At around 4.30 a.m. I leave the others to put the report together and deliver a copy to David Steel's flat, and take off for just over an hour's sleep before a shower and then the morning meeting of the APG at 6.45 a.m. The Leaders join us at 7.45 and we then have the press conference at 8.30. Pardoe, Harris, Ellis, Newby and I then have breakfast at the Royal Horseguards, and return to Cowley Street for the 10.15 meeting of the APG. By then the Leaders are away on their daily tours. I get to bed about 1 p.m. for about three hours' sleep and then do some writing in my room, and watch the early evening news before joining the evening APG meeting at 6.15. From there I will either do an evening meeting for a candidate in or near London, or do some more writing, or perhaps have dinner with one of the team, before starting all over at 10 p.m. The key members of the team are working a minimum 16-hour day and sometimes longer.

Our first party election broadcast (PEB) appeared on television tonight. Harris and Pardoe have been a bit nervous about it all day. I now saw why. It was one of those broadcasts which will either be a big hit or a non-event. It consisted entirely of Rosie Barnes. The opening shot was of her playing with her daughter and the family rabbit, and the rest of the broadcast consisted of a close-up on Rosie's face, and a series of what were obviously answers to questions, with the interviewer edited out, and brief fade-outs between each point. She began by talking about her children, and how parents today have to worry about what will happen to their children – when they were older would they find work and a home? 'Parents are having to worry about what our parents took for granted.' She talked about the Conservatives being uncaring, about factional parties 'cancelling out politics'. She talked about looking for solutions that worked, and not political gimmicks. She talked about life on the streets – crime, vandalism, violence, and suggested that there were deeper changes taking place in Britain than we at the moment understood ... it wasn't enough just to have a stronger police force, although that was necessary – we had to tackle the real causes of these problems. She concluded by talking about why she was in politics – the world was getting a harder place – if you didn't like the way it was you had to get in there and change it – that's why she was there.

The remarkable impact of Rosie Barnes – a combination of innocence and determination, idealism and common sense – was undenialbe. But does it really work for now? I wonder whether it was not a better broadcast for political peace time? Don't we need more punch now that we are at war? I await the reaction with interest.

Saturday, May 23 (P–19)

> 'It all depends on how the party leaders do. If Mrs
> Thatcher is found in bed with a camel three days
> before polling, then the Tories will lose.'
>
> Ken Livingstone

Nigel Lawson claimed today that Labour's manifesto pledges will cost more than £35 billion to implement. 'This would require either a doubling of the basic rate of income tax or VAT at 50% or a mixture of the two. There would be increased borrowing leading inexorably to higher interest rates, sharply higher inflation, a total collapse of confidence in the pound and not lower but higher unemployment.' Roy Hattersley replied that the annual net cost of Labour's programme would be £6 billion and that the money was available. Labour would return the standard rate of tax to last year's level, providing £2.5 billion, and return borrowing to the level originally planned for this year, providing £3.5 billion.

The Tories also claimed that our programme would cost an additional £19 billion a year but Ian Wrigglesworth quickly replied by quoting Coopers and Lyebrand as saying that 'the increase in public spending proposed by the Alliance would be phased over five years, building up from £6 billion a year in year one' and that 'the Alliance programme does not imply any general increase in the rate of taxation'.

Kinnock was asked at his press conference in Cardiff if he could guarantee that if he came to power the Left would not take over in the way that Ken Livingstone took over the GLC. Kinnock snapped: 'Don't you patronise me, son. We don't elect the Leader of the Labour Party in the same way that group leaders are elected. I think that the kind of scenario you paint would make a moderately interesting novel, but it bears no interest or relationship whatsoever to the policies of the Labour Party.'

Kinnock can't hope for an end to this line of attack. It's only too obvious that Labour have decided to reduce the risks to the minimum. Their big rallies are for supporters only. The press conferences out of London are designed to reduce to a minimum the hazards of the big London encounters with the media. The Benns and Skinners, the Livingstones and Bernie Grants are out of sight.

Not that the Tories are much better; their rallies, too, are all-ticket, and they are addressing the nation almost entirely by television.

Our 'Ask the Alliance' rallies may not come across so well on television, but at least any man or woman can walk in off the street, sit in the front row, and have a go at Owen and Steel; at least our Leaders are facing the media every morning at the press conference; and our doors are open, almost too open, to anyone who walks in.

John Pardoe and Paul Tyler both telephoned me at home. I told John I was worried that we were busy debating whether we should attack the Tories or Labour instead of promoting our own policies. John revealed that he, too, felt there was 'a lack of aim and purpose'. What were we really about? We needed a clear theme that people can identify with. I argued that we should try to prioritise the issues at tomorrow's campaign meeting. We were living from day to day, from press conference to press conference and from subject to subject, but we needed these daily activities to inter-relate and to reinforce an overall message. John said he was having difficulty identifying the most attractive message. What made us distinctive was constitutional reform, but the opinion polls showed that what people cared about was education and health and unemployment, and these were as much Labour's issues as ours.

We both acknowledged that the 'play it as it comes' approach of our two Leaders has landed us in an election campaign without a proper strategy. The problem is they are both brilliant opportunists, Owen in particular having fed off the Press Association tapes for years. It had been almost too easy. Perhaps the SDP leader planned the General Election campaign as an exaggerated version of the same game?

Of course, they could be right. Instead of trying to set the agenda, come forward with our worthy policies, and be constructive, perhaps we should be picking up on what the other parties are doing and saying, forcing ourselves into the main debate, appearing to be the sane voice between two warring factions. At least that would be a strategy!

Paul Tyler telephoned to tell me about the background briefing of Sunday journalists. We were emphasising that we were appealing to the thoughtful voter; 30% of the electorate was undecided and maybe 10% of Labour or Tory voters were only loosely attached to those parties. We intended to appeal directly to them, with some emphasis in health, education, and housing. He said that the Rosie Barnes party political broadcast had been the subject of some severe criticism from activists, but that in his view it had some virtue as a simple, clear message to thoughtful voters. He reported that the three opinion polls to be published tomorrow will reveal a stalemate, the

Conservatives holding steady, no real surge to Labour, and the Alliance down one or two points. The 'phoney war' and the first week's campaigning have made no difference. We're back where we started.

Week Two

Sunday, May 24 (P–18)

> *'I will leave the custard pie throwing to Neil Kinnock.'*
>
> David Owen

The Harris poll, conducted on Wednesday and Thursday, shows Conservatives 41, Labour 34, and Alliance 22. Gallup has the Conservatives on 42, Labour 33, the Alliance 23, and MORI shows the Conservatives on 44, Labour 31, and the Alliance 24.

Our careful planning of an up-beat briefing for the Sunday papers proved a waste of time, because when the papers arrived this morning the big story came from David Steel, who revealed to journalists in Scotland his discontent with the TV double act. 'We are not a Tweedledum and Tweedledee partnership' he is quoted as saying. Both Davids have been unenthusiastic about the joint regional TV appearances, mainly because they felt the local stations couldn't cope with them technically, so maybe it does make sense to change the plan, but it makes no sense to announce it in such a way that it looks like a panic response to negative polls.

The practise of both Davids of informally briefing journalists on their respective campaign buses is causing considerable frustration to the planning team in London. No matter what we decide, the Leaders seem to feel free to speculate openly, apparently – and amazingly – oblivious to the effect their remarks will have when published out of context in unsympathetic newspapers.

The papers are full of stories about the need for our campaign meeting tonight to 'breathe fresh life into their flagging campaign'. There is also considerable debate about whether the campaign should concentrate more on attacking Labour. Brian Walden in *The Sunday Times* describes our campaign as staggeringly inept. This is because of the 'serious strategic miscalculation' of not attacking the Labour Party. 'When the Labour Party is down, the sensible thing to do is drive a stake through its heart. Turn aside and it will sink its fangs in your neck.' He argues that the Labour vote is not crumbling and will not do so without an Alliance assault. If Labour keeps climbing in the opinion polls the Alliance is going to have difficulty in winning votes from the Tories and may lose some to them. The threat of a Labour win could harden the Tory vote and squeeze the Alliance to death. He says if the aim is to pick up a few Tory seats on June 11, then we are throwing away the future. 'If Labour does well in this Election then the Alliance is out of business. The Labour Party is its mortal foe, will do no deals with it and desires only its destruction. Labour's weakness is that it depends upon many who vote, simply from habit, for a label. This is fertile ground for Dr Owen and Mr Steel, if only they would wake up and get on to it.'

Walden is right about the long term objective, but only half right about the tactics for achieving it. I too share the view that we should not only go for the Tories but also for Labour, but I also think that wherever possible we should attack them *together*, as the parties that have *shared* power. To persuade people to turn to a *third* force we must be positive. We have to promote ourselves as different, distinctive, the new idea. An alternative to them both.

Marcia Falkender in her Sunday column, suggests an answer: 'I believe the central focus should be on the Great Reform package they have conceived ... guaranteeing that democracy in Britain can be safeguarded and reshaped to suit modern conditions ... yet the Alliance remains unsure of its electoral appeal, only half-heartedly campaigning for it ... what we are suffering from are undemocratic councils being dealt with undemocratically by a central government that itself does not reflect the will of the people. Two hundred years ago in Boston the worthy citizens knew how to respond to a government which treated them in such cavalier fashion. They tipped the cargoes of British tea into the harbour and declared there would be no taxation without representation. That's the sort of gutsy attitude the Alliance should be taking to our present political carve up. That should be their campaign focus ... a campaign with guts.'

Margaret Thatcher has made a bad start to the Election. Her 'going on and on' blunder has cost her dear. The opening Tory press conference did not go well, both because she reportedly dominated it, interrupting her Ministers and attacking journalists who asked difficult questions, and because she got into real trouble on the schools policy. This Election campaign was always going to be partly about Margaret Thatcher but perhaps more so than we realised. The feeling that she is bossy, that she doesn't really care, is fairly deep rooted now. The word from the constituencies is that anti-Thatcherism is a potent factor. I think Peter Jenkins in the *Independent* last Monday hit it on the head when he said 'as a Prime Minister she lacks a reservoir of public affection. When she is up she is very, very up, but when she is down her ratings are awful.'

Labour are bound to attack Thatcher, and I think we should let them do it; we'll benefit too. Unfortunately, knowing Labour, they'll probably go hopelessly over the top and it could be counter-productive. They will, however, probably be helped by Thatcher herself; it looks to me as if she is so out of touch with ordinary people that she no longer knows how to talk to them. I hope our Leaders will concentrate on attacking Thatcherism rather than Thatcher directly, the style rather than the individual. Let her self-destruct.

Frankly, I don't think we can easily dent Kinnock. He looks well protected, and well prepared. I think he could have a good election from start to finish. What we should be doing, therefore, is stressing that he, Bryan Gould, Roy Hattersley and John Smith and one or two of the others are a small handful of goodies but behind them there's a menacing mass of left-wingers who, in power, will be a disaster. Apart from that, there's enough in their manifesto to go on with – the opinion polls show their defence policy is unpopular, and they have committed themselves to unravelling most of the restrictions on trade union excesses, and that's likely to be unpopular too.

Both our Leaders are looking and sounding good out in the country; there were some magnificent pictures of David Owen sailing with Debbie on a rough sea on the television last night; but I think it is right that the two Davids should be seen separately more often and above all we need to get them making big and strong speeches.

There is hardly a word in the papers today about defence. Has our aim of exhausting it in the first week been achieved? The main policy issue dealt with by the Sundays' is education. According to *The Sunday Times* Kenneth Baker has tried frantically to defuse the row over plans to allow schools to opt out of the state system by rushing out a clarifying speech in his Surrey constituency. The speech had been drafted just a few hours before Baker delivered it, 'a culmination of intense behind-the-scenes activity between Downing Street and Baker's office'. In it he stressed that there would be no return to the eleven-plus and that parents would not be charged for their children's education. The Tories were apparently briefing the newspapers that there was no dispute within their camp but the problem had been 'loose words by Thatcher'. Kinnock in Cardiff yesterday accused the Prime Minister of wanting educational opportunity to be governed by the size of the parental pocket, and Paddy Ashdown claimed that the Tory plans have been drawn up on 'the back of a fag packet'.

I called in at my office when I arrived in London just in time to turn on the Channel 4 news. It said we would decide tonight to change strategy – that we intended to go for Labour. Owen appeared saying Labour is unelectable. 'People know a rotten apple when they see one – and this one is rotten to the core.' David Steel was also shown explaining the decision about dual appearances on television and explaining it's a minor change being made simply because of the technical problems with regional programmes. This is not good; we're talking about ourselves, not the issues.

I had to pass a battery of television and newspaper cameras to enter the Royal Horseguards for the Campaign meeting. David Steel opened it by saying that it should be brief, otherwise it would reinforce the reports that it was taking place in an atmosphere of crisis. My heart sank. I felt we needed to re-examine our strategy (or lack of it); such a discussion would now be impossible.

We received a detailed report on the opinion polls. Our support has dropped 2.5 percentage points on the first five days of the campaign, but is 4.5 points up on polls at this time in the 1983 campaign. The Tories have dropped 1.5 points and Labour have risen 3.5. Gallup has showed 26% of the electorate either completely undecided or wavering in support for a preferred party. That, at least, is heartening: there is still a lot of volatility that can work to our advantage.

Reasons given for not voting Alliance are that we aren't sufficiently decisive or united, we are inexperienced, there is uncertainty about what we stand for, and that we can't decide who the leader should be. Owen is recognised for determination, shrewdness, and sticking to principles, Steel for being likeable, caring and listening to reason, and also for determination and sticking to principles.

On the issues, the polls suggest that health care is rising to the top, followed by unemployment, law and order, and education. Defence figures less prominently.

The opinion polls have engendered no sense of panic. Most of those present wanted to see more urgency and passion coming across on television, and it was generally felt that we had to attack both of the other parties equally, although John Cartwright spoke for many when he said that the Labour Party was 'getting away with murder'. We hoped the Tories would now throw themselves into an attack on Labour and that we could chip in when it was tactically wise to do so. We decided to bring education forward for the press conference on Monday to take advantage of Thatcher's gaffe.

On the whole, it was as I feared — a most unsatisfactory

meeting, rushed, and made difficult by the media circus outside the door.

Even more unsatisfactory was the ITN news bulletin. John Pardoe had not realised that David Steel and David Owen had given interviews earlier in the day, and thus we had the ludicrous position of Owen appearing first to say that we would now attack Labour, David Steel appearing to say that we would keep up our attack on the Tories, and then John Pardoe saying that our policy was to attack nobody, but rather to present our own policies positively. The presenter commented (with some justification) that the Alliance appeared to be entering the second week going 'in a number of different directions'.

Monday, May 25 (P–17)

> '*Under the Labour defence policy, mujahideen in
> Penge High Street seem to be expected to deter
> Soviet nuclear blackmail.*'
>
> John Cartwright

We had a gratifyingly sympathetic press this morning. The headline in the *Daily Telegraph*: 'First week sees little change', sums it up. Most of the papers are at this stage going along with our story that we're on course in terms of past General Election history.

The *Daily Telegraph* and the *Daily Express* led today with reports of some extraordinary remarks by Kinnock in an interview with David Frost yesterday morning. Frost had suggested that if we didn't have nuclear weapons, our forces would be subject to an unfair battle. Kinnock replied 'yes, what you're then suggesting is that the alternatives are between the gesture, threat, or the use of nuclear weapons – and surrender. In these circumstances the choices posed, and this is a classical choice, are between exterminating everything you stand for and the flower of your youth, or using all the resources you have to make any occupation

244 Battle for Power

totally untenable. Of course any effort to occupy Western Europe or certainly occupy the United Kingdom would be utterly untenable. Our potential foes know that very well and are not going to be ready to engage in attempting to dominate conditions which they could not dominate.'

Whatever he meant, these remarks were open, at best, to speculation, and, at worst, to misinterpretation or misrepresentation, and in an election it is wise to expect the worst. Commented the *Express* in a leading article: 'there has never been talk (in Britain) of surrender, even as a philosophical option. The history of Britain is built on strength and resolve. The word "surrender" has never entered the defence vocabulary. To tell the British people that he and his CND comrades could defend Britain is breathtaking in its arrogance. Defence is the most vital issue of them all. It is a matter of life and death. It is out of Mr Kinnock's league.'

Given the explosive effect the Frost interview is likely to have on the next few days' campaigning, it is extraordinary that no one picked up on it immediately. No one on our side saw it, and it was not until 1.30 a.m. this morning, when I saw the first editions, that we knew what he had said. I understand the Tories only picked up on it sometime during Sunday afternoon, and it was they who tipped off the *Express* and the *Telegraph*, and set George Younger, the Defence Secretary, in motion. He was quoted in the *Daily Telegraph* as saying that Labour's defence policy appears to be one of 'take to the hills'.

David Owen came to this morning's meeting raring to go. He's been wanting to take on Kinnock on defence at some point and surely 'this is it'. There was little enthusiasm because we had all hoped to move on from defence to domestic issues, but we had no choice but to accept the Kinnock gift. I suggested in a note to David O. that he should say that Labour was planning the recall of Dad's Army ... Russian SS 20s v. Captain Mainwaring and the Home Guard!

At the press conference Paddy Ashdown spoke effectively on education, but it was David O. who stole the television bulletins when he was challenged by the right wing journalist Paul Johnson on the radicalism of our education policies and replied with impressive anger about what was happening to schools. He talked of the education of his own two boys and his daughter, and said that night after night he worried about whether he should use his income to take them out of state schools. This was Owen at his most convincing and impressive. If only we could get him off defence and onto domestic issues in this sort of form . . .

The APG this evening was concerned by the speech David O. was planning to make in Glasgow. It was powerful stuff: 'Labour in this Election is an amalgam of narrow sectional interests. You have a grudge? You have a grievance? Join Mr Kinnock's cavalcade! Pick up your post-dated blank cheque on boarding the magical mystery tour, and the best of luck when you try to cash it after June 11 . . . Labour is not a modern political party in the sense that they are advocating new policies. It is the old policies of failure, packaged, de-odourised and sold like soft tissue paper, appearing harmless and innocent to voters unable or unwilling to unwrap the package. In fact, when the package is unwrapped, what it reveals is not a pretty sight. If anyone thinks the Labour Party in the last parliament was going left, then take a close look at the shape of the future parliamentary Labour Party. Under any conceivable election result, there will be an outright majority for the left. The day of the so-called moderate right are numbered. Seventeen days to be precise. For when the votes are counted we will wake up to find a very different Labour Party in parliament. Mr Kinnock will not find himself uncomfortable in such company, for they are the very people with whom and on whom he built his base in order to become leader of the party.'

He then moved on to a savage attack on Labour defence policy. 'Now we are told by Mr Kinnock we must be ready to fight a Soviet occupation of Britain. Thanks a lot! . . . he wants Dad's Army back and Captain Mainwaring's return to the colours.'

Then came the remark that concerned some members of the

APG: 'Or does his [Kinnock's] confidence stem from his own extensive experience of fifth columnists in the Labour Party?'

Our feeling was that having lambasted Thatcher for waving the patriotic flag, and having taken such exception to being called a 'fellow traveller', he was now opening himself up to a similar response from Kinnock and the Labour Party. However, it is clear from the television bulletins this evening that this angle has not been picked up. The line that has captured the imagination is the one about Dad's Army.

George Younger has also been attacking Kinnock: 'The limit of his ambition would be to organise resistance to an occupation, the first occupation of these islands for over nine hundred years.'

We did extremely well for coverage on tonight's bulletins, apart from an absence of David Steel from the BBC one, and yet I can't help being impressed with the pictures of Kinnock's big rallies. Tonight he also was in Glasgow, and the impression was of a vast and enthusiastic crowd welcoming a popular leader. It may well be the case that Kinnock's rallies are for supporters only and represent an illusion rather than the reality of popular success, but our 'Ask the Alliance' meetings simply can't compete for television impact.

Tuesday, May 26 (P–16)

> 'The Alliance has re-launched its campaign in the
> time-honoured fashion. It announced that it was not
> changing its tactics, and then promptly did so.
> Having earlier indicated that he would not waste
> his time on Labour because they could not win, Dr
> Owen was laying into them with gusto.'
>
> Geoffrey Smith (*The Times*)

We've scored a hit. The 'Dad's Army' line is the quote of the day. The Tory papers have been merciless. Building on the Owen and Younger speeches, they have ridiculed the Labour leader. The

Daily Mail comment is typical: 'The idea of a latter day Dad's Army defying the mightiest military empire our continent has ever seen, beggars belief.'

Anthony Bevins, the political editor of the *Independent*, who lies in wait at the morning press conferences like a hired gunslinger, was the only one to take up Owen's 'fifth columnists' remark. David was well prepared. What were the Militants, many of whom were still in the Labour Party, if not a party within a party — fifth columnists? He named some local Labour parties that are at present disaffiliated, and also one or two Militant-supporting former MPs like Dave Nellist.

Nancy Seear, who was there to talk about pensions, stole the show. Kinnock, she declared, may be a nice guy but that was not enough to be Prime Minister . . . and then, with marvellous eccentricity, she added 'it's not even enough for a cook!' The press conference dissolved in laughter.

There was a strange calm about the campaign headquarters this morning . . . it was that before the battle feeling. I think we all felt that the Election was about to hot up, with the Tories known to be on the point of a savage attack on Labour. In fact it was David Steel who kicked off for the Alliance from the top of his 'battle bus' in the market town of Newtown, Montgomeryshire. 'Turn to the back of Labour's manifesto and you will find three blank pages. Since Neil Kinnock won't tell you what's been left out, I shall perform this service on his behalf.' He then detailed the behaviour of far-left Labour councils before returning to Kinnock's interview with David Frost: 'He said Labour would deter any threatened Soviet invasion by setting up a resistance movement to make Russian occupation untenable. Corporal Kinnock will hold back the might of the Red Army by organising resistance fighters in the South Downs. No wonder Major Healey says Moscow is praying for a Labour victory.' Kinnock's platform was a triumph for the advertising agencies; all image and no substance. The word 'socialism' was expunged from Labour's vocabulary, and even the word 'labour' seemed to be hidden in the small print. His campaign has been Thatcherised. There were photo opportunities by the score, but no words, no discussion of policy. He said that one speech by Kinnock taking on Militant and a handful of expulsions fooled nobody. In the recent parliament there had been 40 hard-left Labour MPs out of a total of 209. If just the same number of Labour MPs was returned there would be 62. But if they won 340 seats, enough to govern, there would be 101 hard-left Labour MPs. He then unveiled the list of 'the 101 damnations'. It had been based on six criteria: membership of the campaign group of Labour MPs; support by or of a left-wing newspaper such as *Labour Briefing*, *Straight Left*, *Campaign Group News*, or *Militant*; supporting opposition to the expulsion of Militant from the Labour Party; support for withdrawal from NATO; backing links with the IRA through Sinn Fein; or support for Labour local authorities breaking the law on rates and spending.

This back-of-the-bus speech led the early evening television news and was headlines in most of the evening newspapers.

Margaret Thatcher joined in the attack on Labour this evening, claiming that Kinnock's line on defence made him unfit to govern the country. 'He has left himself no policy but to yield to invasion and occupation and to trust in the forlorn hope that a guerrilla struggle would eventually persuade the army of occupation to withdraw. I do not understand how anyone who aspires to government can treat the defence of our country so lightly.'

Tebbit attacked Labour even more viciously. 'No doubt Mr Kinnock is well-meaning. But he seems unable to grow up, away from romantic visions of so-called freedom fighters – a rosy-pink memory of Che Guevara or Fidel Castro ... he is a left wing leader of the most left wing Labour Party that there has ever been.'

Tebbit's peroration was devastating: 'From the safety of his carefully prepared and scripted TV extravaganzas he just talks – talks of a runaway victory. But it is Mr Kinnock who is the runaway. He is a runaway from the questioning press. He is a runaway from the questioning voters. He is a runaway from the trade union bosses. He is a runaway into the arms of his own extremists. And he would be a runaway from any bully, however big or small, who threatened this nation.'

Kinnock must be rueing his remarks on the Frost programme and yet today he appears to have compounded the error, for in explanation he used the guerrilla tactics used by Afghan resistance fighters as evidence of the ability of a country to resist invaders.

Still, I'm a little worried the Tory attacks on Kinnock are so savage that it could lead to a sympathy backlash. Maybe we should hold back on Kinnock, and if we have a go at Labour, it should be at their policies and 'the real Labour Party' under the glossy surface. I almost feel guilty about my Dad's Army invention; I don't feel comfortable writing *Daily Mail* headlines!

This morning four consultants wrote to the papers to reply to the junior doctors. Admitting to being supporters of the Tories, they rattle off statistics to show that the Conservatives have been investing in the health service. 'Their statement that the NHS is not safe with this government suggests a political bias not supported by the facts.' The *Daily Mirror* reveals that the signature at the head of the letter is that of Sir Arnold Elton 'who retired from the NHS two years ago, runs a lucrative private practice in Harley Street and is chairman of the Conservative Medical Society'. The junior doctors have immediately replied to the consultants' charge that they had been ungracious: 'We see no reason to be gracious when, as a result of government policies, we are regularly forced to turn patients away.'

The Tories returned to education at their press conference, obviously determined to clarify their proposals and reduce their vulnerability. Kenneth Baker stressed that they were wholly committed to the principle of free education within the state sector. Grant-maintained schools would not be allowed to charge fees. They would be funded by direct grants from the Exchequer at the same cost per pupil as the local education authority schools. 'When a school becomes grant-maintained it will retain the same character as when it was an LEA school. The grammar school will remain a grammar school, a comprehensive school will remain a comprehensive school, and a secondary modern school will remain a secondary modern school.' Parents would decide by a secret postal ballot whether schools should opt out.

Paddy Ashdown, who is having a good campaign, renewed our attack: 'Mr Baker's plans amount to the introduction of the law of the jungle in education planning. They will create sink schools, which, once on the slippery slope, will be condemned to closure. They will create larger and larger comprehensives, whereas they say they have been trying to move towards smaller ones. They will condemn the children of many families without transport to second class schools or they will at least double transport bills to be paid out of limited education budgets.'

———————

Tonight David Steel and David Owen took part in their critical *Panorama* interview with Robin Day. Both performed well and they looked all set for a 100% triumph until with three minutes left Day turned to Owen and asked: 'If either Labour or the Conservatives were to have majority, which would you regard as the lesser evil?' Owen's over-riding obsession with defence got in the way of the obvious answer. If he was pushed, he said, he would have to say that the defence and security of the country came first, and that Labour's position was unacceptable. He may not have intended it this way, but it came across as a clear and damaging signal that, given a choice, he saw the Tories as the desirable coalition partner. Day then turned to Steel, who said that he saw no reason why the country should have to choose between two evils; he would not be pushed into answering the question. Owen, realising his mistake, then attempted to backtrack, saying that he was known to be indiscreet. 'David is much wiser in dealing with these questions.' Between the two of them they then recovered some of the ground, but it had been a penetrating question and it had struck home. A hostage had been given to fortune. Labour could be counted upon to use it. On the other hand, you have to grant Owen his consistency. He doesn't find it easy to dissemble. It was an honest answer.

Wednesday, May 27 (P–15)

> *'I'm quite sure that Mr Kinnock is a patriot, but he
> sees things in a different way to us.'*
>
> Norman Tebbit

Ye Gods, the Tory papers have gone for Kinnock. *The Mail* has a
huge headline: 'Kinnock: the man with a white flag.'

We began a poor day with another bad poll – Marplan in *Today*
shows the Conservatives holding at 42, Labour up to 35, and we
have dropped four points to 20. At the morning meeting David
Owen reflected my own concern, and also Polly's, that the 'Ask
the Alliance' meetings were not coming across well on television
and that the two Davids needed to make more substantial
speeches. I was relieved to hear this; my own view is that the
meetings clearly work in the hall but have no impact on television
at all. We need to hear them making a powerful point on the TV
bulletins night after night.

Our press conference didn't really work; we had Roy Jenkins,
who was magisterial but dull, and two industrialists, David
Sainsbury, and John Harvey-Jones, to whom the journalists
reacted with indifference. In fact, I felt we had a poor day. The
Leaders were made to look silly on television; David Owen with a
handkerchief on his head in a mosque, and David Steel conducting a band, and riding a child's bicycle.

The Tories sustained their attack on Labour's defence policy,
aided by President Reagan who, while insisting he did not wish
to interfere in our Election, said in a Washington interview that
should Labour come to power, 'I would try with all my might to
persuade that government not to make those grievous errors' on
defence. He expressed his admiration for Thatcher's handling of
domestic and international matters, and then paid Labour the
rather back-handed compliment of saying that America's relationship with Britain 'has survived Labour governments in the
past'.

Another recording has come back to hit the Conservatives, this time featuring the Prime Minister. The Scottish National Party has discovered a video of a Conservative PPB in May 1977 when unemployment was at 1.34 million. Thatcher appeared on it saying 'sometimes I have heard it said that the Conservatives have been associated with unemployment. This is absolutely wrong. We would have been drummed out of office if we had this level of unemployment.' Thatcher, confronted with these words while on the campaign trail, looked suitably embarrassed but answered that they were uttered in 'a very different world'.

I am becoming increasingly worried about our Party Election Broadcasts, all the more so after tonight's APG meeting when it emerged that plans are not finalised for our broadcast on Friday night. John Pardoe, who was equally worried, explained that the planned broadcast could not be ready in time, and that David Abbott, the man we are paying to do all this, is talking of putting together a number of interviews that he already has on tape and making a PEB out of them. I am appalled that in the middle of a General Election campaign we should be in such a position. We have been negligent in not appointing a competent member of our Cowley St team to be in overall charge of PEB's.

This evening I went to Wimbledon to speak for Adrian Slade. The meeting was in a small school hall, and it was easy to see how popular Adrian is, and also why. He struck me as the ideal Liberal candidate – decent and direct, with a clear view about national issues, but also in touch with his constituency and able to relate local problems to national issues. His humour and feel for what concerned the audience helped him to make a highly effective speech. Adrian is to be my successor as President of the party and on this performance will be just the man for the hour.

By the time I reached Cowley Street a bad day had become even worse. BBC's *Nine O'Clock News* revealed the latest Gallup opinion poll, a critical one because it was based on a sample of over 2,500, and the interviews had been conducted during the past two days. It showed we had fallen five points to 18, while the Conservatives were up 2.5 to 44.5 and Labour were up 3 to 36.

No matter how you look at it, this is bad news, and it is reinforced by an NOP poll of marginals to be published in tomorrow's *Independent*. We are now two weeks from that optimistic day when we launched our campaign with the 'Great Reform Charter' and, no matter what we do, we are still falling in the polls. It is beginning to look like a real 'squeeze'. Neil Kinnock's rating as a campaigning leader has sky-rocketed, while the ratings for our leaders has fallen.

With every hour, and we are now living from hour to hour, I am convinced that we need to do four things: (a) focus our campaign more positively, (b) decide on our themes for the day and develop them better during the day with all our main speakers, (c) reduce the frivolity of the Leaders' tours and get them coming across more strongly and urgently, (d) demand a higher standard for our remaining three Party Political Broadcasts.

The Tories used their PEB tonight to attack the Labour Party directly, naming and showing photographs of hard-left candidates and quoting their past words. They quoted our list of 101. It reinforced our doubts, including those of David Steel, about the wisdom of the '101 damnations' approach. As John Pardoe said: 'When I saw the Tories quoting us I had a terrible feeling we had got it wrong!'

Thursday, May 28 (P–14)

> 'The essential feature of this Election is that nothing
> is happening . . . so far it seems to be a campaign
> for politicians only.'
>
> Geoffrey Smith (*The Times*)

Another bad start to the day. I was confronted at 2.30 a.m. by the first edition of the *Independent* with a front page lead story headed 'Owen risks rift to revitalise Alliance hopes'. It claims that Owen's frustration with the bland Alliance election manifesto has led him to take 'a calculated risk' of upsetting his Liberal partners by re-stating his belief in the social market economy. 'The SDP Leader believes the Alliance's faltering performance could be due to the lack of a cutting edge to its campaign. He described its manifesto as the most radical reforming programme in living memory but privately he was dismayed by its caution. It failed to carry any specific mention of the market economy. Last night Dr Owen re-launched the Alliance campaign by deliberately discarding the caution forced on him by some of his senior colleagues and Liberal leaders.'

It says, too, that 'the SDP Leader has also been frustrated by the Liberals over defence policy. Although he told journalists yesterday that the Alliance had come through sound on defence, he felt hamstrung by the policy agreed with the Liberals, which prevented him naming a preferred replacement for the Polaris system when the Alliance was accused by the Conservatives of unilateralism by default.'

This is an extremely unfortunate story from two points of view: first, we cannot afford any suggestion of disunity within the Alliance. It will finish us off. Second, the story has either come from David himself or someone close to him, and the implication that if the going gets tough the Liberals will be blamed is intolerable.

David O. was not at the morning meeting because he was appearing on the daily radio–television programme, *Election Call* with Robin Day, but David S. reported that he had spoken to Owen who was angry at the *Independent* article and said it must have come from one of his entourage. We were given the impression the individual would be dealt with firmly. Relief all round!

We immediately began an inquest into the polls. Andy Ellis said that for the first time he was receiving messages from some constituencies suggesting that what was happening in the polls was happening on the ground. Jim Dumsday looked down the table to me and said 'Des, is there any good news in these figures at all?' I couldn't think of any. Neither could anyone else. We took some comfort from a poll in yesterday's *London Daily News* that suggested we had improved our support in London, and also from the Harris rolling poll on TV-AM that showed we were up two points in two days. Nevertheless, there was no reason to believe that the BBC's poll of polls, showing us just below 20%, was not accurate. With two weeks left, we were in trouble.

In David Steel's presence we argued for toughening up the speeches and the rallies, and also for abandoning the plans for the PEB and replacing them with some dynamic film of the two Leaders, and a to-camera appearance by David himself. The following one could feature David Owen, and the last one both Leaders. I argued that we had to try to come in at a higher level than the other parties' PEBs, trying to raise the tone of the election campaign.

I approached the 10.15 meeting with some apprehension, because I felt there was a danger of a split at the centre of our campaign over whether we should continue the powerful attack on Labour ... indeed over whether we should be attacking anybody at all. The 'Attack Labour' advocates would, I knew, be strengthened by two newspaper articles today. The *Independent*, in a leader, said that despite Kinnock's attack on Militant back in 1985, as many as 8,000 Militant supporters remained within Labour's broad church and so did all sorts of other unattractive extremists. 'There is a danger for the Alliance in scrabbling for the votes of some supposed anti-Thatcher majority by signalling that Labour are much of a muchness and that tactical considerations should dictate how best to vote. Such behaviour suggests nothing positive about the philosophy behind the Alliance or its reason for being. Those who left the Labour Party to form the SDP did so because they believed that it had moved beyond the point of no return ... little of substance has changed ... if the Alliance can now demonstrate that it offers a distinctive and credible alternative to an unreformable Labour Party then it could act as a magnet for far more radical, centre-left votes than now seems likely and position itself to replace Labour. The Alliance should concentrate its fire on the Labour Party while expressing more robustly its social market alternative.'

And in the *Guardian* Hugo Young said that 'however much the professional may marvel at Labour's clever campaign, and its droolingly wonderful election commercial, sober voters should remember why the cleverness and the commercial have been so admired: for their evasion, not their substance; their blurring not their sharpness, their power to distract, not their efforts to enlighten'.

He argued that 'Mr Kinnock, Mr Gould and Mr Hattersley know very well that the alien left is stronger than it was, with roots that are impossible to dig up. They've been fighting it for years with only limited success. They know that a fair number of their sworn enemies will reach the Commons if Labour does well: more and tougher people than ever embarrassed Harold Wilson. These characters, in their turn, believe that they alone stand for socialism. They have kept quiet for the duration. Their silence will not last long. All this must now come out and be examined. What are we *really* electing if we elect a Labour government? It's a national, not a party question.'

These are fair points. And they do imply an assault on the Labour Party, rather than personal attacks on Neil Kinnock. But there are problems: first, the more we attack the Labour Party the more many in the anti-Thatcher majority may feel that this reflects greater compatibility with the Tories. Tim Clement-Jones, who heads the team that is briefing and keeping in contact with candidates, says that they are increasingly concerned about this. The polls suggest that the attacks on Labour are not taking us forward; on the contrary, we could end up reinforcing Conservative fears, and thus drive wavering Conservative voters back into their ranks, while at the same time alienating wavering Labour voters, and driving them back to Neil Kinnock. Also, the opinion polls show that the main reason for lack of enthusiasm for the Alliance is 'we don't know what they stand for'; whatever we do, we have to answer that question and we can only do so by campaigning *for* our own programme. There is another point: the more we join in the attack on Labour, particularly when it comes to naming names, the more we abandon our high moral ground, our claim that we represent the new politics of issues rather than personalities, of cooperation and consensus rather than confrontation.

I was impressed by what John Pardoe said over breakfast: that he would rather go down fighting for what he really believed in than fighting negatively on the others' weaknesses.

In any case my fears about a damaging division appear unjustified. It was clear at the APG meeting that a consensus is developing around the more positive approach. For instance, Polly Toynbee, who had felt strongly that we should hit Labour, now felt that it was critical that we should come across as angry about the country's problems and passionate about the failure of both the other parties and about the potential of our policies.

The lunchtime television news was dominated by the Kinnock press conference and the Tories' response. It is fairly clear that Kinnock has coped well. In answer to charges that he has been ducking questions, he pointed out that he had held many more press conferences than the Tories, and had been open to question on his provincial tours. It wasn't his fault that the Westminster reporters didn't want to leave London.

But nearly all of the questioning was on defence policy. He brushed aside the 'Dad's Army' criticisms. 'I have not advocated guerrilla warfare; I have not even inferred that we were talking about armies of resistance, or partisans of any of that novelette stuff. What I did say was that everybody knows, including potential foes, that the domination of the free countries of Western Europe, including the UK, was not a feasible military proposition.'

He conceded little on his unilateralism. On the contrary, he would order the decommissioning of Polaris 'within a couple of weeks' time when we are elected'.

Our advisor on opinion polls came to brief the afternoon APG meeting on some private polling. It showed that if you excluded all people who would not vote, and all people who would definitely vote Conservative, Labour, or Alliance, 37% of electors could be described as wavering or undecided. The Alliance was still coming across reasonably persuasively to them. Of the campaigns this week, Labour's has put off 19%, the Conservatives 15%, and the Alliance only 2%.

Of those questioned, 47% were vague about what the Alliance was about, and 36% clear.

On Labour, the poll suggested that 56% of the public reacted negatively to their nuclear defence policy, and they also were seen as more extreme, and likely to put the economy into worse shape.

The meeting was also cheered up by news of a big Marplan poll, over 1,500 voters, questioned within the last twenty-four hours, that showed no further fall in our position – 21%, with Labour dropping one point to 32%. However the Tories have moved up three points to 44%.

Our problem is that more than the other parties we live by the polls and die by the polls. When they're working for us, they create a kind of bandwagon effect, the momentum we need. But when we're in this position, permanently in third place, almost every story about the polls (and there is a story every day) refers to the Alliance 'trailing in third place', the Alliance 'far behind' etc. As a result, the two Davids have spent a lot of their campaigning time answering questions about polls, looking for the bright side of polls and sounding defensive about polls. And heaven knows what effect it is having on our chances ... this constant repetitive message to the electorate that we are far behind.

Friday, May 29 (P–13)

'*The march of moderates has begun*'
David Steel

By the early hours of this morning morale was rising. The Marplan poll suggested that all was not lost and the headline on the first edition of *The Times* was encouraging: 'Poll shows Tories 12 points ahead of Labour as Alliance hold steady.' David Steel telephoned me at about 12.30 a.m. in good spirits. He had had a good day on tour, and the television coverage had been a lot better. By all accounts his interview on Channel 4 News went particularly well. And he had spent the evening making the party political broadcast for tonight and is happy with it.

Unfortunately the press conference was a disaster. Simon Hughes was there to present our health policies. Beside the table was a mountain of computer print out, eight feet tall, intended to show what the waiting list for hospital beds would look like. Simon was carefully briefed to stress that these were not the real names, as these would be confidential; this was a simulation of the waiting list. Unfortunately, he did the opposite: 'These are real people,' he said, waving the top sheets of the print out at the journalists. I groaned inwardly, and Polly Toynbee who had set up the press conference and briefed Hughes went pale with horror. We both knew there was no way the reporters would let this pass.

Sure enough, hardly had Hughes finished than Robert Carvel asked 'Where did you get the names and what do you intend to do with them?'

Simon then replied that of course they were not real names. The press conference was in uproar. Paul Johnson, scenting blood, started calling out, 'So it's phoney, it's phoney.' Others called out, 'So you're saying it's bogus?'

Too late, Simon tried to explain that the print out was there to represent the size of the list. 'Whose names are they?' cried the reporters. 'The names are irrelevant,' said Simon digging himself ever more deeply into trouble.

The two Davids tried to look good-humoured, but there was no humour in their smiles. Steel deftly subdued the baying journalists by talking about a visit he made to Guy's Hospital last night and the waiting list there, and David Owen joined in talking about the simulated list as if the rumpus had never happened.

But we all know that the 'propaganda newspapers' will take full advantage of it tomorrow.

The coverage of both David Steel and David Owen has been first class today, the new style 'Ask the Alliance' rally came over well on television, and we're now keeping our fingers crossed that the weekend opinion polls will show that we have bottomed out.

The PEB is in my view a considerable improvement. It consists entirely of David Steel talking to camera; an old-fashioned approach maybe, but he speaks quietly, placing his emphasis on the strident nature of the others' campaigns, and on the way that Britain is being changed, not by the people, but by the politicians. The Alliance is an alternative – it would have the country working together. 'The march of the moderates has begun,' he declares.

I'm convinced he has struck the right tone for the right moment; there's no question that the defence issue has run out of steam; there's little more the Tories can say about it at the moment, and Kinnock has at least established his position and does not appear to have dropped in the polls as a result – although it may have been a factor in stopping his advance. As for the Alliance, it may be that our involvement in the issue over the first few days will pay off after all, because we, too, have been left to concentrate on other issues.

If the public have been at all turned off by the defence row, then our appeal now to 'the thoughtful voter' may have a chance to be effective.

Saturday, May 30 (P-12)

> '*It would be a tragedy if defence is all this Election is about . . . for there is also the matter of the country we are becoming and the society we are asked to defend.*'

> David Steel

The *Financial Times* has an interesting leader saying the Alliance is in danger of being squeezed between a reforming Labour Party and the formidable Conservative electoral machine. It claims: 'There is a remarkable confusion about whether the principal Alliance aim is a hung parliament or simply to maximise its percentage share of the vote.' The evidence of the opinion polls is that a hung parliament would not be popular. Also, by going for a hung parliament as its major goal the Alliance will look exceptionally foolish if it fails to achieve it. 'The better aim is to go for every possible vote. It should attack the Labour Party for being reforming but not yet reformed. It should attack the Conservatives for the gaps and inconsistencies in their approach to the social market and the lack of the safety net. In other words, it should put itself forward as the natural repository for those who want Thatcherism with a human face. The Alliance has become too inhibited. In the last ten days of the campaign it should come out fighting. For if it fails now, something very like it will have to be reinvented later.'

I put in a pre-arranged call to David Steel at Ettrick Bridge, briefing him on the morning papers (they don't arrive at Ettrick Bridge till later) and discussing strategy. I told him the response to the PEB from candidates was enthusiastic, and there is broad feeling that we are making the right sounds. I urged upon him that he should keep his speeches over the weekend on the 'high moral plane' of the broadcast, and a possible theme should be 'real answers to real problems'.

David Owen has circulated a memo saying that he intends to focus on six issues: promises to reduce unemployment, spend more on education, and reduce hospital waiting lists (all areas where the Tories could be undermined) and to sustain the trade union reforms, maintain a nuclear deterrent, and strengthen the police (all areas where Labour were open to doubt). This begins to sound like a strategy. It could be good news.

The papers are full of reports of new studies that undermine Tory claims about protecting the health service. One study suggests that the reason there appears to be a record number of patients being treated was because there had been an increase in the numbers being re-admitted to hospital. Another shows that spending on hospital and community health services fell below the target of 2% growth last year. The real purchasing power of health authorities, after allowing for pay and price rises, went up by only 1.8% and 1.5% of this was due to the revenue from efficiency savings. All of this will fuel the debate on the health service.

It's hard to believe that we're at the end of the second week of the real campaign, and twenty days have passed since Thatcher called the Election. The second week has been a better one for us, because Kinnock has been embattled on defence, but we still seem to have the same problem: we are not coming across with an identifiable message. Tomorrow's polls are crucial – we need signs of movement, preferably Labour down and the Alliance up; upward momentum will itself focus sharper attention on us, and hopefully help clarify our image.

Week Three

Sunday, May 31 (P-11)

> 'Her personality, her temperament, her background,
> the narrowness of her outlook and her values cut
> her off from ordinary people.'
>
> Bryan Gould

What are we to make of the opinion polls?

Harris in the *Observer* shows the Conservatives at 41, Labour 37, and the Alliance 21. Given the 4% margin of error, it's possible, on the basis of this poll, that the other two parties are neck and neck. But Gallup in the *Sunday Telegraph* has the Conservatives on 41.5%, Labour 34%, and the Alliance 22.5%

— a Tory lead of 7.5 points. MORI in the *Sunday Times* is best for the Tories — Conservatives 44%, Labour 32%, and the Alliance 23%.

A Marplan poll of marginal seats in the *Sunday Express* shows the Tories strengthening their hold on their own Conservative-held marginals; but a Harris poll of marginals on *Weekend World* shows Labour gaining.

All of the polls show the Conservatives holding steady and Labour apparently not suffering from the hammering they have taken over the past week. Nor, however, have they continued their upward momentum. This at least has been temporarily halted. Our much-needed upward momentum has not begun. We are 5% down on the start of the campaign.

In two respects, however, we are better off today than on the same Sunday in 1983. On that Sunday we were even further down in the polls. And on that Sunday the two Alliance leaders of the time, Roy Jenkins and David Steel, were attending that tense meeting at Ettrick Bridge where, before a room full of senior members of both parties, David Steel had to inform Roy Jenkins that his performance as 'Prime Minister' designate had proved an electoral handicap. He would have to take a back seat. No one who attended that meeting would forget it. There are one or two who to this day have not forgiven those who they believed guilty of an act of treachery. How much better this time: the two Alliance Leaders were together in London, being interviewed by David Frost, both looking tired but still at ease with one another.

Confronted with the polls, their references to 1979 and 1983 were beginning to sound a little unconvincing; I suspect that explanation won't be a runner much longer. Both chose to emphasise their belief that Labour can't win, and that there had to be an attack on the Conservative vote; the real question facing the electors was whether they wanted an uncontrollable Margaret Thatcher back in Downing Street.

From the papers it is clear that Labour is planning to launch a powerful attack on Margaret Thatcher as from today, while the Tories are planning to turn their attack on Labour's trade union links.

The *Sunday Times* reports that Maragaret Thatcher is planning a spectacular eighteen-hour summit appearance at the meeting of Western leaders in Venice on the eve of the General Election. It would allow her to project herself as international stateswoman, above the domestic cut and thrust of the election. The summit communiqué would enable her to claim that her economic policies represented the only realistic way forward for Britain, and she would be able to endorse the proposed deal to eliminate medium and shorter range missiles in Europe, and thus play a trump card in the defence debate. There would then be a four-day climax to the Tory campaign on the theme of 'making Britain great again'. It all sounds frighteningly probable and frighteningly formidable.

There is an article by Simon Jenkins in the *Sunday Times* that makes me feel a little uneasy. His case is that we should release David Owen like a 'charging rhino' to lead the attack. The enforced Alliance with Steel had been a disaster according to Jenkins. It had only worked at a price of all the qualities a campaign should contain: leadership, passion, personality, guts. 'It looks like what it is, an old-fashioned fit up from a smoke-filled room. It suffers from Wordsworth's complaint: no single volume paramount, no code, no master spirit, no determined road.'

Jenkins argues that 'the refreshing thing about this Election is that for once, the British voter is being offered an unambiguous option between the two central ideologies of post-war politics, market freedom versus socialism, the private versus the public sector, high versus low taxes, a competitive society versus a collectivist one. There is no trace of echo in Thatcher versus Kinnock. On June 11, we are offered a massive, crucial choice.'

Quite so, but Jenkins writes as somebody who has already made his choice, and knows his choice will win; in no way does he acknowledge that whichever of the two wins, the *supporters*, the constituency of the other, will also be the loser. It's a fight between two nations, with a prize for only one.

Andrew Neil, editor of the *Sunday Times* also refers to Owen becoming despondent and 'increasingly going his own way, to carping from the Liberals'.

There are danger signs that if we do not begin to rise in the polls over the next few days that considerable pressure will be applied upon Owen by these newspapers, and others who are not our friends, to believe that the fault is everybody's but Owen's, that if only he were the sole leader, if only he were able to follow his instincts, all would be different. To a man with a sense of destiny, this can be seductive.

There have also been a few signs that Liberals are preparing to take up the opposite position: that it is Owen, and in particular the suggestion that he could only make a deal with the Conservatives, that is in fact holding us back. It is vital that we resist pressures to blame each other for setbacks — we are not the Labour Party!

This afternoon we had the expected attacks on Thatcher from Labour. Bryan Gould, who has been Mr Clean in this campaign so far, now revealed for the first time that he is as capable as anyone else of dishing the dirt. He led the attack; according to him she was arrogant, lacking in compassion and understanding, and obsessed — 'particularly with nuclear weapons'.

Gerald Kaufman said her values could be said to be 'want it, own it, get it, grab it'. Commenting on the fact that Thatcher's supporters had taken to chanting 'ten more years' Kaufman said: 'We all want longer sentences for serious crimes, but this is ridiculous.' In the best Labour tradition of going over the top, Tony Blair, speaking of Thatcher's plans for council tenants, said 'they are the product of an unchecked and unbalanced mind'. Kaufman was called in to assure the country that Labour was not actually suggesting Mrs Thatcher was mad.

The campaign meeting this evening was in stark contrast to the famous Ettrick Bridge one of 1983; it was calm, there was no sense of impending disaster, there were no recriminations.

Alec McGivan, the SDP's national organiser, submitted a paper saying that we needed to change the mood of the election, and that we needed to clarify and define our message.

'Essentially there is a need for some passion in our campaign, for some emotional appeal. This election is a massive con trick. It's the cover-up election. The Labour Party is dishonestly hiding away its extreme personalities and its extreme policies. The Conservatives are behaving as if they have improved rather than have destroyed the things we most care about . . . yet in the midst of this Election we appear to be hardly moved by any of it. We almost appear as if we are just going through the motions of yet another rather boring election campaign . . . but we should be angry. We should feel passionately about not only our politics but about what is going on in this particular Election campaign. And if we feel these things, we ought to be capable of conveying these feelings to the British people.'

He proposed that we put our emphasis on three themes: A new way – a new politics, stressing that we are not just another political party but in marked contrast to the old politics. 'Those who vote Labour or Conservative are voting for the old politics. The pendulum will continue to swing from right to left and back again. Our children will experience the same old political battles that we ourselves witnessed . . . in stressing this key point, that we represent the new politics, we should address people's idealism. We should say that we want to reach out and touch people. We should talk about new horizons. We should talk about the Alliance representing the opportunity for the older generation to lay down a new political path, one that the younger generation will be able to tread.'

Second, that Alliance policies add up to plain common sense and that the common sense enshrined in our policies demonstrates that our heart is in the right place but also our head.

Third, that this is a key moment in history. The importance of the hour should be the third key message we communicate to the electorate.

In other words, a unique political moment – a unique political movement presenting the country with commonsense policies.

McGivan's note was backed up by Shirley Williams who was worried that we were becoming part of the slanging match. We were sufficiently distinctive. David Steel took the view that we had reasonably consolidated our position and that the latest polls contained a few hints that we had turned the corner. But he, too, accepted that we had not established a distinctive image and he accepted many of the points in the McGivan paper.

Andy Ellis then reported what he had deduced from candidates, that there were still a lot of undecided voters about and there was a lot of sympathy for us but we needed a positive message if we were to turn that sympathy into votes. The impression in England and Wales was that our vote was holding up in places where we had local credibility and where morale in the constituencies was high, but there was some frustration that we weren't being more innovative nationally.

He was one of a number of speakers who proposed that the two Davids should switch their line of attack, with Owen applying more pressure on the Tories, and Steel on Labour. He said an image problem had been created because of the *Panorama* programme and the impression created that David Owen would rather do a deal with the Tories. This could cause damage when we reached the point of tactical voting.

Dick Newby supported Ellis, but he was worried that the Labour vote was firming up. The Labour activists had been boosted by the early days of the campaign and were working hard. He, too, felt we needed a theme that was uniquely ours, but said we must also be efficiently reactive. We must be seen to be part of the debate, otherwise it would take place without us.

David Alton was also worried about the widespread feeling that we were too easily, too readily open to a deal with Thatcher – not the Tories, but Thatcher. This was a threat in seats where the Alliance was in direct confrontation with Labour.

I read the McGivan paper and listened to all this with rising spirits. It reflected my own feelings, and I hoped (and felt) the two Leaders were open to the argument.

I contented myself merely with expressing my fears about the snippets in the newspapers implying disunity. I said I knew the Leaders had too much sense to encourage it, but there were some who, if we did not start to rise in the polls, could start to look for scapegoats. There could be some Liberals who would blame the image of David Owen. There could be some Social Democrats who would like to imply that it was 'woolly Liberals' who were holding Owen back. The fact was that we had a united campaign and it was vital we kept it that way. Any indication of disunity could be catastrophic electorally, but also for the longer term.

David Owen shared the view that there should be 'no fraying around the edges', and supported Steel in believing that we could be about to turn the corner. The line has to be 'steady as she goes – it'll come later'.

He felt that we had to campaign on a few issues, the ones he had indicated earlier in the weekend – that we would reduce unemployment, spend more on education, maintain trade union legislation, uphold the police and the rule of law, reduce hospital waiting lists, and retain a minimum nuclear deterrent. He did, however, indicate that he felt we should stress these as achievable in a coalition.

David Steel immediately replied that he felt that it was too early to open up the balance of power argument – at least until we had some rise in the polls.

After the campaign meeting the two Leaders, Polly Toynbee and I sat down to discuss the press conference for Monday. I desperately wanted to abandon the 'subject of the day' approach and have the two Leaders talking with some passion about what they wanted to say for the rest of the campaign. The defence issue had run out of steam; Labour was busy attacking Thatcher, in my view counter-productively, and the opportunity existed to seize the moment. I proposed that we should take the paragraph in Simon Jenkins' article as a text and argue that the two choices confronting the country would be equally disastrous. If that were the full picture it would mean that whichever party won, more than half the country would be the loser. We decided that David Steel would adopt this approach, and David Owen would lay his emphasis on the six issues.

In the early hours of the morning I drafted some words for David Steel: 'Whichever of those parties wins, more than half the country will be the loser. That is what the Conservative and Labour parties have come to . . . at best they offer government of *all* the people by *half* the people for *half* the people. Of what value is the choice between two parties, each doctrinely blinded to common sense, committed by their backers to inevitable division? But it isn't the full picture . . . it represents exactly half the picture ... this Election *is* between two options, but those options are not the Labour Party and the Conservative Party; the two options are between the narrowness of both, and the balance, sane, unifying approach of the Alliance.'

I sent it round with the overnight report.

Monday June 1 (P-10)

> 'There has been an effort to deflect the campaign
> from policies to personalities ... what they are
> accusing us of is having the guts and spine to put
> our policies through – and to that we plead guilty.'
> Margaret Thatcher.

David S. has used most of my press release, but added a paragraph of his own: 'Both the other parties are threatening if elected to become narrower still. If the Tories win, to the long list of those we have loved – Carrington, Prior, Pym, Gilmour, St John-Stevas – will be added the names of Biffen and Walker. The shift will be to the right. If Labour were to win they've promised a repeal of the secondary picketing legislation. Scargillism and the scenes at Wapping will once more be the order of the day' (this was the paragraph that made the lunchtime television bulletins; so much for all my headline-catching phrases!).

Our pre-press conference meeting was, however, shaken by the draft of David Owen's press release, for it was an all-out call for coalition. A majority of the APG felt that this was a mistake, mainly because if we said it today, before we were clearly seen to be rising in the polls, it could look as if we were abandoning many of our ambitions – admitting a kind of defeat – and would be interpreted as such by unfriendly commentators and by the other parties. It would also raise all sorts of questions about who we preferred to coalesce with, what the terms would be, etc. Instead of campaigning all-out for our own policies, we would be campaigning for the right to do a deal, and we would be pressured to be more explicit.

It is arguable that we should have settled this strategic question before the Election, but it should be remembered that there were times when we were ahead of Labour in the opinion polls, and Kinnock was in danger of self-destructing. There had been occasions when there was every reason to believe we could make a major advance at this Election, winning more of the popular vote, and setting ourselves up to challenge for power in 1991–92. We had been concerned, too, about the difficulty of persuading people to vote for balance of power – for what would appear a negative result i.e. stopping anyone having overall power. Then there were different pressures from different kinds of constituencies; candidates desperate to squeeze the Labour vote were anxious not to promote the idea of a Conservative–Alliance coalition that could possibly put Thatcher back in Downing Street, while candidates in other constituencies believed they could win over the soft Tories only if they were convinced it would not put Labour in, that there would not be a repeat of the Lib-Lab Pact.

I suspect, too, there are fundamental differences between the two Leaders, that David Steel is not at all enthusiastic about holding the balance of power, that he believes we will be the long-term loser from a power-sharing arrangement, that he would be more than happy to settle for a narrow Tory majority with the Alliance making an advance. Owen, on the other hand, doesn't hide his impatience for power, and genuinely believes that we can negotiate a satisfactory deal. He also believes that people can see we won't win, and that they will respond to an objective they know to be realistic. Even if I mis-read Steel's ambitions, there's no question that he believes that tactically we can only lose from talk of a coalition, because he can see more clearly than Owen the damage caused by the widespread belief that Owen would be happy to work with Thatcher. And even if I mis-read David Owen's personal ambitions, it is beyond question that he believes that our main demand, proportional representation, inevitably leads to coalition, and that we only make sense if we campaign positively for the result that is the logical conclusion of our argument. With every day that we fail to rise in the opinion polls, the more convincing David Owen's case becomes, for the only convincing answer to the question: 'But look where you are in the polls – you have no chance' is to say 'That depends what the objective is; we may not win the Election, but we can stop either of the others winning, and so moderate their policies at Westminster.'

The crux of the matter, however, is timing; we felt this morning we must try to advance further in our own right, and leave the coalition argument until later in the campaign, maybe the last few days. Fortunately David Owen arrived at the meeting exceptionally relaxed and good humoured, and, while not agreeing with the majority, did not demur from holding back on coalition. He made it clear, however, that he would want to begin to argue the case whole-heartedly fairly soon. Less fortunately, this left inadequate time to beef up Owen's press release. Instead of spelling out the importance of each of the six points, his press release was now brief and bland, and because his heart was not in it, the press conference too, was anti-climatic. Instead of seizing the moment we missed the moment.

The two Johns, Pardoe and Harris, the two Secretary-Generals, Andy and Dick, and I went to breakfast at the Royal Horseguards somewhat depressed. No one felt the press conference had been a success. We were all beginning to feel that our failure to unite around a message that the two Davids passionately believed in was becoming a major obstacle. We rehearsed the arguments about coalition a second time. We then went to the APG at 10.15 and rehearsed them a third time. John P. said that we had a PEB on Wednesday, and some money to spend on advertising, and only a few days left, and we had to decide whether we were (a) concentrating on Owen's six points, (b) running a campaign based on changing the system, or (c) stressing the power of the Alliance – its ability to control and limit the excesses of the other parties – coalition.

Paul Tyler argued that if by the middle of the week the polls were edging in the right direction, the coalition case could be credible. But if we were stuck at our present level, it would be incredible. It would sound so much more convincing from a party rising in the polls. Andy Ellis remained opposed to heavily promoting coalition. It raised questions about uncertainty in government; and it dragged us into discussion about with whom we would deal and on what basis.

John Harris' worry about coalition was that people would not see it as a likely outcome on the basis of the current polls. 'It won't happen so what are they going on about?' For that reason it was better to stress our own distinctive message.

Polly Toynbee argued that coalition, partnership, balanced and moderate programmes drawing on the best of the other parties as well as our own, was what the Alliance was about – the end to extremism and the beginning of people working together. All of this was summed up in the coalition argument.

I felt at the end of the meeting that while there was a consensus for not promoting coalition at this point, there was still an understanding that it was a question of timing, not of principle.

Labour's attacks on the Prime Minister and her Cabinet continued. Neil Kinnock described Thatcher as 'the would-be empress who wants to go on and on' and her Cabinet as 'sycophants and doormats'. Denis Healey said that it was fair to compare her with Genghis Khan 'because she has done to British industry what Genghis Khan did to the population of Central Asia'.

David Owen joined in when speaking in Oxford, saying that the University's refusal to award her an hononary doctorate had been a calculated insult – 'the only way it could make known its repugnance for the contempt in which education has been held by her'.

Kenneth Baker replied that Labour leaders were introducing the 'language of hate' to the campaign. The attacks on the Prime Minister added up to concerted villification. Showing he was a competent mud-slinger himself, Baker charged that eighteen out of twenty-one members of Neil Kinnock's Shadow Cabinet had the advantage of selective grammar school or private school education. 'Ninety per cent of the Shadow Cabinet benefited from a system which they now want to deny to everybody else. What a bunch of sanctimonious hypocrites they are.'

The Tories also launched into Labour's manifesto as a 'jobs destruction package', alleging that it would throw at least a million people out of work. A national minimum wage would cost 600,000 jobs as the low-paid were priced out of work, and scrapping nuclear weapons, phasing out atomic power, imposing sanctions on South Africa, and squeezing the private health and education sectors would swell the dole queues by another 400,000. Bryan Gould replied that the Tories wanted to pursue a low wage, low productivity economy. He claimed that phasing in a national minimum wage would have a positive effect on unemployment because employers, unable to fall back on 'scrapheap labour at scrapheap prices', would be forced to become more productive and competitive.

This evening I travelled to Southampton and back to do a television programme. I am now afraid (and I hope I am proved unnecessarily pessimistic) that we are already seeing the results of the Election in the polls. This is not entirely our own fault; the Tories began from a position of considerable electoral strength, and Labour are running a superbly professional campaign. These are dramatically different circumstances than, for instance, surrounded the Greenwich by-election or, for that matter, that have existed nationally for most of the year. We are, however, paying a price for the lack of a clear strategy, and also for the structure of the organisation. We suffer from the mechanism for reaching decisions. We only see the Leaders briefly in the mornings, and much of that time is taken up with discussion of the morning press conference. This would not matter if decision-making was fully delegated, and its implementation properly integrated, so that the two Leaders were spearheading a well-coordinated campaign, operating to clear daily objectives. As it is, we meet in London to discuss the campaign, while the Leaders are already on the road, decisions about what they will say being taken by themselves and their own travelling team, or speech writers in their own offices in London. It's as if there are two election campaigns – one run from Cowley Street, and one run from a couple of buses at opposite ends of the country. This would be bad enough if there was one leader who had a rough idea what he was doing; but two leaders thinking aloud on two different buses in two different parts of the country is a recipe for disaster. It's driving the APG mad with frustration; we all fix a line in the morning and then turn on the television set at lunchtime or in the evening and sometimes can hardly believe our ears. John Pardoe says that if any of us survive for another General Election, we'll be on the bus, and we'll leave the journalists at headquarters. More jocularly (but only fractionally so) he told David Steel's plain clothes policeman, 'don't worry about protecting him from the gunmen; it's the journalists you have to keep away!'

———————————

There was better news when I arrived at Cowley Street around midnight. A Marplan poll showed we had moved up a point over the past week, while Labour had fallen back two points. This is the kind of movement we need. The Tories, however, have also moved up one.

The Marplan poll also shows that some 20% are undecided, and that figure does not take into account the 'soft' Labour and Tory votes.

Tuesday, June 2 (P-9)

> '*I said on television the other night I thought this campaign was the dirtiest of all and that is still my view.*'
>
> Edward Heath

We had a sparkling press conference this morning. Polly had organised an impressive set, with photographs of women candidates behind the speakers. With the two Davids were Nancy Sear, Shirley Williams, and Rosie Barnes. Nancy was in terrific form. When the veteran *Evening Standard* journalist Robert Carvel made a joke about the good-looking women in the photographs, and asked how many women candidates the Alliance had, Nancy replied, 'You're a bit old for 105 of them, Robert.' The presentation of women's issues did well on television throughout the day.

At last a strategy is beginning to emerge. David Owen's list of themes has now been divided on the lines suggested by Alec McGivan in his memo to the Campaign Committee – under 'Head and Heart'.

The suggestion is that if you vote Conservative to maintain a nuclear defence, strengthen the police to deal with crime, and control the trade unions, you could be voting with your head, but not with your heart. You would be voting out of fear. If you vote for Labour to cut hospital waiting lists, to improve schools, and to deal with unemployment, you would be voting with your heart but not your head – you would be voting for a party that would be incapable of delivering the goods. But with the Alliance, you could have both those sets of policies – you could be voting with head *and* heart.

We have decided also to develop the idea of the 'supervote', an idea that originated with David Penhaligon; how extraordinary that six months after his death he should be one of the authors of one of our closing themes for the General Election.

What is clear is that the two Leaders are happy with this theme; thus there is a real chance of disciplining them to stick with it. We plan to take advertising in the national newspapers to develop it further and to stress it in the final PEB.

David Owen ran into trouble today. Speaking in King's Lynn, he said, 'Voters, in voting for us, have a unique, perhaps never-to-occur-again opportunity.' It was picked up as suggesting that the Alliance could not survive failure.

'Alliance may not get another chance – Owen' was the headline in the PA report. In fact, when you read the PA report more closely it did not justify the headline, for it faithfully described a subsequent conversation with journalists. Asked about the now-or-never implications of his speech, he said, 'I don't say it'll never exist again, but it perhaps could be unique where you have this combination of a strong third force and unpopular Conservative and unpopular Labour parties.' If the Alliance failed to achieve the balance of power this time, it might have to drop its mould-breaking stance and settle for being in second place behind the Tories in a two-party system. It could take the place of a fragmented Labour Party.

He then went on to deny the Alliance 'had had it' if it failed to achieve a balance of power this time. 'No, I don't think we've had it,' he said. 'I'm always slightly reticent about saying this is the only opportunity you will ever have or that this is the most important election.'

———————

Tonight the Tories launched an attack on Labour's links with the trade unions. The Prime Minister argued that Labour would restore unrestrained union power by repealing the Tories' trade union reforms. It would mean the return to mass picketing, the enforced closed shop, and violence at the factory gates, with workers being spat at, stoned and victimised.

She said her union reforms had transformed a lame duck economy into a bulldog economy but under Labour the prosperity would vanish like a dream and the nightmare would return. 'Restore union power, as Labour wants, and production lines would grind to a halt, orders would be lost, investment plans would be cancelled, foreigners could no longer rely on prompt delivery of our goods. We would cease to pay our way in the world.'

The *Daily Mail* headline: 'Thatcher's warning to Britain — the tyrants are waiting!'

Kenneth Clarke, her Employment Minister, accused Labour of keeping trade union leaders hidden away during the campaign. 'No leading Labour Party member has appeared with a trade union leader in public throughout this campaign. The big names in the trade union movement have paid into party funds and then vanished from the scene in the hope of a Labour victory to return their old power to them.'

———————

Tonight David Owen went to Islington where George Cunningham and Chris Smith are locked in a battle that the pollsters are finding too close to call. It was the first real old-style political meeting of the election campaign ... with all the drama of hecklers, and a speaker fighting back from the platform. David O. launched a ferocious attack on the 'loony left' — in Islington there were large numbers of Labour people who 'despise, detest and condemn' what is going on in the Borough. The best case for proportional representation was to end extremism in local government. But the Tories were happy to live with the extremist left. 'They like having the lethal left as their target. They like them to be mad-hat, lethal or lunatic.'

At last, confronted with the hecklers and in the atmosphere of the meeting, we saw the kind of passion and power that we had been crying out for in the speeches of the Leaders.

In the early evening David Steel relaxed in his armchair in his Leader's office at the House of Commons and talked to Peter Jenkins and Antony Bevins of the *Independent* about what would happen if parliament was hung by a mathematical freak. He replied that he would not even attempt to negotiate a coalition. 'One of the reasons for the Lib-Lab Pact rather than any attempt to form a coalition at the time was because you need a minimum number of MPs before you can contemplate taking part in a coalition ... I wouldn't like to put a precise figure on it, but I'm talking in terms of 40 or 50, rather than a dozen. So getting the balance of power by an arithmetical fluke with a small number of MPs is not a happy situation, and I frankly don't think that is going to happen, because that presupposes a scale of Labour recovery which I don't think is there. It is not there at this stage of the campaign, and I don't see how the Labour campaign is going to produce it between now and polling day ... but if Labour does manage to close the gap and there is a slender majority, or a hung parliament, the Alliance holding the balance with a small number of seats, I would see that as a mathematical freak ... I would be acutely disappointed ... I don't think we should realistically contemplate negotiations at all in those circumstances. I think that supporting a government with the present number of MPs would be extremely difficult. I don't rule it out if we were invited so to do, but I certainly don't think it would be our top consideration.'

Afterwards I had the welcome chance of a dinner with David Steel in the Dolphin Square restaurant. He looked in surprisingly good shape, although disturbed that once more he had little coverage on television today. I stressed that we needed stronger speeches and more pressure on the news programmes to cover them.

He remains optimistic: 'There are only nine days left – it's still all to play for.'

I asked him how he saw the state of the campaign. 'Well, it still looks good in a lot of our hopeful seats, our target seats . . . but it's bad elsewhere. Given that the Tories will probably win, we could end up with about 25% of the popular vote or even a little less . . . but a handful of extra seats . . . I would settle for that.'

He acknowledged that we needed the campaign to be more upbeat, optimistic, and exciting. Above all, we needed to be winning over Labour tactical votes everywhere. We could only do that by making it clear that we were anti-Thatcher. 'What it needs is for David Owen to say that there is an anti-Thatcher majority out there, and that he is part of it.'

———————————

There's been an interesting *Newsnight* poll tonight. It's a survey of sixty constituencies, all of them marginals. It shows that Tory support is unchanged from when they last did it nearly two weeks back at 40%. Labour have moved up to 35% and we've fallen two points to 23%. In 1983 the Tories polled 44.5% in the same 60 seats, Labour 27.1%, and the Alliance 26.7%

Undoubtedly on these figures a balance of power cannot be ruled out. (This afternoon rumours of the polls started to circulate in the City and there was a sudden plunge in share prices.)

There's a disturbing poll from Scotland that shows we have slipped and the Scottish Nationalists are moving up.

We're still waiting on good news – the beginning of the surge.

Wednesday, June 3 (P-8)

> '*Labour voters . . . need to know that they are not going to wake up next morning and find we have climbed into bed with Mrs Thatcher.*'
>
> David Steel.

This was the day when I came to the conclusion we should never, ever fight another election with two leaders. Politics is complicated enough, without having to live with the risk of putting *four* feet in it ...

David Owen began by having to repair any damage done yesterday. His comments in East Anglia received a mixed press. The *Independent* made it their front page headline: 'Owen describes Election as Alliance's last chance' and the *Daily Express* splashed it as 'A desperate measure'. On the other hand, the *Daily Telegraph* interpreted it entirely differently: 'David Owen yesterday seized triumphantly on an opinion poll which he said pointed to the possibility of a hung parliament. He urged people to throw their support behind the Alliance and take a perhaps unique opportunity to break the two-party mould in British politics.'

With David Steel appearing live on BBC's *Election Call*, Owen had the press conference to himself, and handled the questions comfortably. He denied that he had talked about a 'last chance' and said his reference to a 'unique opportunity' was justified by the rarity of electors choosing between an unpopular Government party, an unpopular Opposition, and a rising third force. Asked about the limit of his ambitions, he said that while he would like the Alliance to be the largest party in the House of Commons, realistically this was unlikely; to achieve a power-sharing government would, in fact, be winning.

No sooner had he defused that particular one, than David Steel, speaking on *Election Call*, lit the fuse of another controversy. Asked whether he would back Mrs Thatcher in a hung parliament, he replied, 'I find it unimaginable that there would be any circumstance in which a minority government led by Mrs Thatcher could be sustained in office by us. Her whole style and the nature of her policies is one which would not lead to the kind of compromise, the kind of search for consensus, the wider agreements, the healing of wounds that is required in this country. She would be disqualified for a whole range of reasons from leading such a government.'

This appeared to go beyond the declared position that, while we found it unimaginable that Mrs Thatcher would *want* to stay on, we would negotiate with the Leader of whichever party had the most seats in the House of Commons. It implied that we would disqualify her, instead of she disqualifying herself.

He was questioned further by journalists on tour with him, and he maintained, and even strengthened this line. She would have lost the confidence of the country and in those circumstances she would not be the right person to lead the new government. She had never shown the slightest intention of dealing with problems such as unemployment and electoral reform which concerned the Alliance.

David Owen, who had always argued that it was not for one party to choose the leader of another, initially responded to questions by saying he refused to discuss personalities or choose other party leaders, insisting that the real issue was forming a government on agreed policies. He acknowledged that David Steel had more determined views on Mrs Thatcher than he, but stuck to the party line that it was very hard to conceive, it was unimaginable, that Mrs Thatcher would want to serve in a coalition having lost a majority of 144 seats and having had her own way for eight years.

This was beginning to look like a split. The two talked on their mobile telephones and when they met in Nottingham issued a joint statement:

'The question of how we will use the balance of power is now fast moving up the agenda of this election. It is a relatively new political concept for many and we, unlike Mrs Thatcher or Mr Kinnock, are ready to tell the electorate where we stand.

'We are ready to negotiate with either the Labour or the Conservative Party and we will talk first to whichever has the largest number of MPs. We are not in the business of propping up either Mr Kinnock or Mrs Thatcher and if they are not ready to listen to reason, if they are not ready to take account of the judgement of the voters, then let their parties find other leaders who are ready.

'We are not in the business of choosing the leader of another political party. But nor are we in the business of negotiating with a leader that stubbornly refuses to change policies that the voters have rejected or are not supported by a majority of the electorate.

'If the Labour Party has the largest number of MPs, we will

talk to them first. But there is no way that we would form a coalition government with them if they demand that Polaris be decommissioned and the United States be kicked out of nuclear bases in this country.

'If the Conservative Party have the largest number of MPs we will talk to them first. But there is no way that we would form a coalition government with them if they demand that their economic policy remain unchanged and refuse to substantially reduce unemployment.'

But in answering questions David Steel continued to take a tougher line. He dismissed the idea that Thatcher would stay on in these circumstances as 'wonderland' but said that if she did 'one of the things we would have to make clear to her is that she has been rejected by the British people. She is not the most suitable person to head up a new government. People will have voted for a change of government and you can't simply re-run the Thatcher government after that.'

According to a number of newspaper reports, David at one point actually said 'I would refuse to serve under her.'

In the meantime, Neil Kinnock was rubbishing the idea of a post-election deal. He said in Bristol 'there will be no deal, no horse-trading, no cooperation which involved them in any way'. He also attempted to exploit the differences on Thatcher.

Determined to attract tactical voters from the Labour Party, David Steel continued his assault on Thatcher at the 'Ask the Alliance' rally in Nottingham: 'Extremes meet. Arthur Scargill and Margaret Thatcher have a lot in common. They both want to go on and on, and on, in office. They both believe in their divine right not to negotiate with their colleagues, let alone their critics. They both prefer confrontation to compromise, whatever the cost to their country. They are both shrill to denounce rather than calm to consider a problem. And they have both left a trail of destruction behind them in their own organisation: Mr Scargill in the National Union of Mineworkers and Mrs Thatcher in the Conservative Party.

'Nottingham miners rightly said enough is enough and refused to put up with "King" Arthur's authoritarianism any longer. It is time too for the many caring Conservatives, worried by the authoritarianism of Mrs Thatcher, to stand up and be counted, while they still have voices on the Tory Front Bench.

'After all, they do not have much to lose. Mrs Thatcher is ruthless in rejecting people whose faces don't fit ...

'This is serious for British parliamentary democracy. The very word "parliament" derives from the French word *parler* – to speak. Democracy depends on dialogue, but Mrs Thatcher does not speak to persuade, she shouts to dominate. Mrs Thatcher believes in monologue not dialogue.

'The result is a more and more divided Britain – Britain where the spirit of Scargillism is positively encouraged.

'We shall not rebuild British industry by re-establishing the abuse of mass picketing, which the Labour Party proposes. But neither shall we heal our country's wounds by continuing to exalt division as a way of life, which is what Mrs Thatcher does: division between classes; division between regions; division between rival dogmatisms; division between political parties even when agreement between them could be achieved. A sharply divided rather than a balanced Parliament whatever the votes of the electorate show the British people want. The Conservative leader has a great liking for division. It is time people woke up as to why. She likes to divide because it makes it easier for her to rule.'

Earlier in Chelmsford, David Steel had equated Thatcher and Lawson with 'drug-pushers' for the way they promoted consumer credit: 'Mrs Thatcher preaches the Victorian values of "honest money" and "good housekeeping" in keeping tight control of the government's borrowing. But she turns a blind eye to the huge rise in plastic card borrowing. The reasons are obvious. With industrial investment still 15% below the 1979 level, any recovery in the economy has depended on stimulating consumer spending with more and more injections of credit. The trouble is that, like heroin addicts, the consumers are taking more and more when the doses are already at a critical level. Total consumer debt has soared from 9 billion pounds in 1979 to almost 31 billion by 1986. In the first three months of this year, it has risen even further, with plastic card addicts paying interest rates so high that the Office of Fair Trading has stepped in. The fact is the consumer credit boom is out of control . . . under the Tories, more and more people are now hooked on monthly credit injections. The real culprits are the pushers, Mrs Thatcher and Mr Lawson, who have created an economy kept alive by short term fixes while industrial investment suffers.'

All of this led maximum television exposure for David Steel throughout the day and evening, and must have done much to lift Liberal spirits, for David Owen had dominated the bulletins over the last couple of days.

Those bulletins led tonight with news of a major Gallup poll that showed the Election getting closer. Conservatives were on 40.5%, Labour within four points at 36.5%, and we were up from the 18% in the equivalent poll last week to 21.5%. Despite the fact this was balanced by a NOP poll of marginals showing Conservative 43%, Labour 34%, and Alliance 20%, the Gallup poll revived talk of a balance of power, setting the scene for David Owen's party political broadcast on television.

Like the Steel one last Friday it consisted entirely of Owen talking, but whereas Steel spoke to camera, Owen was clearly talking to an unheard and unseen interviewer. The tougher style contrasted well with Steel's, and it was also upbeat in tone. He began by making it clear that no one would win, if either the Tories or Labour achieved a majority. 'If Mrs Thatcher wins, unemployment will stay far too high. This country will remain divided between north and south; between those who are in a job and those who are out of a job. The health service would be neglected, some of our best scientists would leave the country, and we would end up worse off, poorer and more divided than we've ever been before.' If Kinnock won the Election, it would deeply damage the defences of the country. 'It will make us a tragic laughing stock of the world . . . we will be felt to have acted totally out of character. It is out of character for this country to be unilaterist; to abandon its responsibilities.' It would also be a country which would be giving too much power to the trade unions, in which there would be at least a hundred Members of Parliament from the hard left, who loathed the police, did not really believe in civil liberties, and were prepared to trample on people, who wanted the power of the state to grow. 'If you really care about this country, the national health service and education, you shouldn't have to vote Labour and then have to accept unilaterism, anti-police attitudes, and reversing the legislation over the trade unions.' He didn't see why people should have to have this choice. It was the old politics. They could have something different, something better. 'All they've got to have is the confidence, the courage if you like, the conviction to vote for what they want. That means voting for the Alliance, letting the Alliance in and forming a coalition government in which the Alliance voice is strong.' He listed the priorities we had decided to promote: dealing with unemployment, education, law and order, trade unions, the health service, and defence, and said that we wouldn't enter a coalition unless these were on the agenda. He concluded that people had not yet really realised the potential. 'It's already clear that a quarter, and probably a third, are ready to vote for the Alliance. Vote for us and you'd be surprised at what could be achieved. Trust us and you'd be amazed at what we can do.'

The effect of all this is that a hung parliament is now firmly on the election agenda, and the possibility, and the permutations are likely to dominate the next few days.

Thursday, June 4 (P-7)

'*I pay insurance to enable me to go into hospital on the day I want, at the time I want, under the doctor I want.*'

Margaret Thatcher

The *Independent*'s headline is 'Alliance split over coalition with Thatcher'. There are other similar ones.

These disunity stories will not help; on the other hand, I

suspect Steel knows what he is doing. As he said to me at dinner, the message is coming to him loud and clear that, particularly in Scotland and the North, Thatcher's unpopularity is a major factor; if our candidates there are to win over the soft Labour vote, we must not be seen to be identified with her. My guess is he would rather risk a few 'rift' headlines than fail to achieve a clear distinction in peoples' minds between Thatcher-led Tories and the Alliance.

Hugo Young, in his column in the *Guardian* this morning, has identified a growing problem, namely that with the Tories and Labour so polarised, and with Labour so much stronger than in 1983, the Election is beginning to have a two-party look about it and that this is reinforced by the television coverage, because television thrives on the head-on clash.

'This apparent yearning, throughout the political system and perhaps in the very psyche of the British, to replicate the two-party model has also been noticeable especially in the second half of the campaign, in the television news coverage. I've seen half a dozen items in the last few days in which the Alliance contribution has looked like an after thought. Especially when their spokesmen are beamed down the line from some celtic fringe, the interviewer, suddenly recalling a statutory duty, drags them in to break up the real argument in the studio. So the Alliance has become marginalised.'

We are facing a real danger of a squeeze, and we've also been a little unlucky. For instance, we had planned to deal with trade unions at our press conference this morning, but have missed yesterday's main clash between the two parties on the issue. Now they are moving onto health today, while we appear to be tagging behind on yesterday's issue.

Unfortunately, too, our 'moles' at the Labour and Conservative press conferences report that Labour have scored a direct hit on the Prime Minister on the subject of health. It all arose from a superb piece of campaigning by Labour. First, they had Kinnock having breakfast at a hospital, talking to nurses. Then they produced a ten-year-old boy whose admission to hospital last Monday for open-heart surgery they claimed had been cancelled because of Tory health cuts. Mark Burgess promptly became one of the personalities of the Election, making widespread television appearances, and having his photograph in all the newspapers.

At their press conference Kinnock and Michael Meacher savaged the Tory record on health. It so happened that Norman Fowler was due at the Tory Party press conference to talk about the elderly, and he and Thatcher found themselves on the defensive. Instead of immediately responding sympathetically and saying she would look into the case, she began aggressively talking about the million cases the NHS was dealing with every week, and pointing out (rightly) that she could not possibly run every hospital. She eventually said that 'we'll have a look at it, of course we will, because anyone who has a child in that condition will be almost desperate if they cannot get treatment.' But it was a bit late.

Things went from bad to worse for her. She was questioned about her use of private health care and launched into a powerful defence. 'I, along with something like five million other people, do insure to enable me to go into hospital on the day I want, at the time I want and with the doctor I want. And for me that is absolutely vital ... I exercise my right as a free citizen to spend my own money in my own way, so that I can go on the day, the time, to the doctor I choose and get out fast.'

Things now went from worse to even worse. She went on to say that of course 'the day may come when we have to have a very, very complicated operation. I hope it never happens, but if it does, I'm afraid that one could not, of course, possibly bear that on private insurance.'

It was clear from the television pictures that Norman Tebbit, sitting beside her, was hating every minute of it, and rightly so, because it came across dreadfully on television.

We were all quick to follow up. David Owen labelled her 'the Marie Antoinette of British politics'. Owen said 'She behaves as if you have to be richly sick in this country. She tells us the NHS is safe in her hands and then goes on to take her own operations out of the health service and have them privately.' That was no way to lead the country, 97% of whom used the NHS family practitioner service. The health service was one of the most unifying forces in Britain.

There is no question that Labour will now make a real issue of this. At their press conference yesterday they not only promised significant cuts in prescription charges and an annual 3% increase in health service spending in real terms, but said that pay beds in NHS hospitals would be gradually phased out and consultants and surgeons on full health service salaries would have to spend less of their time on private work. The private health sector would face strict regulation.

Labour tonight repeated the Kinnock party political broadcast, claiming that it was by public demand.

Bryan May has defected to the Labour Party. He has written an article for the *Guardian* saying that it was David Owen's warmongering jibe that Britons' preferred 'the sandbag to the windbag' – a reference to Neil Kinnock, that had finally caused his outrage to overflow. Owen's remark, says May, is 'transparent electioneering on a matter of such grave importance.' I'm afraid May completely misreads Owen. Whatever you may say about his emphasis on defence in this election, it is not electioneering; he feels as strongly as May, but on the other side of the argument.

Graham Watson has written some fighting stuff for David Steel's speech in Newcastle tonight: 'Nowhere is the failure of Thatcherism more apparent than in the north of England and here in the north-east in particular. Unemployment is an unacceptable 17% higher than in any other region. One in five of those unmployed in the north have now been out of work for over three years. And youth unemployment continues to rise faster than the expansion of the youth training scheme. Do you hear that, Mrs Thatcher? Do you see that, Lord Young? Can you imagine what that feels like, Mr Tebbit? Of course you can't, because your policies towards the north-east have been a crude economic version of the three wise monkeys: you hear no unemployment, you see no unemployment, and you speak no unemployment.'

David Steel was involved in a hard-hitting interview with David Dimbleby on the *Nine O'Clock News*. Asked if he would never serve under Thatcher, he said he would never use the word 'never' but that it was unimaginable. 'If she had lost the election, she would be unqualified and almost definitely would not wish to continue. She would have lost the election. She would go. You must give Mrs Thatcher some credit — she's a democrat.'

Friday, June 5 (P-6)

> '*As I understand it, the right to choose is the essence of Christianity.*'
>
> Margaret Thatcher

Encouraged by the APG, John Pardoe read the riot act to the two Leaders this morning. 'I don't care what you say, as long as you're both saying the same thing,' he said. The Leaders were asked if it was necessary to do so much briefing of journalists on the campaign buses. They appeared to think it was, although it was clear their colleagues around the table did not share the view.

———————————

A Marplan poll shows the Conservatives steady at 44, Labour up two to 34, a full ten points behind, and ourselves on 20, down one, not before the City had apparently gone mad with billions of pounds wiped off share values and a fall in sterling because of rumours yesterday that Marplan would show a cut in the Tory lead to two points.

———————————

Geoffrey Smith in *The Times* talks of the problems in promoting constitutional reform. 'Its constitutional proposals seem arid when set out as simple propositions. They have totally failed to capture the imagination of the country. To have stood a chance of doing so they needed to be presented in a broader context.

Specific reforms needed to be related to the concentration of power and secrecy in government which then needed to be related to the quality of decision-making, which in turn needed to be related to economic performance and the quality of social services.

'It is not a train of thought which can easily be presented in one minute on television. The line of argument may reasonably be disputed. But the very nature of the appeal required a thoughtful campaign.'

Not even the 'Ask the Alliance' sessions helped to develop an argument. 'That would require a series of major speeches, which would lead less time for competing in purely media events. But while the Alliance is not good enough at the new style of electioneering, it has not dared to put its faith in the old style.'

I think we did make a serious mistake in choosing to repeat the 1983 formula. If Labour have captured the attention of the anti-Thatcher majority, it is because they have been crusading with vigour and spectacle; we are simply being drowned out. We needed to develop our arguments in big speeches, with passion and enthusiasm. It's not enough for the Leaders to come back and tell us how well they are being received on the ground, or talk of the warmth of their reception: the country has to see it on television. But Geoffrey Smith is wrong to suggest that it is the format of our campaign that has made our distinctive policies on constitutional reform a loser; since the week of the phoney war we have not attempted to promote them at all. We conceded defeat on them as an electoral asset from the start.

I know we're all trying to capture the high moral ground, but Margaret Thatcher went over the top today, linking the Conservative Party with Christianity. Speaking on Jimmy Young's radio show she said. 'The essence of human rights is that each person can choose, choose between right and wrong. Choice is the essence of morality. It is the essence of religion. If you are to take away so much in tax that people don't have a choice, to take away from them responsibility for their families and their children. I would say that was the immoral route. And as I understand it, the right to choose is the essence of Christianity.'

The Bishop of Manchester is quoted in the *Independent* as saying 'the heart of Christianity is the ability to love, including loving our neighbours. Most people don't have the power to choose.'

Labour are now so confident that they have established themselves as the opposition that are appealing to Alliance supporters to desert. At this morning's press conference Kinnock said. 'Many know by now that a vote for the SDP, the Liberals, Nationalist and other minor parties would be simply a wasted vote. It would be a vote that would divide the anti-Conservative majority and bring the result which all of those non-Conservatives most want to avoid.'

David Steel has apparntly been maintaining his line on a deal with Thatcher. According to Allan Travis of the *Guardian* he said on the bus that the joint statement of he and David Owen on Wednesday night was 'a little weak'. Confronted in the street by a student who challenged him directly on whether he would work with Thatcher, he replied 'No, I wouldn't.

It's all getting terribly confusing. Because according to other reporters, he said, 'I cannot say that there are absolutely no circumstances ever in creation when Mrs Thatcher and I would be in the same government. Let's live in the world of political reality – it isn't going to happen and I'm not going to be part of a Thatcher government.'

I know what he is trying to convey – that he finds the idea of Thatcher wanting to continue if she loses her majority of 144 as inconceivable; but its coming across in a very confused way. Is it deliberate? Is he trying to counter-balance the Owen–Thatcher factor? I think so.

The Tories have now launched themselves on a wholesale attack on Labour's tax plans, one made easier by some confusion within the Labour leadership. Labour is being reticent about the detail of its proposals, and actually excluded from its manifesto one or two of its policies, including abolition of the ceiling on national insurance contributions and the abolition of the married man's allowance, and this has enabled the Tories to talk about a conver up.

Roy Hattersley has admitted that there are 'no easy answers' to who will gain and lose under the party's proposals.

Neil Kinnock appeared to admit that anyone earning more than £15,000 could be worse off under their proposals, but Bryan Gould subsequently stated 'an intention of our radical restructuring will be to ensure that there is no significant group outside the richest 5% whose tax burden will rise.'

The Tories promise to return to this over the weekend.

It is now clear that we are about to see an unprecedented advertising blitz. The Tories are spending millions, taking page after page in the same newspapers, to hammer home the theme that 'Britain is great again — don't let Labour wreck it'. Labour are also planning a savage advertising campaign intended to expose uncaring Thatcherism. Even we plan to join in, with a pitiful £250,000 compared with their millions, our theme will be that you can now vote with head *and* heart'.

Saturday, June 6 (P-5)

> '*Any reading of the polls now suggests that the*
> *Conservatives are on course for victory. Any rational*
> *person would say that.*'
>
> David Steel

John Pardoe rang me at home with news of the three big opinion polls to be published tomorrow. There is some cause for optimism. Gallup has the Conservatives on 41.5, Labour 34.5, and the Alliance 22.5 — no change from last week. Marplan has the Tories up one to 43, Labour steady on 32, and the Alliance up one to 23.

Harris has the Conservatives up three to 44, Labour down four to 33, and the Alliance steady on 21.

John has been comparing these with the same polls on the same Sunday before the 1983 General Election, and the comparison is fascinating – we are up half a point of Gallup compared with our position on this day in 1983, down one on Marplan, and down two on Harris.

But, averaging out the polls, we are only one point lower than we were on this day in 1983. And that is well within the margin of error.

While the chances of improving on our 1983 popular vote are not good, we could now equal it.

We decided John should talk it up and create an 'Alliance set to move . . .' atmosphere around the campaign.

Week Four

Sunday, June 7 (P-4)

> *'There are only four more days of hope-destroying, unemploying, care-cutting, factory-shutting, nation-splitting, poor-hitting, truth-mangling, freedom-strangling Toryism left to go.'*
>
> Neil Kinnock

All the papers are predicting a comfortable Tory win, but the Alliance is not completely written-off. The *Sunday Times* reports that 'the Alliance rose strongly in 1983 from a not dissimilar base five days from polling' but it qualifies this by noting that in 1983 we hit a rising trend, benefiting from a collapsing Labour campaign.

The *Sunday Telegraph* draws the conclusion from its Gallup poll that the Alliance campaign has been the only one to have created an overall favourable impression during the past week. 'The Alliance is locked in the 21–24% bracket. It could poll at the top end of that bracket, if only because second-placed Alliance candidates will be doing their utmost to squeeze weak, third-placed Labour candidates in the last three days of the campaign.'

That newspaper also says that at the outset Mrs Thatcher wanted the polls to show the Conservatives at 40% or more before she went to the country; since May 13 there have been 30 national polls, and every one had shown the Tories at 40.5–45%.

It argues that one of the effects of Labour's advance being halted is that more people may vote tactically; 'there may be a few spectacular anti-Conservative constituency results'.

Unfortunately the most pessimistic voice has been that of David Steel, whose comment yesterday that 'any reading of the polls now suggests that the Conservatives are on course for victory. Any rational person would say that', may indeed be rational, but was hardly wise. Though he qualified this pessimism, there are vultures out there waiting to swoop on any single word that can be taken out of context to our disadvantage. Thus, the *Mail on Sunday's* front page claims 'Despair for Alliance as Steel says: Maggie's the winner!' and the *Sunday Telegraph* has a story in bold type headlined 'Steel accepts Tory victory'.

Owen is maintaining an upbeat line, attacking 'Doom watchers' who predict we will fail to achieve our final surge and saying 'I'm not going to let the Alliance be written off by all those Fleet Street pundits'.

The *Mail on Sunday* has up to now been fairly sympathetic to us, and its leader is therefore depressing: 'This newspaper has been a consistent supporter of the SDP-Liberal Alliance', it begins, but 'alas, during this election campaign the Alliance has shown that it is not yet fit to govern.'

For me, its main criticism is particularly depressing: 'The Alliance lost confidence in the one policy that separated them from their rivals. What they had to offer was reform – of all of our institutions; reform of the way we are governed; reform of the very essence of parliamentary government.

'No doubt their marketing man told them that the great British public was only interested in issues of unemployment, pensions, the economy and so on.

'But on these issues where it had to compete with Thatcherism and socialism, it made no impact.'

It concludes: 'The Alliance, far from breaking the mould, became just another political party.'

I'm afraid that's fair comment.

We did begin with an emphasis on constitutional reform, literally launching the campaign with the 'Great Reform Charter', but it was hardly mentioned thereafter. It was almost as if we had deliberately got it out of the way so that we could move on to the real issues. I became almost embarrassed to raise it, because it seemed to others that I was promoting a personal hobby-horse in the face of the realism of the polls showing people really care about health, education, unemployment etc. Sarah Horack, our private pollster, more than once suggested that the reform issues should come higher on our agenda, but she too went unheard.

David Abbott, the advertising man, who I felt never got within a hundred miles of what the Alliance is really all about, said from the start that he didn't think people cared about these issues and that he saw no reason to promote them. It is, of course, possible he is right. After all, I have no evidence whatsoever that we would have gained by promoting our fundamental reforms. But the real point is that if we fail at this election while *not* promoting them, we will have lost twice, because we will have lost while fighting on others' terms and won't even have the consolation that we stood up to be counted for what we're really about.

Most of the other leading articles are predictable, with the *Observer* coming down for tactical voting as a way of controlling rampant Thatcherism, and the *Sunday Times* arguing that the rest of the world will think we are mad if we don't return the Conservatives.

All three parties turned on the razamatazz today – Labour and the Conservatives much more effectively than us, but then it's all a question of money!

The Kinnocks were given a terrific reception by a couple of thousand supporters at their show in Islington, but a few hecklers got in and were quickly chucked out. The Tory one at Wembley was almost as repulsive as their one in 1983 – a set of seedy comedians followed by Margaret Thatcher.

Our Leaders travelled up the Thames on a boat, and then addressed an enthusiastic crowd of a few hundred at Richmond.

Thank heavens Owen was still talking up the result — 'This election has a lot of steam in it yet, and the steam and the fire power, and the engine and the drive and the momentum is going to come from the Alliance' — and he also scored with the crowd by saying of the so-called split between the two of them over 'whether or not our dear Prime Minister can listen to anyone else' that 'David thinks she can listen to no one and I don't think she can listen to anyone. On that remarkable difference the BBC and ITN managed to hang a great many newscasting programmes.'

David Steel accused Thatcher of creating an 'apartheid of the pocket'. The Tory manifesto had set out a comprehensive system of separate development. 'Private health schemes, private schools, private transport — the Tories love them all, while those who can't afford them find the public services cut and cut again. The message is clear: if you can pay, then go your separate way. The Prime Minister has created an apartheid of the pocket. There are now two classes of people in this country: the haves and the have nots. Those who count in Tory eyes and those who don't.'

The Tories have launched an onslaught of Labour's tax plans, helped by conflicting promises from Neil Kinnock and Roy Hattersley. Hattersley had been reassuring voters that no individual earning £500 per week (£26,000 per year) or less would lose out as a result of Labour's proposals, but Neil Kinnock appears to have said that people earning more than £300 per week (£15,000 per year) would be affected.

It's clear that there is genuine confusion within the Labour leadership on this, and the Tories are moving in for the kill. Nigel Lawson has said they are 'making up policies as they go along' and Norman Fowler has accused them of 'shiftiness'. Needless to say the Tory papers are hammering Labour: 'Labour's tax plans are beginning to smack of a gigantic hoax', the *Daily Mail*'s front page story begins.

We have now only three campaigning days left. As I drove the Brighton-London road for the last time in this campaign I tried to stand back (if you can do that while you're driving!) and consider our position.

The opinion polls have remained so steady from the day Margaret Thatcher called the Election that it's difficult to hope we are not now looking at the result. I would now happily settle for thirty or more seats and an increase, no matter how small, in our vote, and I think that's still possible.

For all our ups and downs, I think our campaign has finally come together. At last we have both the Leaders and the campaign team committed to a theme; the programme for the last three days is full of variety and the word coming back from the constituencies is still positive.

I wonder, however, whether if we had been more effective, had a more coherent strategy, and even had a bit more luck, it really would have made a lot of difference. I feel there are factors operating out there that are beyond any campaign we could run ... they are to do with self-interest, polarisation, feelings about Thatcher and Kinnock, the alienation of the Scots and the Welsh, and none of them will work for the Alliance.

Monday, June 8 (P-3)

> 'A gondola on the Grand Canal and a serenade by
> President Reagan is no substitute for real leadership
> – her trip is a "one cornetto" publicity stunt.'
>
> David Owen

We took advantage of the morning meeting to spell out in unmistakable terms what we hoped the Leaders would do over the last three days – talk up the result, and go for the moral high ground.

A TV South poll (the same one I was confronted with in Southampton last week) showed we were up seven points and we decided to maximise its propaganda potential.

The difference of opinion over coalition surfaced once more.

The press conference was to be on constitutional reform, and David Owen argued cogently that we really could not keep talking about proportional representation as if it would not lead to coalition. Coalition was an inevitable result of PR, so we should argue the case for it positively. David Steel was still concerned, however, by the negative factor in the marginal seats where we need tactical voting to take place. My guess is the leaders are each going to do their own thing.

Ian Wrigglesworth and Malcolm Bruce made worthy contributions on the chosen theme, the waste of North Sea oil, but once more it was David Owen who seized the moment, talking about the intellectual vandalism of Thatcherism, and arguing that the Election had failed to lift peoples' sights to look to the future, to realise the fundamental and basic neglect of science, research, and education. In how we invested North Sea Oil could be seen the respective values of the different parties. His opportunistic skills are remarkable.

Both the Labour Party and we have been doing our best to mock Thatcher's trip to the Venice summit today. She plans to spend only sixteen hours there, and there's little question that it is being played for its electoral advantages. David Owen had been particularly effective: 'It has been easier to persuade Mrs Thatcher to catch a plane to an international summit than to catch a plane to one of Britain's deprived or depressed regions . . . yet she is one of the least internationalist of the leaders of the Western World.'

Neil Kinnock said she would just have enough time in Venice 'for a sandwich, a sermon, and a photo session'.

Kinnock also talked about the trip providing new meaning to the phrase 'Venetian blind' and Denis Healey talked about her going on the 'Grand Banal'.

The row over Labour's tax plans hotted up still further today with Nigel Lawson accusing Roy Hattersley of 'lying through his teeth'.

Neil Kinnock replied that he did not believe Mrs Thatcher's denials about extensions of VAT. When asked if there were any other matters he did not take the Prime Minister's word on, he replied 'we have only got the rest of the day.'

I'm convinced these bruising attacks on Labour over tax are doing as much damage to them as their problems on defence, and as much as the Tories suffered over the health service.

Labour at least now appears to have united around its claim that there would be no losers on incomes around £500 a week. It believes that it can achieve this by the redistribution of 3.6 billion pounds raised from the richest 5%. Labour will not, however, say how it would achieve this income. 'We can raise 3.6 billion from that group of tax payers with a range of different measures, which we are certainly not going to alert them to, given their proclivities for evasion,' Bryan Gould said.

Tonight I went to Greenwich to speak at Rosie Barnes' last meeting. David Owen had arranged to come for the opening twenty minutes, mainly to make a speech that would catch the evening television bulletins, and as a result of a misunderstanding, was left walking up and down in the street outside the hall while Rosie and I were chatting at headquarters. We entered the hall to enthusiastic cheering. It was a typical Owen performance. Uncompromising, rambling, at times brilliant and at times boring. He was at his best when sticking to the theme – 'you can vote for the Alliance with head and heart.'

Rosie's performance was formidable. Referring to Labour's tendency to describe it as 'their seat' she told the audience 'this seat belongs to the people of Greenwich and they will give it where they will'. She talked about people wanting practical solutions to practical problems – solutions that would work.

She was particularly effective on education – 'there is nothing wrong with the intellect of our children – there is something very wrong with their education'.

She has an extraordinary capacity to strike home with telling phrases, while never indulging in rhetoric.

Her supporters clearly love her.

But sitting at the back was a small woman, I should think about sixty, who rose to ask whether Labour was telling the truth when it said that Rosie had missed a number of vital votes in the House of Commons.

Uncharacteristically, Rosie began her reply by listing figures for votes that Neil Kinnock and others had missed. The woman was on her feet like a prosecuting attorney: 'I'm asking about you – not them – you.'

Rosie then replied that she had come to the House of Commons near the end of a parliament, and had inherited a vast number of constituency problems. She would always spend a lot of her time in the constituency – she had no intention of hanging around the House of Commons just to cast a vote in the face of a Tory majority of 140.

'This is just waffle,' shouted the woman. She was now doing some real damage, but, fortunately for Rosie, she then stormed out of the hall, thus losing whatever moral advantage she had in the argument.

I was particularly struck by this exchange, because it illustrates a real problem. With so few MPs, it is crazy that they should become prisoners of House of Commons procedures. We need them out in the country campaigning, and we need to use them selectively in the House of Commons, not demand of them that they try to shadow more than a hundred ministers and junior ministers. It makes no sense to have Rosie Barnes pinned down at the House of Commons night after night in order to maintain a meaningless voting record when she could be out speaking for the Alliance, or working in her constituency.

The trouble is that come election time, these voting records can be embarrassing, especially if circulated to every household by your opponents, and it is difficult to reply effectively to charges of negligence. The only solution is for the parliamentary party to announce and make a virtue of the fact that it only intends to vote when it really matters, or on a number of stated priority issues.

Tuesday, June 9 (P-2)

> *'You brought me in here to talk about the summit and you decided to talk about my wife.'*
>
> Denis Healey

This morning I found myself sitting between the TV AM presenter Anne Diamond and Denis Healey discussing the Venice summit when she suddenly asked the old entertainer to comment on a story in the *Sun* that his wife Edna had once had a private hip operation.

After explaining the circumstances, he suddenly became heated, accusing her of a classic dirty trick, and asking her where she planned to have her baby. She replied she was not a politician, and Healey said that his wife was not a politician either.

The row continued for some minutes, with Michael Heseltine and I as open-mouthed witnesses, and when there was a commercial break Healey stood up and said to her, 'You're a shit!' He repeated it, and after a few more exchanges, proceeded to have another row with the political editor, Adam Boulton, while Heseltine and I fled the building.

By this evening it was front page headlines and the episode was being repeated on the television news bulletins.

I thought I'd seen it all from the propaganda newspapers, but their treatment of this was mind-boggling. Said The *Express*: "What is frightening is that this disgusting bruiser could be Foreign Secretary in forty-eight hours if Labour win power.' Said The *Sun*: 'When he can behave like a geriatric bovver boy, is he really to be trusted as Foreign Secretary? If he took to clobbering foreigners, it could mean war!'

It really is all hopelessly over the top.

In any case, my sympathies were divided: on one hand, Labour can hardly complain if such questions are raised after the way Margaret Thatcher has been pilloried on the issue. On the other hand, I was with Healey when he specifically asked a programme editor about the subject matter and was told it was the Venice summit. I see no reason why he should not have been warned that the question would be asked; he would have probably accepted the validity of it and dealt with it more calmly had he not felt he had been set up.

The whole episode was a storm in a teacup and it says a lot about the coverage of this Election by the mass circulation newspapers that it has been given such astonishing publicity.

Tonight the two Leaders spoke to a crowded rally in the Central Hall, Westminster, making their last major appeal to the voters. Thatcher did the same at a rally in Harrogate, and Kinnock in Leeds.

Kinnock was speaking exactly four years after his famous 1983 speech at Bridgend when he warned that if Thatcher was re-elected people should not be ordinary, young, or old. Now he once more spoke emotively, saying Britain's children needed to live in a country that was not divided by privilege, poverty, or poisoned by conflict.

'The question is always, what will the outcome of this Election mean for my children, what will it mean for the future of the country?'

He continued: 'When we know that we have to face the choice, each person of all politics and no politics has to ask themselves: "Am I prepared to offer to the rising generation unemployment, under-spending on education, shortages in training? Am I prepared to offer the young an environment that is abused and endangered, the tensions between races, the deepening divisions between rich and poor? Should Britain's youngsters face a society where full opportunity was dependent on the ability to pay, where housing was priced beyond reach, where women were greater in number but permanently smaller in income and status? They are the questions. They pose themselves with a starkness not known to any post-war generation of voters."'

Thatcher also told her audience that Britain had to make its starkest election choice ever, between a country willing to defend itself and one on the brink of surrender. Labour would destroy prosperity and bring a 'strife-torn, strike-ridden, divided society'. Labour was a party of the past which would condemn the present generation and their children to a second class life in a third class country. The prosperity built up by the Conservatives in eight years could be destroyed by Labour in a few short weeks.

At the Central Hall, David Steel said that there were two days to go and one thing was clear: 'Labour cannot win this Election. Yet there must be a progressive alternative to Thatcher. There must be a government which gives ordinary people a chance to make a success of their own lives and ensures they are cared for when they need to be. The ideology of Thatcherism must be driven out – and the people of this country must be enabled to take power for themselves.

'Britain in this decade is becoming an ever more divided nation. True, the majority still enjoys a comfortable existence in prosperous areas; but a growing minority is trapped in the twilight zones of our old industrial cities or the bleak overspill council estates, where crime is up, drug addiction is up, and the ratings in despair among the ranks of the new dispossessed have soared. The new right in the Conservative Party have taken one nation and split it into two.'

He concluded: 'As we go into the final days of this campaign, the question is this. Will the clash of the class warriors go on to the crack of doom? Is our country to be divided forever? Is there to be no greater common good than the triumph of one minority over the other?

'The voters know that only our Alliance, two parties united in a common cause, can now revive our country . . . we do not stand for more of the same: more division, more decline, more callousness and more bossiness. We stand for a nobler and greater ideal – one United Kingdom where the government trusts the people and the people, at long weary last have reason to trust their government.

'The power of the Alliance is to deliver in government more of the policies people want, less of the policies they fear.'

For Owen, as ever, this was 'the thoughtful Election'. A vote for the Alliance was a precious vote for it could change not just the shape of the government, but the shape of all future governments. It could be the Election that ensures that never again can a party without the support of the majority of people impose its own ideology on the nation. People voted for Thatcher out of fear, not out of enthusiasm. They did not vote with their hearts. The Conservatives were in the lead today because people were afraid of what Labour would do.

'But there does not have to be five more years of no jobs, bad schools, and hospitals buckling under the strain put upon them. We do not have to remain divided by class. We do not have to be split between those doing well and those doing nothing. We do not have to fear crime in our homes or on the streets. We do not have to go on tolerating a generation of youth on the dole.

'The Alliance says to the voters, "Use you heads and your hearts, you can have the sound market economy, conventional and nuclear deterrents, the responsible trade unionism that your head tells you that Britain needs. You can have people back in work, with every pensioner enjoying a decent retirement, all our children fulfilling their potential, and with no one waiting years in pain for a routine operation – that your heart tells you Britain needs.

"You don't have to make the impossible choice. You don't have to cut yourself in two – half head, half heart."'

Apart from a radio and a television interview tomorrow, my campaign ended with speeches in support of Shirley Williams and Gavin Grant.

I arrived in Cambridge to be met by an open-deck van, bedecked with Alliance posters and balloons, and playing the Purcell Trumpet Tune repetitively over a scratchy loudspeaker. From there we paraded across Cambridge to a meeting of about 200 people.

I abandoned my notes and talked to them about what I felt the General Election should have been about – that because major decisions these days are so far-reaching, it was not just about 1987, but about the turn of the century, the prospects for our children beyond the year 2000.

I asked them what they believed historians would say about our generation – about the waste of North Sea oil, about the environmental destruction, about the erosion of the quality of our democracy, about our diminished and mean-minded role in the world, about the accentuation of class and economic divisions.

I talked of the 'supervote' – a vote not just for 1987 but for the year 2000, not just for ourselves but for generations to come, not just for a change of government but a change in the whole system of government, not just for one of two outdated alternatives but for an entirely different political concept.

And I asked them to work hard in the last two days for Shirley. I hope they do. If she doesn't win this one, I think she may call it a day. And that would be a pity.

I was then driven down to Southend to speak for Gavin Grant who appears to stand a real chance of beating Paul Channon. Southend is a sea of orange posters — you can almost see a bright orange glow from a couple of miles out of town! There were 150 people in the hall and I spoke on similar lines to my speech in Cambridge. Gavin has not just fought Southend for three weeks — he's fought it hard for a number of years, and I hope he wins too.

Wednesday, June 10 (P-1)

After appearing on LBC's AM programme and BBC's *Breakfast Time*, I joined the two Johns, Andy and Dick, for the last breakfast we will have at the Royal Horseguards, where we have gathered after the press conference every morning, arguing fiercely about campaign tactics, but also having a lot of laughs. I will miss these breakfasts.

From there to the last meeting of the APG.

David Owen flew down to the West Country, and David Steel to Scotland. I cleared my desk at Cowley Street and drove down to Brighton thinking many thoughts. Of how quickly the campaign had passed by . . . of all the ups and downs. And it struck me that during the whole campaign I had hardly met one candidate or one voter. Somewhere all over Britain, in 650 constituencies, there are Alliance candidates, many of them full of hope, using every minute of this last campaigning day, encouraged on by their agents and their families, their friends and party workers, wearing out shoes, spending their own money, calling on their last reserves of stamina and spirit, fighting our fight. These are the front line troops, each engaged in their own campaign, some of them hundreds of miles from Cowley Street and the morning meetings and the press conferences. How uncomplainingly they have accepted our efforts. Nearly all the messages we have received have been constructive or encouraging. These are the real heroes of our Alliance, people who never see a television studio, or read their name in a national newspaper, or see a party leader during the campaign, or even have a supporting visit from a minor celebrity, many of them knowing that their only reward will be a fleeting few seconds of fame as their name is flashed on a screen as a losing candidate on June 11.

They *are* the Liberal Party. They *are* the Alliance. They are what this Election has really been about.

Have we let them down? I guess the answer is both yes and no. Yes, our campaign could have been better. There's no doubt about that. But no, not for the lack of trying. Heaven knows, we have worked.

Tonight I put my feet up at home and watched the closing hours of the election on television ... Neil Kinnock, back in Wales, receiving a hero's welcome, promising that this was the last day of Thatcherism.

'We have taken the politics of this country by storm. We've won the arguments. We've won them on the grounds of making common cause in this divided nation.'

And there was Margaret Thatcher, in a final bad interview with David Dimbleby. As she reeled off statistics about the achievements of the Conservatives, Dimbleby interrupted to say, "Isn't it that people think you yourself accept that level of unemployment; you don't mind about people being out of work; you never say you care about people being out of work?"

Thatcher replied: 'If people just drool and drivel that they care I turn round and say "Right, I'd also like to see what you'd do"'.

Dimbleby said: 'Why do you use the words "drool and divel that they care"? Is that what you think saying you care about people's plight amounts to?' Thatcher looked stunned, 'No, I don't. I'm sorry I used those words. But I think some people talk a good deal about caring, about the policies which they pursue, and I am sorry I used those words.'

It was a striking moment, all the more so because having briefly let her guard slip once more, and suggested impatience with calls for compassion, she was at last looking vulnerable, saying she was sorry, admitting error. Asked if she had learnt any lessons from the last three weeks, she replied: 'Perhaps you have taught me one – that it is not enough to do things which result in caring. You also have to talk about it.'

At a school in his constituency in Plymouth David Owen appeared on television still talking of his hopes of a coalition. 'On the anvil of the Cabinet table a new political metal will be forged. The Alliance will weld together the best government this country has seen for many a decade.'

Finally there was David Steel, pictured in a rather bare hall in his own constituency with Judy at his side, saying 'Labour cannot win; the Tories must not win.

'Floating voters are struggling towards the Alliance rescue ship as Mr Kinnock's boat founders. To those who come from the shark-infested waters of the Tory Party, we say "Welcome aboard".'

And of course, there was news of the last opinion polls: Marplan in the *Guardian* showing the Conservatives 42 (−3), Labour 35 (+3), and the Alliance 21 (no change), an NOP survey of marginals in the *Independent* suggesting Conservatives 42, Labour 35, and the Alliance 21; and a MORI poll in *The Times* showing the Conservatives 44, Labour 32, and the Alliance 22.

So, as I sat exhausted before the box and drank more than one glass of duty-free Chivas Regal, the Channel 4 *News at 7* turned into the *Nine O'clock News* on BBC 1, turned into the *News at Ten* on ITN, turned into *Newsnight*, turned into the hustings programme, turned into midnight, turned into June 11. The 1987 General Election campaign was over.

Thursday, June 11

My local polling station in Brighton Kemptown is a school

gymnasium. Checking names was a Tory woman, dressed all in blue, her huge bosom blocking the door when I arrived. I struggled past and was given a flimsy piece of paper with three names on it. I put a cross beside the name Chris Berry (Liberal/SDP Alliance) and put it in a box.

Chris Berry does not stand a chance. But if his name was not there, and he and his handful of workers had not done their bit, there would have been nowhere to put that cross to keep the alternative afloat, the dream alive.

Epilogue: Picking up the Pieces

Towards a real Alliance

In a corner of the Insider's study is a mountain of paper — minutes of Joint Strategy Committees, minutes of the APG, minutes of the Liberal General Election Committee, memos, letters, draft articles and speeches, leaflets, opinion poll statistics, newspaper cuttings, all memorabilia of the 1987 General Election. Little of it is worth keeping; most of it was outdated within hours of the writing. It was that kind of year. Let's, therefore, leave the Insider to build his bonfire, and consider the state of our democracy and what lies in store for the Alliance.

Judged by Abraham Lincoln's criteria — 'government of the people, by the people, for the people' — British democracy is in poor shape. It may be 'of the people' in the sense that the people *are* governed, but it is not government 'by the people' and not always government 'for the people'. This is not a bitter response to the General Election. Our democracy has been deteriorating for years, but particularly under Margaret Thatcher. Power has become increasingly centralised. In so far as there is more choice, it is based on the ability to pay; in so much as power is shared, it is economic power not political power. Public accountability has been reduced; secrecy is all-pervasive. Power is wielded by people 'elected' on a minority of votes, and in many cases by people who have never been elected at all, with arrogance and cynicism. The nation has been divided and polarised, and opposition and protest made more difficult. The concessions to public opinion in the run-up to the General Election — the sudden decision to abandon four nuclear waste dumps in Conservative-held seats, and increases in public spending on services that had for years been starved — only serve to remind us how little public opinion has been respected over the last few years.

Mrs Thatcher portrays herself as an ardent defender of democracy, but the first test of a representative democracy is that when people enter the polling booth they should know the result of the election will at least approximate to the way they cast their votes. In the 1987 General Election the Conservative Party attracted 42.3% of the popular vote, i.e. the support of roughly two people out of five, but obtained 57.6% of the parliamentary seats – a minority vote but an overall majority of 100. The Tories 42.3% of the popular vote compares with the Alliance's 22.5%, yet the Tories have 375 seats and the Alliance 22 – i.e. the Tories had less than double the popular vote of the Alliance but 17.5 times the number of seats.

No wonder an Alliance voter who could have expected nearly 150 seats in the House of Commons under proportional representation said to me the day after the Election: 'I feel disenfranchised today.'

How can it be right that three parties can enter a General Election knowing the rules are such that even if all three begin with an equal level of support, only two have any chance of winning? In his Northampton speech in late April the Labour leader demonstrated his cynicism by saying that despite the fact that Labour and the Alliance were almost equal in the opinion polls, only Labour could hope to defeat the Conservatives? And he said it unashamedly. He was in effect saying: 'Look folks, they may be as popular, or even more popular than we are, but the dice are loaded . . . we and the Tories have seen to that . . . they can't win . . . so no matter how much you want them, forget it . . . no matter how much you don't like us, or don't like the Tories, it's we you have to choose from . . . because your vote does not have the strength you thought it did . . . your votes may be a free voucher in the supermarket of politics, but the voucher applies to only two of the brands on display.'

Now, I know my anger on this issue is predictable but it is no less justified for that. Not only did the electoral system cheat us of the number of parliamentary seats earned by our votes, but it actually denied us *more* votes, for an opinion poll carried out on Election Day showed that more than 40% of non-Alliance voters were discouraged because they believed their vote would be wasted.

What can be done about it? First, I believe that we in the Alliance have to persuade the public that it is not just we, but they, who are cheated. Over seven million men and women chose to vote Alliance at the General Election — the will of the vast majority of those seven million was frustrated by the system. That frustration must be expressed, their anger mobilised. Then there is the Labour Party. Blinkered as some of its leaders are, it is inconceivable that at some point it will not see that it too is increasingly becoming a victim of the electoral system. Irrespective of other differences, these three forces — the Alliance, the Labour Party, and their respective voters — well over half the country — need to be mobilised together on this issue.

Equally serious is the further evidence from this General Election that the electoral system and the concentration of power at the centre is placing control over the whole nation in the hands of people who have no mandate to govern substantial parts of it. The Conservatives won only 24% of the vote in Scotland, only ten of Scotland's seventy-two parliamentary seats. They achieved only 29.5% of the vote in Wales, only eight of the thirty-eight seats. To add insult to injury, Mrs Thatcher then appointed an Englishman as Secretary of State for Wales. On what basis can the Conservatives claim the right to rule in Scotland or Wales? While the Welsh may be more divided on the question, there is no doubt that a majority of Scots wish more power over Scottish affairs to be vested in Scotland. Both the Labour Party and the Alliance promised this in their manifestos. The Alliance would devolve power to a Scottish Assembly with legislative powers. The Conservative party made no such promise and will continue to govern Scotland from London (the existence of a Scottish office does not alter that reality), despite its rejection by three-quarters of Scottish voters. This is not democratic — it *is* elective dictatorship.

The words 'elective dictatorship' were first spoken by Lord Hailsham, until recently the Tory Lord Chancellor, who once said 'since an election can nowadays be won on a small minority of votes . . . it follows that the majority is then free to impose on the country a series of relatively unpopular measures, not related to current needs, using the whole powers of the elective dictatorship to carry them through. And in doing so, it is not effectively controlled ... it is idle to pretend that such a system is rational, necessary, or just ...'

He also said: 'What is ultimately unfair about our present constitution is that it gives absolute power, when all reason and experience tend to show that unlimited powers are intolerable.'

The importance of electoral reform is not just that it will create a fair voting system, but that it will lead to a series of other measures such as decentralisation, and freedom of information, each designed to strengthen our democracy.

In my view this issue – the salvation of our democracy – is, together with our divided economy, one of the major political issues for the last decade or so of this century. That is why I was saddened by the failure of our Alliance to force it into the forefront of the 1987 General Election campaign. It is, of course, partly my failure too; I have no wish to suggest that I was the only one in step. But it is a fact that our constitutional reforms both *make* the Alliance distinctive, and, as I have argued, are crucial to the solution of many of Britain's other problems, yet we were diverted by opinion polls that told us people were more concerned about *practical* issues, such as health and education, housing and unemployment. We were advised by the advertising men that it made no sense to appeal to people on issues that did not seem to them a priority. Maybe, too, we were persuaded that with our limited resources we simply could not force these complex issues into the forefront of a black and white general election campaign. But I will always wish that we had tried harder ... and it is just possible it could have made a difference.

I do believe another essential reform is to deprive the Prime Minister of the right to choose the date of an election. Never has that right been so cynically manipulated as it was this time, and I believe it would be both fairer, and lead to more sensible planning and greater stability, if we had fixed-term parliaments. Each election should take place five years after its predecessor, unless the Prime Minister is defeated on a vote of confidence in the House of Commons.

There were other trends during the 1987 General Election that should cause concern, all the more so because it is difficult to imagine how they can be reversed, in particular the domination of the opinion polls, the way some of our mass circulation newspapers became no more than propaganda sheets, and the influence of the advertising and public relations men, the packagers.

There were more opinion polls than ever before. One, the Harris poll for TV AM, being published daily. I will leave discussion of their accuracy, methodology, etc to others, but, without being able to offer any solution to the problem (because a ban on opinion polls has to be unacceptable to any democrat), I must record that they put the Alliance at a huge disadvantage during the campaign. Day after day after day polls were published showing the Alliance in third place, trailing by a number of percentage points, and repeatedly people heard on radio and television, or read in newspapers of 'Further setback for the Alliance', 'The Alliance trailing badly', etc, and this inevitably had a depressing effect on our ultimate vote. The drip-drip-drip effect of the opinion polls, appearing to reinforce the message that a vote for the Alliance could be a wasted vote, also had a devasting effect on the coverage of our campaign and on the morale of candidates and party workers as well as on the public.

It is arguable that we were also affected by what appeared to be happening to Labour in the opinion polls. The misleading impression given that Labour could pull off an unexpected victory led to many 'soft' Tory voters returning to the fold to thwart such a result, and many 'soft' Labour voters hardening their support in the belief that they could help to get Thatcher out.

The pollsters would no doubt argue that it is not the polls that are at fault, but people's perception of the polls, that they are only a snapshot of public opinion on the day the questions are asked, and that they should not have the impact on voter behaviour that they do. They may even add that there is little point in blaming the messenger if you don't like the message. There is some validity in all this. Yet – and as I have said, I don't see what can be done about it – the pollsters should not pretend they have no effect on the result; in 1987 adverse effects *were* felt, and felt almost entirely by the Alliance.

There is also little we can do about our newspapers, yet some of them sank during the General Election to lower depths than ever before. So determined were some to undermine Labour and the Alliance that they adopted from the start a 'no holds barred' philosophy, covering hardly a word of the political debate, but instead trying to stir up prejudice by exposure of the private lives of leading politicians or indulging in unrestrained abuse. They came unstuck with their smear on David Steel, and I suspect even they were surprised by the contempt for their tactics expressed by politicians of all parties, by the more serious newspapers, and even by the public. Roy Hattersley was another victim of totally unnecessary publicity of his private life. Apart from these tactics, I do believe that the Labour Party and Neil Kinnock had every reason for fury at their treatment in the run-up to the General Election, and during it. Goebbels himself would have been proud of some of the abusive and one-sided coverage. In a democracy these so-called newspapers are safe; their contribution to the health of that democracy is almost totally negative.

Another feature of the campaign was the packaging, particularly of the two main parties. I have no objection to the employment of professionals in helping parties to communicate their message and present their policies – this makes sense. But this was an election of the 'photo opportunity', with tours by leaders designed for minimum contact with people, minimum debate and discussion, and the maximum number of sympathetic pictures on television and in the newspapers. The big Thatcher and Kinnock rallies were all-ticket affairs; whereas former Labour leaders like Harold Wilson would take on hecklers in open-air crowds of several thousand in our major cities, hecklers at the closed Kinnock meetings were thrown out. Only at the Alliance meetings could anyone attend and ask questions, and it is no coincidence that the campaign appeared to come alive on television on the occasions when David Owen stood up to hecklers and argued back, and it is no coincidence that his own standing rose as a result.

The packaging went beyond the rallies. Labour's manifesto, for instance, was as notable for what it did not contain as for what it did. Personalities believed to be unpopular with the public were ruthlessly marginalised; I did not see Tony Benn on television once during the entire campaign, nor Arthur Scargill (who later complained that he had been forced out of the front line by the Labour leadership), and Ken Livingstone only escaped his shackles in the closing days.

I have no doubt the packaging and the professionalism will continue. After all, despite failing to achieve even a third of the popular vote, the Labour Party was widely applauded for its brilliant campaign. Just how a campaign can be deemed to be 'brilliant' when it leads to such a disastrous result is not explained. But for me this General Election campaign was summed up by the tendency of even our serious newspapers to report the packaging instead of the content. For instance, one would have imagined that the weekly profile in the *Observer* would have been devoted during the General Election campaign to either the party leaders or to key figures in each of the main parties. Instead the three profiles during the campaign were devoted to the three parties' advertising men. Peter Jenkins, the senior columnist on the *Independent*, identified as the hero of the earlier part of the campaign the Labour Party's director of communications. General Elections are supposed to be about politics and politicians; they have now become the playground of the professionals who make a living out of superficiality.

The truth about the 1987 General Election is that, despite an appalling campaign, and an unpopular Prime Minister, the Tories failed to lose it. They were saved by the fear factor. The 'don't let Labour spoil it' message was a powerful one, even to many who did not have much to lose. Does all this sound like sour grapes? If so, I don't feel that way. I accept that under the system as it is the Conservatives won, and that, the Alliance apart, this was a considerable triumph over their traditional opponents, the Labour Party. I would, however, be more impressed if I believed they won well – that they won after a genuine debate, within a genuinely democratic system. As it is, I do not respect their achievement. I am angry that our democracy has become so unconvincing. And I, and I know the majority of Liberal and Social Democrats, remain defiant – all the more determined to fight on in order to change not just the so-called leadership of our country but also the 'system' itself.

The 1987 General Election showed our country to be more

politically divided than ever before. It would require another book to discuss what can and should be done. Let me, instead, devote the remaining pages of this book to the Alliance. Paradoxically, I have to begin with the Labour Party. Within hours of the Election, its leading members, Neil Kinnock, Roy Hattersley, Bryan Gould, and John Smith, all took the opportunity to demonstrate one of their party's outstanding deficiencies — its staggering inability to learn from history.

Labour should have performed well. It was, after all, the main opponent to an unpopular Prime Minister. There were many who accepted Labour's message that we were 'crying out for a change'. On all the main domestic issues they were judged to be more caring and their policies were judged to be the best. They had a highly professional campaign, and a highly presentable leader. They were presenting a remarkably united front. And if there was a surge in the early days of the campaign, it was towards them. And yet the result for Labour was catastrophic — 31.6% of the popular vote. This was a small increase on 1983, when Michael Foot's campaign was probably the worst ever, but otherwise it continues their fall in popular support from 43% in 1970, to 37% in 1979, and now to just over 30%.

Labour lost for two reasons. First, because in the last resort it did not win the confidence of the people in its ability to run the economy or to manage our foreign affairs. It lost, secondly, because it can no longer ever win on its own. Labour may have learned the first lesson; it undoubtedly has not learned the second. Labour likes to talk about an anti-Thatcher majority, but it fails to understand there is also an anti-Labour majority. If Labour continues to act and think as it does, the Tories are home and dry for the rest of the century, yet Messrs Kinnock, Hattersley, Gould, and Smith, within hours of the disaster, were stating that (1) the lesson of the General Election was that only Labour could remove the Tories, (2) there was no need even to consider a common front with the Alliance over the next four years, let alone beyond — on the contrary — the Alliance must be brushed aside, and (3) that they would not consider support for electoral reform.

There was a time when Labour triumphantly claimed 'we are the governors now'. Labour must accept they are a minority now.

Welcome to the club and welcome to two realities of minority life: first, minorities, while they are minorities, can only influence the majority if they work together; second, minorities stay minorities if injustice is built into the system (as it is in the case of first-past-the-post).

Their arrogance and cynicism, their ignorance, their blinkered thinking, will help to strengthen the resolve of the Alliance and its supporters to establish an effective third force in British politics.

Let me spell out to them why their hopes that they can sweep the Alliance aside, or that we will fade away, are fantasies:

First, they underestimate our strength. For the second successive General Election the Alliance polled more than 20% of the popular vote – more than seven million – and, as I have said, opinion polls showed that we would have done much better if people had believed we could win. If we had a fair voting system, we would have nearly 150 MPs in the House of Commons and Labour's whole disreputable case – that in some way the Alliance stands between it and its rightful place – would be demolished beyond even its ability to pretend otherwise.

Second, the two-party system is and always will be bad for the country. Two-party confrontation, with its polarising effect, its attraction to and dependency on conflicting vested interests, its need to glean votes by dividing people, fostering envy and fear and hate, its denial of the virtues of consensus, is not only no solution to our national problem – it *is* the problem.

A healthy third force is also an essential antidote to the corrupting influence of power itself, for it ensures diversity in our political life, exposure of the self-serving deals the major parties make, and a voice for minorities.

But to achieve our objectives we need to realise the full potential of our combined resources, to achieve greater unity both in public and in private, and to clarify our role and philosophy and to sharpen up our message. This is not achievable while we are two parties. This is why, whatever happens in the short term, I believe merger to be inevitable.

I cannot believe there is anybody who was centrally involved in the Alliance campaign who would wish to repeat the experience of having two leaders in two buses in two different parts of the country with two different views on the strategy, effectively conducting two different campaigns. How can it make sense to tolerate the duplication and waste involved in having two headquarters, two secretariats, two lots of print material, two of this, and two of that, adding up to human and financial resources being directed inwards when they could more effectively be directed to campaigning in the country?

The sheer practical benefits of merger are so substantial that there would have to be an overwhelming philosophical difference between the two parties for it to be postponed. No such difference exists. In 'The Time Has Come' we described the Alliance as the coming together of two major reforming traditions in British politics – as a synthesis of our beliefs in individual freedom, pluralism and diversity with the desire for social reform and justice. We are both committed to enhancing the democratic process, to protecting individual rights in balance with the rule of law, to the redistribution of political, social and economic power, to being an internationalist party. We bring together ideas the other parties believe to be mutually exclusive: enterprise *and* welfare, a market economy *and* social justice, economic growth *and* environmental integrity, British achievement *and* international cooperation.

In the preamble to the Liberal Party constitution we say we 'exist to build a Liberal society in which every citizen shall possess liberty, property and security, and none shall be enslaved by poverty, ignorance or conformity. Its chief care is for the rights and opportunities of the individual and in all spheres it sets freedom first'. No member of the SDP says it exists 'to create and defend an open, classless and more equal society which rejects prejudice based on sex, race, colour or religion'. No Liberal would reject that view either.

Of course there are differences between the two parties on specific policies, but then there are differences *within* the two parties. That is inevitable. But the difference between disputes on issues of principle and over policy is that while principles can be justifiable sticking points, few *policies* are worth dying for. Few policies are even one hundred per cent right. Policies should always be open to adaptation and change, and compromise according to circumstances. No two parties should be afraid to unite because some policies differ.

In my view there are only three non-negotiable features for a merged party.

First, it must be committed to the broad philosophical position outlined above.

Second, it must be genuinely democratic and decentralised. This can't be a matter of lip-service. Both parties have stressed the importance of enhancing our democracy, of decentralisation of power, of devolution, of strengthening the individual in relation to the state. We can and must start with our own structure.

Third, it must not only be about changing the government, but the nature of government. Smashing the system. Sharing power in a real sense, both nationally and locally. Roy Jenkins' suggestion at Harrogate last year that we must be 'the anti-party party' sums it up.

I also believe that if we are to merge, we must merge wholeheartedly. Talk of 'federalism' (a mis-use of the word) and other options is really talk about another two-party arrangement with a different name. None of the fundamental problems will be solved. We will only be a genuine partnership when people cease to think as Liberals and Social Democrats and instead think and act as partners together in a common cause. There can be no compromise on this. We would be far better to separate and pursue our own course than to come up with an arrangement that is, in effect, — 'fudge and mudge'!

I am happy to leave constitutional issues for discussion, but clearly to be effective and democratic the merged party must be one member — one vote, have one representative conference, have one democratic and accountable policy-making process, have one leader, have one campaigning organisation, and be decentralised in its structure.

It was Roy Jenkins, who some would describe as the 'father' of the Alliance, who first raised the question of merger after the General Election, and David Steel then took the initiative by drafting a memo to the party officers suggesting a merger. Before he could approach the SDP it was necessary to obtain support from his own party, and this could not be done secretly; he had to publicise his proposal. This was seen by some Social Democrats as a hasty and unnecessary attempt to force them into a corner. Yet I believe the case for moving quickly was a powerful one: first, it meant that instead of lengthy and depressing inquests into our problems during the General Election, we could move forward positively, both tackling the main cause of those problems and creating fresh hope. Second, there were bound to be lengthy negotiations on the detail, and if we were to achieve a decision in principle at our respective conferences in the Autumn we had to move quickly.

Second, I believe we were actually capturing the mood of the overwhelming majority of members of both parties. In many parts of the country, merger has happened in all but name. During the General Election, despite all the difficulties, Liberals and Social Democrats worked harmoniously together locally and centrally, as we have done during numerous by-elections. Immediately after the Election some local Liberals and Social Democrats virtually declared UDI, saying they would merge locally, irrespective of what happened at the centre. There is a real danger for both parties that those who operate nationally, many of us based on London, become out of touch with the feelings and mood of our members in other parts of the country. If we do not forge ahead in a spirit of generosity and optimism towards partnership at the centre, we will in my view anger and frustrate thousands of party members who want merger to happen.

As I complete this book, the National Committee of the SDP have yet to meet to decide on their response to the Liberal initiative. Some of its members have, however, responded truculently, apparently in a fit of pique at what they feel to be public pressure from the Liberal Party. Even if this were justified – and for the reasons I have given, I do not believe it is – it would be no reason for blocking what is right. Nor can conflicting ambitions or egos of individuals be allowed to stand in the path of history, to frustrate what makes sense for both parties and for British politics. The decision to merge will have lasting effect beyond the lives of any of the present-day participants. That is not to say that we should not try to accommodate the abilities and talents of everybody currently involved. Let me address directly the question of David Owen. I have described earlier some of the difficulties of working with David Owen, but there are difficulties associated with working with any political leader. I believe that David Owen made some misjudgements during the General

Election, but we all made some, and they were borne of conviction, not of ill-intent. I believe many Liberals are unfair to David Owen; they underestimate his radicalism, they over-simplify his motives, they under-appreciate his value to the Alliance cause. As I have said earlier, he doesn't wear his heart on his sleeve, he doesn't try to be loved, and yet anyone of perception can see that the passion is there — it's there in the determination, it's there in the courage, and it's there in the sacrifices he has made. It must also be said that no one was more frustrated during the campaign than David Owen himself; he, as much as David Steel, was operating at half-power because he could not carry all of his colleagues with him on strategy. I have no doubt that he must feel now that if he is to be condemned for his strategy, he would at least have liked to put it to the full test. Abrasive and impatient, and, yes, sometimes difficult, as he is, David Owen is also a man of formidable talent and power and we should do all we can to encourage him to play a major part in a merged party.

There is a negative point that has to be addressed: what if we do not merge? For, whether we like it or not, and even if the SDP leadership does try to apply the brakes, merger is now at the top of our agenda and will remain so. If we fail to merge, we will be publicly saying 'we are incapable of uniting; we've considered our respective philosophies, policies, and personalities, and there simply is insufficient common ground'. What would the other parties, the political commentators, the public make of that? Down would tumble the whole edifice of the Alliance as a movement that can govern the country, that genuinely believes in cooperation and partnership and people working together.

Apart from that, what would be the point in continuing a partnership that has been proved to be so flimsy? There is in my view also no compromise on this: we either merge, or we separate, and in our failure lies the Labour Party's only hope. What does the Labour Party want to happen? Does it hope we will merge? Or that we will remain divided? The answer is obvious, and its fear is eloquent testimony in support of merger.

David Steel once quoted to the Liberal Party the words of Burke: 'When bad men combine, the good must associate, else they will fall one by one, an unpitied sacrifice in a contemptible struggle'. Therein lies the challenge. If we merge, we will be saying that no matter how much we love party, we love country more; that if it comes to a choice between a Liberal Party or the creation of a Liberal society, the latter wins every time.

I have no doubt there are months of lengthy meetings and hard negotiations ahead, and that the engagement will have many ups and down before the marriage is a reality. But I cannot believe it will not happen. What follows then? We will be a more effective campaigning party. We will look and sound fresh and the public, desperate for an alternative to the older parties, will respond positively. But we will still have only 22 MPs and we will still be confronted with a corrupt electoral system. We will still have limited resources compared with those poured into the other parties by their vested interests. So how can we capture the imagination of the British people and so convince them that we can win that they put aside fears of a wasted vote and commit themselves in the polling booth?

I do not believe we can do it by apeing the existing parties within the present system. If we believe the system is fundamentally flawed, why keep operating it? That way we become its prisoners. Our MPs are trapped in the House of Commons until the early hours of the morning, voting in the face of a huge majority just to show that they are there, spending hours on a show of strength that convinces no one. I know I am fighting an uphill battle on this, there are parliamentarians who believe strongly that if we are to look capable of governing the country, we have to be seen to be effectively shadowing and opposing where necessary the government of the day. And, of course, we *do* have to be effective in the House of Commons – but do we have to be effective on every issue? It would be ideal, but is it realistic? In attempting to be effective on every issue, are we really being ineffective? I would like to see fifteen of our MPs formed into five teams of three, each operating in a particular priority area – the economy, constitutional reform, inner cities, maintenance of the welfare state, and the like, hammering away on these issues day after day, spearheading corresponding campaigns at every level of the party, so that the themes we plan to put before the British people at the next General Election emerge in the intervening period in all that we say and do.

I know that this is a radical break with the past, but the past has not worked. We are either a campaigning party or we are not. We are either breaking the rules of an unworkable system or we are not. If we are to excite people, if we are to shake up British politics, we need an exciting and different approach to politics. We will not have it if our spearhead – our Members of Parliament – become so bogged down in trying to shadow a government of more than a hundred ministers that they disappear from view.

To sum up, one lesson from the 1987 General Election is that while we presented the country with a coherent set of policies, there was no clear message, no clear theme. We must put that lesson into effect now, by (1) deciding on no more than six broad political themes that we intend to pursue from now to polling day in 1991–2, (2) campaigning persistently, with determination, but also entertainingly, out in the country, on those themes, and (3) deploying our small number of parliamentarians as a campaigning spearhead, relieving them of the necessity to play the constitutional and institutional game, and encouraging them to use the House of Commons effectively as a campaigning base.

We have to use the next four years to convince the country that there is no point in just changing the names and faces of those in power – we have to change the whole system. We have to show how an antiquated, self-serving administration adversely affects the economy and people's everyday lives. We have to prove that the concept of 'British democracy and fair play' is becoming a myth.

We must focus on the division within our country – this is another area where we can be distinctive, because the other parties divide the country – we can hope to unite it. All people of common sense can see the damage done by the traditional war between management and labour, and the dangers for the country in the north-south divide. We must put together all of our ideas and proposals for bringing people together, and campaign for them.

We should take as a theme Britain in the 21st century and the need to invest so that our children inherit a country capable of withstanding almost unimaginable challenges and pressures.

If we combine the strengths of our two parties, if we focus our activities in this way, I believe we can become a great campaigning force that by 1991–92 will be set to make the impact in that General Election that we failed to do this year.

We in the Alliance know that we could have done better in the 1987 Election – *if* we had devised a strategy we could sustain with passion and urgency until the end of the campaign, *if* we had, as Richard Holmes said in a *Guardian* article, 'sharpened and clarified the Alliance's appeal to all those on the centre/left of British politics where most of us believe we belong', *if* we had run a more dramatic and exciting campaign with a more exciting objective than balance of power. But we *have* all come out of the campaign in remarkable shape. We *do* have those seven million votes. We *do* have a force in the House of Commons that can command attention. We *do* have the opinion poll evidence that there are millions in Britain who wish the Alliance well, who want to believe that it is electable, and are there to be won. What matters now . . . what matters above all else . . . is that we develop further a live political movement that has the potential to unite and realise the ambitions of our children, our communities, and our country as we approach the end of the 20th century. To everyone in the Alliance I say: let's learn the lessons of the past, but let's put aside the differences; let's hammer out a merger that will work, but let's do it in a spirit of generosity and hope; let's give the people what the people need and deserve – their own political party.

Acknowledgements

I would like to thank Andy Ellis, Paul Hannon, and Alan Leaman for their constructive comments on some draft chapters, and in particular I would like to thank Paul Tyler for the many hours he devoted to reading the manuscript and providing much-valued advice.

Barbara Boote has been a most helpful and sympathetic publisher.

I owe special thanks to Anne Paintin who patiently and uncomplainingly typed all the drafts and the final manuscript.

Without the support of my friend and fellow director of *Citizen Action*, Godfrey Bradman, my freedom to serve the Liberal Party as well as my other campaigning organisations would not have been possible. I will always be in his debt.

Finally, I thank those members of the Liberal Party who entrusted me with the office of President. I have held it with pride.

D.W. 1987

Appendix

1987 General Election

	Seats	(% of popular vote)
Conservative	375	(43.3)
Labour	229	(31.6)
Liberal/SDP Alliance	22	(23.1)
Others	23	(2)
The Speaker	1	

Of the Liberal MPs, Clement Freud, Michael Meadowcroft, and Elizabeth Shields lost their seats, and the two seats vacated by Richard Wainwright and Stephen Ross were also lost. The party gained three seats, Menzies Campbell winning Fife North-East, Rae Michie winning Argyll and Bute, and Ronnie Fearn winning Southport.

Three SDP MPs, Roy Jenkins, Ian Wrigglesworth, and Mike Hancock, lost their seats.

FROM THE WINNER OF
THE WORLD FANTASY AWARD

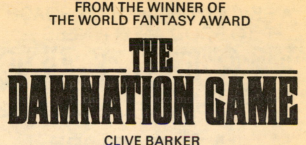

THE DAMNATION GAME

CLIVE BARKER

A CHILLINGLY BRILLIANT NOVEL FROM THE NEW
STEPHEN KING OF HORROR

'I have seen the future of horror . . . and his name is Clive
Barker'
STEPHEN KING

'I think Clive Barker is so good that I am almost literally
tongue-tied'
STEPHEN KING

'Clive Barker writes about horrors most of us would
scarcely dare imagine'
RAMSEY CAMPBELL

'The most impressive first novel I've read for a long, long
time. Touches of sheer brilliance throughout'
JAMES HERBERT

0 7221 1416 8 HORROR £3.50

**Also by Clive Barker in Sphere Books:
BOOKS OF BLOOD Volumes 1–6**

A REVOLUTIONARY APPROACH TO FOOD AND FITNESS

TASTE of LIFE

JULIE STAFFORD

THE DIET THAT SAVED A LIFE

Julie and Bruce Stafford thought they had the perfect life and family until, out-of-the-blue, 30 year-old Bruce, who had never missed a day's work through illness in his life, was struck down by cancer.

As Bruce's health steadily deteriorated, Julie decided to investigate the link between diet and disease. She came up with an eating plan based on the principle of low-fat, salt-free and sugar-free foods but applied it to inventive, delicious and mouth-watering recipes. The result? A miraculous recovery. Within two weeks Bruce's health improved and now he is completely cured.

Julie Stafford shows you how to eat like a gourmet and be healthy too. TASTE OF LIFE is truly a revolutionary, life-sustaining breakthrough.

0 7221 8105 1   HEALTH/COOKERY   £3.50

"A sparkling, penetrating biography" *Sunday Express*

BURTON

The man behind the myth

PENNY JUNOR

He was born Richard Walter Jenkins on 10 November 1925, a miner's son. But by the age of seventeen he had a new name, a new father and a new life before him. By twenty-seven he was in Hollywood, by thirty-seven he was the most acclaimed young actor of his time.

He could have been the greatest actor of his day, the successor to Olivier, but he squandered his talent in second-rate films, threw away his career on drink and women and his own legend.

What went wrong? The question has been asked a thousand times . . . now Penny Junor gives us the answer.

BIOGRAPHY   **0 7221 5212 4**   **£2.95**

A selection of bestsellers from Sphere

FICTION

BIRTHRIGHT	Joseph Amiel	£3.50 ☐
TALES OF THE WOLF	Lawrence Sanders	£2.50 ☐
MALIBU SUMMER	Stuart Buchan	£2.95 ☐
THE SECRETS OF HARRY BRIGHT	Joseph Wambaugh	£2.95 ☐
CYCLOPS	Clive Cussler	£3.50 ☐

FILM AND TV TIE-IN

INTIMATE CONTACT	Jacqueline Osborne	£2.50 ☐
BEST OF BRITISH	Maurice Sellar	£8.95 ☐
SEX WITH PAULA YATES	Paula Yates	£2.95 ☐
RAW DEAL	Walter Wager	£2.50 ☐

NON-FICTION

SOLDIERS	John Keegan & Richard Holmes	£5.95 ☐
URI GELLER'S FORTUNE SECRETS	Uri Geller	£2.50 ☐
A TASTE OF LIFE	Julie Stafford	£3.50 ☐
HOLLYWOOD A' GO-GO	Andrew Yule	£3.50 ☐
THE OXFORD CHILDREN'S THESAURUS		£3.95 ☐

All Sphere books are available at your local bookshop or newsagent, or can be ordered direct from the publisher. Just tick the titles you want and fill in the form below.

Name _____

Address _____

_____

Write to Sphere Books, Cash Sales Department, P.O. Box 11, Falmouth, Cornwall TR10 9EN

Please enclose a cheque or postal order to the value of the cover price plus:

UK: 60p for the first book, 25p for the second book and 15p for each additional book ordered to a maximum chrge of £1.90.

OVERSEAS & EIRE: £1.25 for the first book, 75p for the second book and 28p for each subsequent title ordered.

BFPO: 60p for the first book, 25p for the second book plus 15p per copy for the next 7 books, thereafter 9p per book.

Sphere Books reserve the right to show new retail prices on covers which may differ from those previously advertised in the text elsewhere, and to increase postal rates in accordance with the P.O.